WAR IN THE AGE OF TRUMP

Patrick Cockburn is currently Middle East correspondent for *The Independent* and worked previously for the *Financial Times*. He has written four books on Iraq's recent history—*The Rise of Islamic State, Muqtada al-Sadr and the Fall of Iraq, The Occupation*, and *Saddam Hussein: An American Obsession* (with Andrew Cockburn)—as well as a memoir, *The Broken Boy* and, with his son, a book on schizophrenia, *Henry's Demons*, which was shortlisted for a Costa Award. He won the Martha Gellhorn Prize in 2005, the James Cameron Prize in 2006, the Orwell Prize for Journalism in 2009, the Foreign Commentator of the Year in 2013, and the Foreign Affairs Journalist of the Year in 2014.

WAR IN THE AGE OF TRUMP

*The Defeat of Isis, the Fall of the Kurds,
the Conflict with Iran*

Patrick Cockburn

VERSO
London • New York

This edition first published by Verso 2020
© Patrick Cockburn 2020
First published in the United States by OR Books LLC,
New York © Patrick Cockburn 2020

1 3 5 7 9 10 8 6 4 2

Verso
UK: 6 Meard Street, London W1F 0EG
US: 20 Jay Street, Suite 1010, Brooklyn, NY 11201
versobooks.com

Verso is the imprint of New Left Books

ISBN-13: 978-1-83976-040-2
ISBN-13: 978-1-83976-042-6 (US EBK)
ISBN-13: 978-1-83976-041-9 (UK EBK)

British Library Cataloguing in Publication Data
A catalogue record for this book is available from the British Library

Library of Congress Cataloging-in-Publication Data
A catalog record for this book is available from the Library of Congress

Printed in the UK by CPI Group (UK) Ltd, Croydon, CR0 4YY

Contents

PREFACE

This book covers the critical three years after the election of Donald Trump as US president in 2016. Its central themes are the US-Iran confrontation, the defeat of Isis and the fall—some say betrayal—of the Kurds. The election of Trump coincided almost exactly with the start of the nine-month siege of Mosul by the Iraqi army, which was to be the decisive battle in the defeat of Isis. The terminal date of the book is early 2020 with the assassination of Iranian General Qasem Soleimani by the US in Iraq and the impact of this in Iraq and Iran. This followed closely on Trump's announcement in the fall of 2020 of US military withdrawal from Syria and opened the door to a Turkish invasion of northern Syria. At the same time, mass street protests in Iraq and Lebanon were beginning to shake the political dominance of Iran and its allies in the Shia heartlands. Much that I wrote during this period concerned the rise and fall of the de facto Kurdish states in Iraq and Syria and the final elimination of the self-declared Isis caliphate, which culminated in death of Abu Bakr al-Baghdadi.

As in a previous volume, I look at events from two angles. One is contemporary description using writings and diaries I produced at the time; the other is retrospective explanation and analysis from the perspective of today. Both have their advantages: it is important to know what events looked like when they were still happening, but also to see retrospectively "how things panned out" and what was their true significance. As historians have often said, it is important to remember that past events were once in the future.

I have tried to give a voice to what Syrians, Iraqis, and Kurds felt about events as they unfolded around them. Their instincts, honed by decades of danger to themselves and their families, were often sharper, or at least different from mine. I always try to keep in mind the warning of an Iraqi friend who told me, as we drove through a particularly violent district north of Baghdad, "Take off your seatbelt—no Iraqi ever wears one and it identifies you as a foreigner."

Canterbury
14 January 2019

INTRODUCTION

ONE

The Assassination

At the time of his assassination, General Qasem Soleimani's strategy in Iraq and in other Middle Eastern countries with large Shia populations, had become counterproductive. He is now guaranteed the status of an Iranian and Shia warrior-martyr, in spite of the mistakes he made in the last years of his life, the effects of which may, to some extent, have been reversed by President Donald Trump's decision to kill him. Beginning last October in Iraq, Soleimani orchestrated the violent repression of small-scale protests about social and economic grievances, which turned them into something close to a mass uprising by the Shia community. Iran and its proxies were blamed for the death of more than 500 protesters and injuries to 15,000 others; demonstrators chanting anti-Iranian slogans burned the Iranian consulates in the Shia holy cities of Karbala and Najaf. Later the same month in Lebanon, vast crowds filled the streets of Beirut, demanding an end to a political status quo that Hezbollah, Iran's local ally, had fought for decades to create. In Iran itself, the government ruthlessly suppressed November protests over fuel price rises; according to Amnesty International 304 people were killed. At home and abroad, the Shia coalition, which Iran had built up with immense effort since the 1979 revolution, was falling apart; the Iranian state and its two most powerful regional allies, Hezbollah in Lebanon and the Hashd al-Shaabi, or Popular Mobilisation Forces, in Iraq, were losing their legitimacy as defenders of their communities and the opponents of foreign interference in their countries.

The Iranian leadership faced a political crisis long before President Trump ordered the assassination by American drone of Soleimani at Baghdad airport on 3 January. Trump ignored the old military saying "Never interrupt your enemy when he is in the middle of making a mistake," at a time when Soleimani, and those who thought like him in Iran, Iraq, and Lebanon, had made a grave misjudgment in choosing violent repression to deal with opponents of the political status quo. As the largest crowds since the funeral of Ayatollah Khomeini in 1989 filled the streets of Tehran and other cities to mourn Soleimani, senior members of the Iranian government appeared astonished by a renewed sense of national solidarity. Demands by demonstrators that the government stop wasting money on foreign adventures, like those organised by Soleimani, were replaced with cries for vengeance against the US. Since he withdrew from the Iran nuclear deal in 2018, the purpose of Trump's Iran policy and, crucially, the imposition of sanctions has been to ramp up popular pressure on the Iranian leadership, forcing them to give in to US demands if they want to stay in power. There was strong evidence that this approach was working until the Soleimani killing revived support for the government in Tehran.

But Trump is not the only leader who makes unforced errors. Just when the Iranian government was riding a wave of re-awakened nationalism, an Islamic Revolutionary Guard unit near Tehran airport shot down a Ukrainian passenger aircraft, killing all 176 passengers, including eighty-two Iranians and sixty-three Canadians. The Revolutionary Guards lied about their responsibility for the incident for three days until finally admitting that the crew manning the anti-aircraft missile battery had mistaken the civilian plane for a US cruise missile. Within hours, demonstrators were back in the streets of Tehran and other cities. But this time they were shouting anti-government slogans, demanding the punishment of the Revolutionary Guard commanders, and blaming the regime for everything that had gone wrong. Student protesters chanted: "Guards, you are our dictator. You are our Isis," while others called for the resignation of the Supreme Leader Ali Khamenei and an end to forty years of clerical rule. Iranians noted that their military had taken great care not to kill any Americans in retaliation for the death of Soleimani when they fired ballistic missiles on 8 January at US bases at Erbil and Ain al-Assad in Iraq. They asked why their generals did not pay equal attention to keeping their own people alive. Iran is a deeply polarised country of eighty-two million people, and though not all of them will have felt that way, the popular mood swiftly changed; a week that began with the government basking in new-found popularity ended with it being denounced for its incompetence, mendacity, and brutality. These feelings of outrage and contempt were expressed in an angry joke on Iranian social media: "The Revolutionary Guards have sent a message to the US that, if you attack us once again, we will level Iran to the ground."

In Iraq, the effect of the assassination is less straightforward: protesters involved in the last round of demonstrations are not likely to shed tears for a man who has spent the last three months trying to kill them, and yet, perversely, his death does undermine the protests. The Iraqi political elite, that had begun to look as if it might buckle under popular pressure, can now claim that it is defending Iraqi independence, and that the greatest threat to Iraqi sovereignty comes from the US, and not Iran. Iraqi leaders sympathetic to the protesters will be more cautious: President Barham Salih, for instance, had rejected two interim prime minister nominees (to replace the discredited Adel Abdul-Mahdi) for being too close to the pro-Iranian camp. Grand Ayatollah Ali al-Sistani, whose support or tolerance is essential for any Shia-dominated government in Baghdad, was backing fresh elections. These moves may continue, but in a less major key: "no Iraqi leader," said one Iraqi commentator, "will want to open himself up to accusations of being too pro-American." Already there are signs that Mahdi may stay on as prime minister. From the start of the protests, pro-Iranian paramilitary groups have claimed that the movement was a plot by the US, Israel, the United Arab Emirates, and Saudi Arabia to stage a "velvet revolution" to overthrow the government. These conspiracy theories will be pushed harder and repression will intensify: On 5 January protesters in the southern city of Nasiriyah, who were refusing to take part in funerary rites for Abu Mahdi al-Muhandis, the Kata'ib Hezbollah leader who was killed alongside Soleimani, were shot at and their tents set ablaze.

Since Soleimani's death, Trump and his cabinet have been demonising him as the terrorist mastermind responsible for the deaths of hundreds of American soldiers. On the contrary, in Iran and in Shia communities across the world, he has been presented as the supreme national and religious martyr who died for his country and his faith. The two narratives combine into a somewhat exaggerated picture of Soleimani's significance. They distort the image of his twin-track role as the head of Quds Force, the foreign branch of the Islamic Revolutionary Guard Corps, carrying out covert operations and open diplomacy in parts of the Middle East with significant Shia populations: Iraq, Syria, Lebanon, Yemen, Afghanistan, and the Gulf states. He certainly would have given the orders for the drone and missile attack on Saudi oil facilities at Abqaiq and al-Khurais last September, but he was also a highly visible regional politician. He manoeuvred and acted as an intermediary between different national, ethnic, and religious leaders. Iraqi Prime Minister Mahdi says that Soleimani had flown into Baghdad International Airport to discuss measures to reduce hostility between Iran and Saudi Arabia: "I was supposed to meet him in the morning the day he was killed; he came to deliver a message from Iran in response to the message we had delivered from the Saudis to Iran." Trump, who wants to portray Soleimani as a monster, denies this, but it is highly likely that what Mahdi says is true.

The US has always been keen to hide the degree to which it has been Iran's de facto partner, as well as its rival, in Iraq ever since Saddam Hussein (effectively allied to the US during the Iran-Iraq War) invaded Kuwait in 1990. The Iranians, for their part, have also been discreet about their co-operation with Washington. For much of the time after the US invasion of 2003, the Americans were dealing with Soleimani—knowingly, but at a distance. Both Washington and Tehran had to agree on the appointments of all Iraqi presidents and prime ministers. In 2006, the US ambassador proposed Nouri al-Maliki as prime minister: at first he was thought to be close to the Americans, but later shifted towards Iran. The same system was operating up to 2018. The basis for this co-operation was that both sides had an interest in keeping a stable Shia-dominated government in power in Baghdad, even if they vied to bring it under their own respective influence. The link between Tehran and Washington was closest after Isis captured Mosul in 2014 and its fighters were advancing on Baghdad, something both governments were determined to stop. "They shake their fists at each other over the table, but shake hands under it," was the cynical Iraqi saying about the US-Iran relationship.

Soleimani was important in Iraqi and regional politics, but not quite as significant as he liked to pretend. Iraqi politicians in Baghdad were irritated by his grandstanding, especially his habit of having himself photographed with pro-Iranian paramilitaries and implicitly crediting himself for victories over Isis that leaders in Baghdad saw as their own. Iraqi leaders were not alone in their criticism: last year the online magazine *The Intercept* published secret cables from officers of the Iranian Ministry of Intelligence and Security (MOIS) stationed in Iraq between 2013 and 2015. Many of these documents concern Soleimani, and one of them speculates that his high profile on the battlefield was a way of preparing for a future presidential bid in Iran. Of course, feuding between rival intelligence agencies like Quds and MOIS is notorious in every country, but in this case the contemporary portrait of Soleimani drawn by the MOIS agents looks convincing. They were particularly troubled about the degree to which Soleimani's reliance on Shia militias fighting in Sunni areas in Iraq was fuelling sectarianism and leading Sunnis to blame Iran for atrocities. An intelligence agent described a successful attack on Jurf al-Saqr, a strategically crucial Isis-held town close to the main road south of Baghdad. Among those taking part were fighters from Asaib Ahl al-Haq, a paramilitary group close to Iran. But victory had been followed by a massacre of Sunni inhabitants. "It is mandatory and necessary to put some limits ... on the violence being inflicted against innocent Sunni people in Iraq and the things that Mr. Soleimani is doing," wrote the agent. He added that whatever happened to Sunnis, directly or indirectly, would be blamed on Iran. In the event, the surviving Sunni were driven out of Jurf al-Saqr and have not been allowed to return.

Soleimani was certainly a good tactician in the fields of militarised politics and low-level guerrilla warfare in which Iran has always specialised. "They have a PhD in that type of war," commented one Iraqi politician. But Soleimani was not the first or the only commander in the Middle East to specialise in asymmetric warfare, which differs little from old-fashioned guerrilla strategy of attacking a militarily superior enemy at their weakest point. In the case of its confrontation with the US, Iran was eager to militarise the conflict and maintain a continuing sense of crisis, but to stay just below the level of an all-out military conflict which they want to avoid. The limited Iranian ballistic missile strikes on US bases in Iraq in January shows that this is still the Iranian strategy. Iran may want to halt, or at any rate reduce the pinprick attacks on Saudi Arabia and UAE, and concentrate instead on forcing US forces out of Iraq through political pressure. But in the long run Iran probably has no choice but to resume low-level warfare, whatever the risks, as its only viable response to sanctions.

How that might unfold is unclear for the moment but Soleimani's death makes it easier to adapt his failed policies in Iraq to new circumstances. His vice-regal airs, high visibility, the arrogance of the pro-Iran Hashd, and their unrestrained violence towards protesters, have seriously damaged Iran's reputation, particularly in the Shia community that had only recently looked on Iran as its saviour from Isis. Polls show that the proportion of Iraqis with a favourable attitude towards Iran fell from 90 percent in 2015 to less than 50 per cent in 2018. Those who said they saw Iran as a threat to Iraqi sovereignty rose from 25 percent to 58 percent over the same period. One Iraqi analyst in Baghdad was quoted at the end of last year as saying that he thought the Iranian supreme leader Ali Khamenei should put Soleimani in jail because of the damage he had done to Iran's reputation in Iraq.

Soleimani miscalculated the response to repression of the Iraqi protesters, who refused to leave the streets or respond in kind to gunfire—because every Iraq family owns a gun, this showed great restraint. He similarly underestimated the likelihood that Trump would eventually react strongly. And that he would even be prepared to go to war if Iran kept up its needling attacks, such as limpet mines attached to oil tankers off the UAE coast, or allowing pro-Iran protesters to penetrate the outer gates of the US embassy in Baghdad as they did in December. The belief that Trump would avoid doing anything that might lead to war had become conventional wisdom among Iranian leaders and their Iraqi allies. When I interviewed Qais al-Khazali, the leader of Asaib Ahl al-Haq in September, he said confidently that "Trump will not go to war," and that Iran knew how to keep any confrontation below the level of a full-scale military conflict. It may be true that Trump does not want war, but he is impulsive, ill-informed, and keen not to appear weak. He is surrounded by neo-conservative interventionists, equally ignorant, but instinctively aggressive. The result is that US policy in the Middle East is a chaotic compromise between different factions in Washington. The on/off US withdrawal from Syria last year was a typical consequence.

Iraqis have an acute sense of when danger is approaching. They were predicting last summer that a new crisis was on the way, even though the country was more peaceful than at any time since 2003. After Trump withdrew the US from the Iran nuclear deal in May 2018, they argued that Iraq was bound to be the arena for an Iran-US confrontation. Some friends in Baghdad were already making plans to buy a house or apartment in Turkey. Iraqis tend to take a pessimistic view of the political future thanks to forty years of crisis and war, but their forecasts rapidly turned out to be correct. They understood that any quarrel fought out in Iraq is necessarily confused, unpredictable, and unlikely to produce a decisive victory for either side because power in Iraq is so fragmented: Iraqis say that the four dominant authorities in the country are the government, religious hierarchy, the paramilitary forces, and the tribes. But even this is an over-simplification as Iraq is split between Shia, Sunni, and Kurds. The latter two communities will try to exploit any breakdown of relations between the US and the

Shia to increase their own power. On the other hand, they will not want to be used by the US as pawns to exert leverage against Baghdad—and then abandoned, as they strongly expect they would be.

It does not take very much to destabilise Iraq and the signs are that Trump does not care if he does. Certainly, the consequences for Iraq of assassinating Soleimani does not seem to have bothered Trump. The US approach today is much like the mindless hubris shown by the Americans in Baghdad after the 2003 invasion, when they did not know what they were doing or care who they were offending.

Could the whole Shia coalition in the Middle East led by Iran, which Soleimani is credited with creating, now begin to unravel after his death? Iraq and Lebanon are clearly shaky, and in none of the Shia-controlled states has power been successfully institutionalised in a way acceptable to the entire population.

At the same time, it is a mistake to forget the strong sense of solidarity among Shia developed down the centuries because they were one of the most persecuted religious minorities in the Middle East, quite separate from Iranian influence. In the wake of the Soleimani assassination, they fear that once again they are being demonised and potentially targeted, as Donald Trump denounces all who oppose the US in the Middle East as Iranian proxies.

Yousif al-Khoei, the grandson of the Grand Ayatollah al-Khoei, told me that the confrontation between Iran and the US was already leading to "the rise of anti-Shia sentiment." He receives many calls from non-political albeit very worried Shia who interpret Washington's rhetoric as crude anti-Shia propaganda. "The threat to demolish 'cultural sites' in Iran was shocking to hear from a US president," said Khoei. "Ordinary Shia express fear that this may mean attacking our holy places and institutions where faith and culture are intertwined." One of the most significant developments in the Middle East since 1945 has been the rise of the previously marginalised and impoverished Shia communities in many—though not all—of the region's countries; above all Lebanon and Iraq, the latter becoming the first Shia-ruled state in the Arab world since Saladin overthrew the Fatimid dynasty in Egypt in 1171.

Yet American and British politicians too often treat the rise of the Shia as purely the outcome of unjustifiable Iranian interference. Western leaders find it convenient to adopt the anti-Shia propaganda line pumped out by Sunni states like Saudi Arabia, which persecutes its own Shia minority, and Bahrain, which has an even more oppressed Shia majority. In both countries, Shia who demand civil rights are punished as terrorists and alleged Iranian proxies. Often, the Sunni authorities are convinced by their own propaganda: when the Bahraini government, backed by Saudi troops, crushed the Arab Spring protests on the island in 2011, Shia doctors in a nearby hospital were tortured to make them admit that they were receiving orders from Iran. A high-level international investigation, however, found no evidence of Iranian involvement in the protests. Bahraini officials even became convinced that a sophisticated piece of medical equipment in the hospital, used for monitoring heart conditions, was a high-powered radio used for keeping in touch with Tehran.

After the invasion of Iraq in 2003, American and British military commanders were paranoid about alleged Iranian plots to foster resistance to the occupation. In fact, it needed no fostering, because neither Shia nor Sunni wanted Iraq to be occupied by a foreign military force. Old propaganda claims have resurfaced over the last week about Iran assisting the predominantly Saudi 9/11 bombers, or being the driving force behind the largely Sunni resistance to the occupation.

Such self-serving conspiracy theories, whether they are being peddled in Washington, London, Riyadh, or Abu Dhabi, are counterproductive. They foster a sense of Shia solidarity that is to the benefit of Iran. We saw this over the last week in Iran, as anti-government protests in 2019 were replaced this year by crowds numbering millions, jamming the streets of Iranian cities to mourn that very same government's top military commander. At the time of writing, the pendulum has swung the other way again, thanks to the dysfunctional and authoritarian nature of the Iranian government that led to the shooting down of the Ukrainian plane and the abortive cover-up.

One advantage for Trump in Soleimani's assassination is that the Iranians are likely to be more cautious in launching limited attacks on the US and its allies. But this does not mean they will discontinue entirely. Iran does not have many cards in its hand and sees this guerrilla-type campaign as one of them. It is unlikely to de-escalate without some relaxation of sanctions, which are strangling its economy. At the same time, Trump and his administration are peculiarly ill-equipped to judge the likely outcome of any new phase of the conflict, or predict how the Iranians will respond. This makes blundering into war a prospect more likely than usual, though neither side wants it.

TWO

America's On/Off Retreat

On 7 October 2001 I was standing on a rocky hillside in Afghanistan forty miles north of Kabul watching bombs and missiles explode on Taliban frontline positions to the south. It was the start of the first of the post-9/11 wars and of the US air campaign to overthrow the Taliban in retaliation for them helping Osama bin Laden and al-Qaeda. There was the twinkle of ineffective anti-aircraft fire in the distance, but I saw no other signs of resistance to the US attack. A few weeks later the Taliban fighters melted away and opposition militiamen captured Kabul without a fight. The easy victory appeared to be proof of America's status as the one true superpower in the world.

Compare what I witnessed that night on a hillside in Afghanistan with a somewhat similar scene viewed from a road in eastern Saudi Arabia on 14 September 2019. Travellers saw, as I had done eighteen years earlier, explosions and plumes of fire on the horizon, but this time it was Iranian cruise missiles and drones that were smashing into the giant Abqaiq oil facility. They caused destruction sufficient to cut Saudi oil output in half and raise the world price of oil by 20 percent. This time around it was not the Taliban but a US ally, Saudi Arabia, that was on the receiving end of the air strikes, which its vastly expensive US air defence systems failed to detect or prevent. The pathetic excuse advanced to explain this was that such systems had been designed to combat high flying aircraft while the Iranian drones and missiles were unfairly flying too close to the ground. Though the US and Saudi Arabia blamed Iran for the strikes—discounting a claim by the Houthis in Yemen to have carried them out—they showed no inclination to retaliate militarily against the perpetrator, though the Iranian action was a blatant act of war. This lack of reaction was as significant as the original air strikes, indicating an awareness that what had happened once could happen again. This caution on the part of Trump was over-interpreted by Iran as a sign that he was averse at all times to a military response. This over-confidence was certainly true of Iranian General Qasem Soleimani who would have ordered the attack. Despite this, he continued to travel openly on scheduled flights until he was killed at Baghdad International Airport by a US drone on 3 January 2020.

The attack in Saudi Arabia, nevertheless, indicated a significant change in the political and military balance of power in the Middle East that is to the disadvantage of the US and its Gulf allies. Its shock effect was enhanced because of the unexpected nature and accuracy of the air strikes, but it was not a one-off event. It was rather the culmination of multiple trends that have eroded US superiority over its rivals and enemies in the region since 2001. Some of these negative developments, as seen from the American point of view, are self-evident: those initial victories in Afghanistan, and later in Iraq, were not as conclusive as the US believed at the time. Instead, they opened the door to the "endless wars" that President Trump complains of and from which he says he wants the US to withdraw.

One reason why the US was less able to get its way in the region was a global phenomenon: the collapse of the Soviet Union in 1991 left the US as the sole superpower, but this status has been increasingly threatened by authoritarian nationalist leaders like Vladimir Putin in Russia and Recep Tayyip Erdogan in Turkey. Old enemies of the US, like Iran and Syria, showed themselves more resilient and adept at combating US hostility than had been expected. Old friends like Saudi Arabia under Crown Prince Mohammed bin Salman—a monarchical version of the trend towards authoritarian nationalists—turned out to be peculiarly disaster prone, starting a horrendous war in Yemen in 2015 and allegedly ordering the grisly murder and dismemberment of Saudi journalist Jamal al-Khashoggi in Istanbul in 2018.

But the ebbing of US political and military power—and the economic strength that underlies it—is not so conclusive as to end all argument about whether or not it is happening and, if so, what to do about it. The US failed to achieve its objectives in wars in Afghanistan, Iraq, and Syria, but it did not suffer decisive military defeats, like the French in the siege of Dien Bien Phu in 1954, or an overwhelming political reverse, like Britain in the Suez Crisis in 1956. It might have been better for the US if it had suffered a similarly traumatic experience, because then its withdrawal from imperial power might be less hesitant and divisive. As it is, there is room left for influential people to argue that repeated setbacks are the result of a culpable weakness of will on the part of those in charge. President Obama, a frequent target for such criticism, lamented how the foreign policy establishment in Washington invariably favoured US military action in Syria, Libya, Afghanistan, and Iraq, ignoring past failures and current risks. He dismissed this way of thinking with resigned contempt, because he had been forced on occasion to go along with it, as "the Washington Playbook." Trump, despite his bellicose rhetoric and denunciations of Obama's supposed timidity, has shown similar caution when faced with the threat of being sucked into messy wars in the Middle East. Almost three years into his presidency, he has yet to start a war, though he has often appeared to be been on verge of doing so.

He has seldom got his own way entirely as US foreign policy becomes a confused compromise between warring factions in Washington. Distrust and loathing between supporters and opponents of Trump are so intense as to preclude a coherent foreign policy. Both Trump and anti-Trump forces have become similarly detached from reality on the ground. Even when Trump's actions have a core of realism they are often encased in layers of craziness, ignorance, and personal abuse. His institutional opponents, by way of contrast, are gently portrayed by the media as clear-eyed public servants and "the only grown-ups in the room," though they are more usually bureaucrat warriors fighting to preserve their fiefdoms with no more idea of what America should be doing in the world than Trump himself.

An example of the way in which domestic factional battles in the Trump era weaken the US as a state is the on/off withdrawal from Syria in 2019. Trump touched off the crisis on 3 October with a tweet greenlighting the Turkish invasion of northern Syria, announcing the immediate pull out of US troops. The timing of the withdrawal was a surprise and its implementation shambolic, maximising the likelihood of the Syrian Kurds being ethnically cleansed by Turkish-led forces. Yet the decision to withdrawal US troops was more realistic than it was given credit for at the time because the US was a small and vulnerable player in north-east Syria at the mercy of decisions taken by leaders in Ankara, Moscow, Tehran, and

Damascus, not to mention the Syrian Kurds themselves. Proponents of keeping US troops in Syria argued that this was necessary to protect the Kurds, deter the Turks, weaken Syrian President Bashar al-Assad, and curb Iranian influence. These may or may not be good things for the US to do, but those advocating them never admitted that to carry out such an ambitious agenda successfully would require a large field US army with tens of thousands of soldiers, as in Iraq in 2003, or, at the very least, a prolonged air campaign in support of dubious jihadi allies on the ground, as in Libya in 2011.

Looked at from the point of view of cold-hearted American self-interest, a US retreat from Syria after the final defeat of Isis in early 2019 was justifiable. But it was announced and carried through with grotesque ineptitude so that the Syrian Kurds, who had lost 11,000 fighting Isis in alliance with the US, found that they were being left to the mercy of Syrian Arab jihadis who acted as the vanguard for the Turkish advance. Soon there were 132,000 refugees on the roads, while those who tried to keep their homes were menaced on every side. And even the US did not make a clean break with what Trump himself had called the Syrian mess. Opposition from the Pentagon, State Department, Republican senators, and media got the decision partially reversed. Trump ordered 500 US troops with armoured vehicles to remain in or to re-enter Syria to occupy the Deir Ezzor oil fields. They did so ostensibly to stop Isis taking them over, though there is no reason to suppose this would happen, and in practice to prevent Assad seizing them back. This weird policy is to be carried out with the US in de facto alliance with the Syrian Kurdish fighters of the People's Protection Units (YPG), who are themselves newly dependent on Syrian government and Russian goodwill to defend them from the Turks. Through such comic opera manoeuvres, the US had ended up with the worst of all possible worlds, having betrayed the Kurds by the manner of its withdrawal, but still failing to extract itself from the Syrian morass. Two months after Trump had announced that US troops would be leaving north-east Syria, the US commander in the Middle East, General Kenneth McKenzie, was quoted as saying: "I don't have an end date [for his troops' departure]."

Debate about how far the Syrian crisis affected US interests and what should be the degree of US engagement there long predates the Trump presidency: Obama and Trump both deciding, in their very different ways, that the risks were high and US interests low. But neither Obama nor Trump had any doubts about the importance of Saudi Arabia to the US, even though Obama had chilly relations with its rulers and Trump warmly embraced them. It is this that makes the Iranian/Houthi attack on the Abqaiq and Khurais oil facilities, and the lack of a US military response, such a political and military turning point.

The success of the Iranian air strikes in hitting such valuable and supposedly well-defended targets gave disconcerting proof to Saudi Arabia and the other Gulf oil states that their US security guarantee is not what it used to be. They are vulnerable to new generations of missiles and drones and vast sums spent by them on air defence systems, mostly sold by US companies, had failed to provide the promised protection. The Pentagon, with an annual budget of $750 billion, and the intelligence services, with a budget of $85 billion, knew nothing about the attacks until they were over. Saudi Arabia was due to spend $58 billion on its military in 2019, but drones costing tens of thousands of dollars had inflicted devastating damage.

If the US and Saudi Arabia are hesitant today to retaliate against Iran, it is because they know, contrary to what they might have believed a year ago, that such a counter-attack might not be the cost-free exercise it once was. Iran has become a "drone superpower" and oil and gas production facilities, along with desalination plants producing much of the fresh water in Saudi Arabia, provide conveniently concentrated high-value targets for precision guided drones and small missiles.

In other words, the military playing field will be a lot more level in any future conflict between a country boasting a sophisticated air force and air defence system and one that lacks them. The trump card for the US, NATO powers, and Israel has hitherto been their overwhelming superiority in airpower over any likely enemy. In the first Gulf War in 1991, the US air force was able to destroy much of the Iraqi infrastructure without fear of retaliation. But this long-standing calculus has been fatally up-ended because drones allow almost anybody to be a player on the cheap when it comes to air strikes.

Anthony Cordesman, a military expert at the Center for Strategic and International Studies in Washington, succinctly sums up the importance of this change, writing that "the strikes on Saudi Arabia provide a clear strategic warning that the US era of air supremacy in the Gulf, and the near US monopoly on precision strike capability, is rapidly fading." He explains that a new generation of drones, cruise missiles, and precision strike ballistic missiles are entering the Iranian inventories and have begun to spread to the Houthis in Yemen and Hezbollah in Lebanon.

These changes in the military balance are significant, but so too are their political counterparts. As events in the second half of 2019 demonstrated, the US is no longer willing to or capable of defending a small temporary ally, like the Syrian Kurds, or big permanent ones like Saudi Arabia. Trump's strain of American nationalism is genuinely isolationist in the sense of suspecting foreign alliances to be costly entanglements. His inaction after Abqaiq should not have been a surprise because it had been telegraphed ahead over the summer as Iran engaged in pinprick attacks on Saudi Arabia, UAE, and their allies. Over the course of a few months, Iran placed limpet mines on an oil tanker in UAE waters, hijacked a UK flagged ship in retaliation for the UK seizing one of its vessels, and most tellingly of all, fired a surface-to-air missile to shoot down a $130 million US surveillance drone over the Strait of Hormuz on 20 June. It is fair to assume that the Iranians orchestrated all these attacks, calculating carefully what they could get away with without provoking massive retaliation or an all-out war. Transparent though their responsibility was, they sought to retain deniability and avoided killing anybody, the intention being to send a warning message rather to inflict maximum damage. They got their calculations wrong in the end, but it remains unclear how the US would respond to a resumption of attacks on US allies as opposed to US troops or embassies. In the wake of the Soleimani assassination, Iran might be less aggressive, but in the long term this type of irregular warfare is Iran's main counter to the US policy of "maximum pressure" on Iran—effectively a tight economic siege—and will not be abandoned while sanctions continue.

THREE

The Death of al-Baghdadi

21 November 2019

America's first act in the war on Iraq was an attempt to kill Saddam Hussein. In the early hours of the morning of 20 March 2003, forty cruise missiles were launched and bunker-buster bombs dropped on a compound on the outskirts of Baghdad where US intelligence wrongly believed him to be staying. Three years later a US air strike succeeded in killing Abu Musab al-Zarqawi, the founder of al-Qaeda in Iraq, the organisation that would become Isis. Neither Saddam's survival nor al-Zarqawi's death had much impact on the course of events, but the White House remained convinced that eliminating leaders and other high-value targets was a war-winning strategy. There is little evidence to support this theory; but still, the assassination of demonic opponents is clearly good politics, allowing American presidents to impress voters with decisive action amid what have been messy, inconclusive wars.

The death last month of Abu Bakr al-Baghdadi, who had led Isis since 2010, in a US raid in north-west Syria was celebrated in a self-glorifying speech by Donald Trump as proof that Isis had been definitively destroyed. The claim had some substance: al-Baghdadi, who five years earlier had declared himself caliph in the al-Nuri mosque in Mosul, was the most important surviving symbol of Isis as a territorial state. The possession of an actual state—at its height it stretched across Syria and Iraq, from west of the Euphrates to east of the Tigris—distinguished Isis from other militarised Islamic cults, like Osama bin Laden's al-Qaeda. For a brief, astonishing period, this reborn caliphate governed, in brutal but well-organised fashion, a population of ten million, claiming divine inspiration in its pursuit of true Islamic principles. Its rise was spectacular, but so was its fall: it lost its final piece of territory, a village in the desert on the Syrian side of the border, six months before al-Baghdadi's death. He was reduced to moving from hideout to hideout in Idlib province, near the Turkish border, far from the Isis heartlands, with little control over Isis strategy or tactics—though it was always unclear whether he actually exercised full command.

The process of Isis decision-making over the last ten years—and al-Baghdadi's role in it—is a mystery. If he was in total control of operations between 2011 and 2014, he can take credit for rebuilding Isis: he took advantage of the opportunities offered by the disintegration of Syria, and of Sunni resistance to a sectarian Shia government in Iraq. But after Isis captured Mosul in June 2014, almost every decision taken or endorsed by al-Baghdadi was disastrous. The caliphate in any case posed too much of a threat to other powers to last for long, but al-Baghdadi accelerated its demise by effectively declaring war against the entire world. Not everyone thought it in their interests to fight the new theocratic quasi-state: Kurds in both Syria and Iraq at first stayed neutral, opportunistically expanding their own territories as Isis battled the central governments in Baghdad and Damascus. But at the peak of Isis success, its fighters attacked the Kurds in both countries without provocation, making enemies of them—and, fatally, guaranteeing US involvement on the Kurdish side. In al-Baghdadi's vision, to be outside Isis was to be an infidel by definition. Inevitably, the list of his opponents was all-encompassing: both the Americans and the Russians; both the Syrian government and the non-Isis armed opposition to that government. Countries which had once tolerated Isis—Turkey allowed 40,000 Isis fighters to cross the border into Isis territory—found that such covert co-operation was no guarantee that they themselves wouldn't become a target.

Isis systematically publicised its atrocities on the internet in order to terrorise its opponents, a tactic which at first worked well but ended up mobilising those it threatened—such as the Shia in Iraq, who outnumber the Sunni population three to one. Outnumbered and outgunned, Isis would inevitably be ground down and crushed, with the Sunni community as a whole in the northern tier of the Middle East between the Iranian border and the Mediterranean suffering by association in the wake of their defeat.

The terror inflicted by Isis attacks around the world is not easily forgotten: 142 killed in Yemen when two Shia mosques were bombed; 103 peace protesters killed by a suicide bomber in Ankara; 224 blown up on a Metrojet flight to St Petersburg; 131 shot or bombed in the Paris attacks of 2015; 86 run down by a truck in Nice the following year; 593 killed in an operation in the Philippines the year after that; 311 killed when attackers opened fire during Friday prayers at a mosque in Sinai; 149 killed by a suicide bomber at an election rally in Pakistan—not to mention the eight killed in the UK in 2017 after a van drove into pedestrians on London Bridge.

So the prospect that Isis may still fight on remains a live concern around the world. Americans and Europeans may not care what happens to the Kurds, or who rules in Damascus and Baghdad, but they do worry about Isis—because Isis is a threat to themselves. In the coming presidential election campaign, Trump will try to capitalise on the assassination of al-Baghdadi, as Hillary Clinton tried to capitalise on the killing of Osama bin Laden in 2011, however little she had to do with it. It's a dangerous strategy: it takes only one spectacular attack, like the co-ordinated series of suicide bombings at churches and hotels in Sri Lanka in April this year, for Isis yet again to contradict claims of its demise. Its defeats on the battlefield—especially the loss of Mosul and Raqqa after the sieges of 2017—have destroyed it as a territorial entity. But al-Baghdadi's death makes its resurrection in new forms no less likely—perhaps more. Al-Qaeda franchises had greater success after the killing of bin Laden than they did during the years of his holdout in Abbottabad. Al-Baghdadi was a symbol of Isis in victory, but also of Isis in defeat. If it is to be revived, it will have to be with new methods and modified ideology: no longer seeking self-isolation above all, no longer punishing anyone not wholeheartedly in its own camp. Al-Baghdadi's removal may make such a transformation easier to carry out.

That said, the obstacles are formidable. Until its apotheosis in 2014, opponents of Isis were willfully blind to its growing power, or thought they could turn it to their own advantage. They did not find it ominous that Isis had seized Fallujah, thirty miles west of Baghdad, and that the Iraqi army could not get them out. Earlier that month, Barak Obama had told David Remnick of the *New Yorker* that, compared to al-Qaeda, Isis was a junior varsity basketball team playing out of its league; a few months later, its fighters emerged from the desert to defeat six Iraqi army divisions and capture Mosul.

Wary of making the same mistake again, the US and its allies have remained on the alert for any sign that Isis may be back in business. But it is easy also to overestimate the threat it poses. If it is to do more than launch sporadic guerrilla attacks in isolated rural areas and stage periodic massacres of civilians abroad—if it is to re-emerge as a serious force in the region— Isis would have to persuade shattered Sunni communities and tribes in its former centres of power in Syria and Iraq that armed resistance is once again both feasible and necessary. Over the last decade, millions of them have had to flee their homes as cities from Aleppo and Homs to Mosul and Ramadi have been pounded into rubble by air strikes and artillery fire. US Central Command reports that between 2014 and 2019, it carried out a total of 34,573 air strikes on targets in Syria and Iraq, almost all of them in Sunni areas. Ferocious resistance by Isis fighters in Mosul and Raqqa resulted in unthinkable numbers of civilian dead. During the last months of the siege, I spoke to many people trapped in the Old City of Mosul. By the time the siege was over, everyone I had been in contact with was dead: killed by coalition air strikes if they stayed in their houses, or by Isis snipers if they tried to escape.

Until recently, then, the chances of an Isis revival looked slim. Friends and enemies had both suffered the murderous violence of its rule and had no wish to repeat the experience. An organisation as ruthless as Isis isn't going to seek popular approval before it acts, but it can't rely wholly on intimidation to gather recruits for a new campaign: it needs to retain some sympathy among the Sunni community at large. More important, it has always thrived on chaos: with its rivals at one another's throats, it could exploit the vacuum of political and military power. For much of this year, chaos seemed to be on the way out, as normal life gradually returned to former battle zones in both Syria and Iraq—unpropitious conditions for Isis. But in October, the situation changed.

I was in Baghdad on the evening of 1 October, staying at the Baghdad Hotel near Tahrir Square in the city centre. I was planning to visit Diyala Governorate, north of Baghdad, the following day. The area had once been an Isis stronghold, and I wanted to see whether it was making a comeback. From my hotel, I heard the distant sound of shots. They could have been in celebration of a wedding, or victory in a football match, but the gunfire went on too long for those things to make sense, so I went down to the lobby to find out what was happening. As I reached the front door, a man came in from the street to say that the security services were shooting at protesters;

ten of them had been killed. Later in the evening, I got in touch with a doctor at Medical City, a hospital complex not far from Tahrir Square, who said that ten dead was an underestimate and that he himself had seen four bodies. Meanwhile, the government was claiming a death toll of one.

Nobody had been expecting violence. By Baghdad standards, it was a small protest—some 3,000 people on the streets—and it was motivated by social and economic issues: unemployment, government corruption, and inadequate electricity and water supply. I had been told about it the previous day by a group of young men demonstrating opposite the foreign ministry, where they were demanding jobs appropriate to their status as university graduates. They said they had been camped out there for forty-three days and were intending to go to the rally in Tahrir Square, but they didn't seem to be expecting trouble. Street protests have become a familiar part of Iraqi politics over the last few years. In 2016, demonstrators broke into the Green Zone and ransacked parliament and the prime minister's office. Last year in Basra, protests over water and electricity shortages led to the setting ablaze of government and party offices, though only twelve people were reported killed.

Last month in Baghdad, the response of the security forces was very different. And, as it turned out, not only of the security forces: also patrolling the streets were the pro-Iranian factions of the predominantly Shia paramilitary Hashd al-Shaabi, or Popular Mobilisation Units. When the protesters tried to cross the al-Jumhuriya bridge leading from Tahrir Square towards the Green Zone, they were met with live fire.

The next day I drove through Tahrir Square, where protesters and soldiers were eyeing each other nervously during a lull in the demonstrations. A man was lying on the pavement on a slip road leading up to the square, but I couldn't see whether he was injured or dead. Shortly afterwards the government declared a twenty-four-hour curfew in Baghdad, a city of seven million people, as well as in towns and cities in the overwhelmingly Shia southern part of Iraq. It cut off access to the internet in the hope of making it impossible to organise protests—but the effect was that smaller rallies began popping up all over Baghdad. My contact in Medical City reported that his hospital had been invaded by pro-Iranian Shia paramilitaries—members of either Kata'ib Hezbollah or Asa'ib Ahl al-Haq—who were beating injured protesters as they lay in their beds. He complained to one of the paramilitary commanders, who hit him with a baton and told him to mind his own business.

News of the protests was being broadcast by local media. In an attempt to put an end to the publicity, members of a group called Saraya Talia al-Khurusani invaded TV stations, wrecking studios and smashing equipment. In the streets, riot police fired heavy-duty tear gas grenades directly at protesters, inflicting serious and, in some cases, fatal injuries. According to surgeons who treated the wounded, paramilitary snipers were aiming for the head or chest. The government announced that these tactics were prohibited and would not be repeated—but it was clearly no longer in control of the way the protests were being policed. The use of maximum force proved counterproductive since, over the next few days, the demonstrations gathered in size, but whoever was issuing the orders was apparently determined that this was the only way to deal with them.

That person was reportedly the Iranian general Qasem Soleimani, head of Iran's elite al-Quds Brigade. Soleimani had flown into Baghdad airport on 2 October and taken a helicopter to the Green Zone to chair a security meeting—taking the place of the usual chair, Iraq's prime minister. There could be no plainer demonstration of Iranian power over Iraqi policy, or of the arrogance with which it has been exercised. Soleimani is the architect of Iran's regional security policy, determined to maintain Iranian influence by every means available as the US struggles to realise Trump's declared ambition of containing it. In recent confrontations, Soleimani, who has a reputation for being a skilled commander, has repeatedly outmanoeuvred the US and its Gulf allies. But success appears to have gone to his head. At the meeting in the Green Zone, he made clear his belief that there was only one way to respond to the protests. "This happened in Iran and we got it under control," he is reported as having said. He was presumably referring to Iran's successful repression of the Green Movement that sprang up there in 2009—but then there had been no indiscriminate shooting into crowds, or singling out of movement leaders by snipers. By the end of October, the strategy as implemented in Iraq had resulted in the deaths of at least 250 protesters—the actual figure is probably much higher—with no sign of the demonstrations slowing. What's more, they have taken an increasingly anti-Iranian turn: on 3 November, protesters set fire to the Iranian consulate in the Shia holy city of Karbala.

Like so many security chiefs down the centuries, Soleimani has helped fuel the revolutionary situation he was trying to prevent. As an Iraqi friend told me, "shooting people isn't going to work because too many of them have nothing left to lose." Repression on this scale was unexpected, as well as unwise. In the days before the rally that led to the first shootings, I spoke to the commanders of several of the pro-Iranian paramilitary groups, none of whom seemed to be anticipating a crisis. I asked them how they thought the US-Iran face-off would affect Iraq. Qais al-Khazali, the leader of Asa'ib Ahl al-Haq, was confident that in Iraq as elsewhere, Iran knew how to handle tensions in a way that would stop short of full-scale military confrontation. There would be no war, he said, "because Trump does not want one." Abu Ala al-Walai, the leader of Kata'ib Sayyid al-Shuhada, was more apprehensive: a recent drone attack, which he blamed on Israel, had destroyed fifty tonnes of arms at al-Saqr, a base under his command on the outskirts of Baghdad. I went to see it; evidently, a giant blast had torn the place apart. "The big new development," Abu Ala said, "is that Israel has come to Iraq." But the reaction—the overreaction—of the Iranians and their paramilitary allies to the protests in Baghdad may be a sign that they interpret events on the ground in the light of their struggle with the US. At the end of October, Iran's supreme leader, Ayatollah Ali Khamenei, declared that "the US and western intelligence agencies, with the help of money from regional countries, are instigating unrest in the region. I advise Lebanon and Iraq to make it a priority to stabilise these security threats."

Mass protests erupted in Lebanon on 17 October after the government tried to introduce a tax on the use of voice messaging systems like WhatsApp and FaceTime. As in Iraq, economic and social grievances have gradually escalated into generalised opposition towards a corrupt and dysfunctional political system. As in Iraq, pro-Iranian militias—in this case, supporters of Hezbollah—have used force against demonstrators, attacking protest camps in central Beirut. In both Iraq and Lebanon, Iran and its Shia allies feel that the political status quo they have fought for is at risk. Paranoid that the US may be playing its part in encouraging dissent, they have opted for repression. If sustained for long enough, this strategy may succeed, not because force will necessarily win out but because in neither Iraq nor Lebanon have protesters given much indication that they have any concrete ideas about how to replace the present discredited system—or with what.

As these events were unfolding in Lebanon and Iraq, there was similar unrest in Syria—but for entirely different reasons. Trump had long declared his intention to bring home American troops, or at least to extract them from the Syrian "mess," and the withdrawal of the 2,000-strong US military force in the north-east of the country began on 6 October. The time had come: the troops were there to fight Isis and Isis had been defeated. The idea—pushed by Washington's foreign policy establishment—that this small force could simultaneously protect the Kurds, defend against Iranian influence, weaken Bashar al-Assad, and deter Russia had always been unrealistic. Recep Tayyip Erdogan in Ankara and Assad in Damascus, much though they dislike each other, were united in their determination to eliminate Rojava, the Syrian Kurdish mini-state which—with the assistance of American airpower and a limited number of US troops on the ground—had been established after the Syrian army withdrew from the area in 2012.

A US withdrawal may have been inevitable, but its shambolic on/off nature was not. Unlike the White House, the Pentagon wanted to keep a presence in Syria—however unclear its purpose in a region now under the sway of Russia, Iran, and Assad—and had not prepared contingency plans for withdrawal. In the ensuing shambles, the US military bombed its former headquarters in a cement factory near the city of Manbij and abandoned other bases to the Russians and the Syrian army. Trump's tweet greenlighting a Turkish invasion of Rojava was—understandably—portrayed in the US media as gross treachery towards America's brave allies, but it was no surprise to anyone in the region. In early 2018 Turkey invaded the Kurdish enclave of Afrin, north of Aleppo, and engaged in ethnic cleansing—no objection was raised in the US or elsewhere. Erdogan made it clear then that Rojava would be next. I was in Rojava at the time of Afrin's fall and spoke to Kurdish leaders, who knew that fending off both Erdogan and Assad would be next to impossible. The area they controlled was flat and indefensible, so they had no real military option. Much of the population lived close to the Turkish border and even a small-scale Turkish incursion would turn them into refugees. These fears have now been realised, with some 132,000 Kurds displaced from the border region.

There was clearly a degree of complicity between the main players in Syria after Trump's withdrawal of US protection from the Kurds, though all sides publicly expressed shock at what was happening. The Turkish invasion was limited to the area between the towns of Ras al-Ayn and Tal Abyad, involving only about 6,000 regular Turkish troops alongside a much larger force of irregular troops nominally belonging to the opposition Syrian National Army but operating under the authority of the Turkish army. In the event, the carve-up went smoothly from the point of view of its beneficiaries: the Turks took a couple of border towns; Russian and Syrian forces raced into cities like Manbij, Raqqa, and Kobani. Erdogan achieved his main aim: the break-up of Rojava and an end to the US-Kurdish military alliance. Both events have also benefited Iran, which faces problems with the Kurds within its own borders, while Russia has reinforced its position as the most important player in the Syrian conflict. The Kurds are the losers they always feared they would be. They are now trying to rescue whatever they can from the wreckage and to limit the ethnic cleansing of their communities by Turkey.

How much does Isis stand to gain from the collapse of the US-Kurdish coalition it has been fighting for the last five years? The turmoil will be all the greater because of Trump's bizarre decision to reverse course and increase the number of US troops in the oil fields of eastern Syria. All this adds up to the sort of confusion that Isis has traditionally taken advantage of. Will it similarly be able to benefit from the situation in Iraq, as a disintegrating government grapples with an incipient uprising among its own Shia supporters? It may be that Isis no longer has the strength to exploit the division among its enemies. Movements that combine ideological fanaticism with military expertise can be lethally effective in warfare, but they need victories to validate the justness of their cause. Such victories now seem far off, but the removal of al-Baghdadi may make it easier for Isis to adapt to circumstances that are moving in its favour.

FOUR

Could Isis Have Won? Could It Return?

11 November 2019

Could Isis have won the war in Iraq and Syria? Was it always inevitable that the reborn caliphate declared in 2014 after the capture of Mosul would be eliminated as a territorial entity less than five years later? These are important questions that are seldom asked because many observers condemn Isis as an unmitigated evil and fail to analyse its strengths and weaknesses. But these are important if we are to understand the chances of Isis resurrecting itself in Syria and Iraq or re-emerging under a different name with ostensibly different objectives. It is worth asking: what were the religious, military, political, social, and economic ingredients that went into creating and sustaining this extraordinary militarised cult that for a considerable amount of time controlled a state that extended from the outskirts of Baghdad to the hills overlooking the Mediterranean.

In retrospect, military defeats and victories acquire a false sense of inevitability about them, whether we are looking at the German defeat of France in 1940 or the claimed elimination of the last vestiges of Isis in 2019. Historians study long-term trends, but contemporary witnesses are more aware of the degree to which good or bad decisions determined the outcome of a conflict and that the result might have gone the other way. For instance, what would have happened if Isis had not attacked the Kurds, who would have been happy to stay neutral in both Iraq and Syria in the second half of 2014? This diverted Isis from its spectacularly successful assault on central government forces in both countries and precipitated the devastating intervention of US airpower. If the Isis leader Abu Bakr al-Baghdadi had not split the jihadi movement in Syria in 2013 by seeking to absorb his former proxy, the al-Nusra Front, back into the mother organisation, then Isis would have been in a much stronger position to fight a long war. Probably its very fanaticism—and its belief that it had a monopoly of divine support—prevented it showing greater political adroitness, but we cannot be sure.

As surviving Isis fighters staggered out of the ruins of their last stronghold at Baghuz on the Euphrates River on 23 March 2019, it was difficult to recapture the sense of dread that they had spread at the height of their success. I was in Baghdad in June 2014 when their columns of vehicles packed with gunmen were sweeping south as the regular Iraqi army divisions broke into fragments and fled before them. Some Iraqis, with a sense of history, compared the onslaught to that of the Mongol horsemen who captured and sacked Baghdad in 1258. Official spokesmen on television would stay silent or announce fictitious victories, so I would call policemen in towns in the path of Isis and ask what was happening. Often the calls revealed that it was advancing with frightening speed against crumbling or non-existent opposition. I remember thinking that reporters in Paris in May and June 1940 must have tracked the advance of German panzer divisions towards Paris with similar trepidation.

I learned that Isis had captured without resistance Saddam Hussein's home city of Tikrit and had occupied the town of Baiji next to Iraq's biggest oil refinery. Their fighters were going house-to-house examining identity cards and, to the dismay of inhabitants, taking away the IDs of unmarried women to be photocopied, presumably as prospective brides. I did not know at that stage the full details of what became known as the Camp Speicher massacre that Isis had carried out, slaughtering 1,700 Shia air force recruits outside Tikrit. Later I saw a horrible video of an executioner shooting the terrified young men in the head with a pistol on a landing stage by the Tigris, so their bodies fell into the water. On a bluff overlooking the river, the jihadis had dumped the bodies into pits amid old half-ruined palaces of Saddam Hussein.

Isis might have made a quick dash for Baghdad in a bid to create a mass panic among the capital's Shia majority. There were rumours that the Sunni minority inside the city would rise up in coordination with Isis units attacking from the outside. I suspected that talk of Isis "sleeper cells" was exaggerated and that it was outrunning its military resources.

Moreover, the Shia Grand Ayatollah Ali al-Sistani had called on 13 June for a mass levy of all Iraqis to support what was left of the Iraqi armed forces. There were negative signs as well: the Iraqi government seemed paralysed by its surprise defeat in Mosul and state TV was broadcasting undiluted propaganda, though viewers noticed that there were no pictures of the morale-boosting but non-existent successes. Isis might not be able to seize Baghdad, but that did not mean they would not try. Hotels in Jordan were reported to be full of Iraqi MPs and ministers. Hoshyar Zebari, the foreign minister, told me to look closely at the entrances to other ministries: if there were new sandbags visible, as was the case with his own ministry, that meant that the minister was still there. But, if the sandbags were old and torn and had not been renewed, then the probability was that the minister had already sought safety elsewhere.

The moment of opportunity for Isis lasted for about two months in the summer of 2014, when they were carrying all before them in both Iraq and Syria. They had captured the largest oil and gas fields in Syria and inflicted a string of defeats on the Syrian army. Their atrocities, well publicised on social media, created real terror among their opponents. Then on 6 August, they made a strategic change of direction, the motives for which are still one of the great mysteries of the war: they shifted the weight of their attack away from the Iraqi armies and invaded the territory held by the Kurdistan Regional Government, which would have been happy to stay on the by-lines and exploit the weakness of the central government to its own advantage. Two days later, President Barack Obama ordered US jets to start "targeted air strikes" on Isis artillery units.

The following month Isis launched a full-scale assault on the Kurdish city of Kobani and, in ferocious fighting in September and October, captured most of it. But the Syrian Kurds fought hard and the US launched air strikes that reduced Isis-held Kobani to rubble and may have killed as many as 2,000 Isis fighters during the four-month siege. It was the movement's first failure and it persuaded the White House and the Pentagon that in the Syrian Kurdish People's Protection Units, they had at last found an effective ally on the ground in Syria. The US-Kurdish alliance forged in 2014 lasted for five years until the last strongholds of Isis were over-run when it was ruthlessly discarded by Donald Trump, who gave the green light to a Turkish invasion.

Isis military capacity always exceeded its political ability. Its assault on the Kurds may have been encouraged by Turkey, which was allowing volunteers and supplies to move freely across the Turkish-Syrian border. The Turkish consulate stayed in Mosul after Isis stormed the city, though its diplomats came to regret this. Another explanation, though the two do not contradict each other, is arrogance and belief in divine support that had apparently been confirmed by miraculous victories in 2014. Cult-like military movements with the belief that they have a monopoly of truth and righteousness are a potent force on the battlefield because their members are willing to die for the cause. But because they divide the world into black and white, right and wrong, they have a self-defeating pattern of treating all the world as their enemies and are incapable of creating alliances: It may be that as a militarised Islamic cult, which saw the world in terms of friends and enemies, Isis was ideologically incapable of the flexibility necessary to make even a temporary accommodation with anybody outside its camp. A similar mistake was made by two movements that somewhat resemble Isis: the Khmer Rouge, who took over in Cambodia in the 1970s despite being bombed by American B-52s, and the Shining Path movement in Peru in the 1980s. The Khmer Rouge won their war against government forces but then turned on their former mentors in Vietnam, with disastrous consequences for themselves. The Shining Path came from nowhere, had few resources and no allies, but held a large part of the Peruvian highlands for years using unrelenting violence against all comers. Isis was a similarly self-isolating fanatical movement that was ultimately overwhelmed by the sheer number of its enemies: Iraqi and Syrian governments, Iraqi and Syrian Kurds, the US and Russia, Iran and Turkey.

Isis went down, but it did not go down without a fight. It developed a form of warfare which enabled it to withstand for a long time the attack of its better-equipped and far more numerous enemies. Isis units were mobile light infantry specialising in irregular warfare of a type in which suicide bombers, snipers, and Improvised Explosive Devices (IEDs) played a central role. "I cannot think of a single successful armed opposition attack in Syria that did not use suicide bombers," a foreign military specialist in Damascus told me. The same was true of Iraq where even after the Iraqi army was receiving close ground support from US air strikes, Isis was able to capture the main government stronghold in Ramadi, the capital of Anbar province, on 17 May 2015, and, a few days later, seize the famed city of Palmyra in Syria.

Religious fanaticism wedded to military efficiency is a formidable weapon, but the two do not automatically come together. Isis was the lineal descendent of al-Qaeda in Iraq, established by Abu Musab al-Zarqawi in 2004. It was notorious for its ferocity and sectarianism, but US officers did not rate its infantry skills very highly. This was to change after its resurrection on the back of what was essentially a Sunni Arab uprising starting in Syria and spreading to Iraq in 2012–13. Some commentators have argued that the military expertise of Isis shows the influence of highly trained men who had once belonged to Saddam Hussein's Republican Guard and Special Forces. Isis doubtless benefited from their experience: the predominantly Sunni Arab city of Mosul was the main recruiting ground for the Iraqi officer corps under Saddam and his defence ministers normally came from Mosul and Nineveh province that surrounded it.

A more convincing explanation for the military effectiveness of Isis is simply that it had experience. By the time a few thousand of its fighters took Mosul in June 2014, some of its commanders would have been fighting for a decade. Considering this, I was reminded of the reply of a UN military expert in Lebanon whom I had asked why the Hezbollah fighters were such good soldiers. He said: "If you have been fighting the Israeli army for a dozen years and you are still alive, you are probably pretty good at your job."

The same was true of Isis: It had fought the Americans and a chaotic but still numerous and well-armed Iraqi army and assorted militias. Its tactics were fluid and sophisticated: its motorised columns attacked unexpectedly from different directions at the same time, while its local commanders (emirs) were given objectives at the last moment, but would decide themselves on the best mode of attack. Fighting in the open became too costly in the face of US air superiority, so Isis tactics changed accordingly. In the sieges of Mosul and Raqqa—main topics in this book—Isis deployed swiftly moving squads in built-up areas, sometimes with a guide on a motorcycle. They would set up a sniping position in a house, break through its walls to enable quick entry and escape, and then, after opening fire, rapidly retreat before their position was identified and hit by a retaliatory air strike. Often, the only casualties were the civilians who lived in the house who had been locked in a room and could not get out in time. US and other western air forces boasted of the accuracy of their missiles and smart bombs, but this was beside the point if they did not know where Isis fighters were hiding. Despite the vaunted concern about civilian casualties—and condemnation of the Russians and Syrian government for targeting civilians—the US air force turned Raqqa and the Old City of Mosul into heaps of ruins, much as the Russians and Syrian government had done in east Aleppo and Homs, along with Daraya, Barzeh, and eastern Ghouta in Damascus.

The military prowess of Isis was flattered by the weaknesses and divisions of its enemies, particularly during the early years of its resurgence between 2011 and 2014. This was certainly true of Iraq, where the state was thoroughly criminalised and its army so corrupt that colonels would pay $200,000 and generals $1 million for their jobs. They paid so much because they knew that they could turn a profit by pocketing the pay of "ghost" battalions that never existed or half the salaries of soldiers who never went near a barracks. On top of that, there was the flow of protection money from checkpoints that acted like customs posts and levied a charge on every passing vehicle.

I had written a series of articles about the state of Iraq in 2013, ten years after the US-led invasion and the overthrow of Saddam Hussein. I thought I was shockproof when it came to corruption in the Middle East, but, even so, I found that the kleptocracy in Iraq beggared belief: during my first days in Baghdad while writing the series mentioned above, there was heavy rain. This led to streets in large parts of the city turning into dirty grey lakes of floodwater and sewage, though the authorities had supposedly spent $7 billion on building a new drainage system for the capital. It turned out not to exist and the money allocated to it had all been stolen.

At the end of the day, an Isis blitzkrieg and a dysfunctional Iraqi military were not enough to give Isis victory. Its use of mass terror, publicised by the internet, as a strategic weapon was successful in intimidating many people, but it made even more of them determined to fight to the death. For a fleeting moment after the fall of Mosul, Isis might have generated enough panic to break into Baghdad, but the opportunity was soon gone and would never return.

FIVE

2016: Three States on the Edge of Disaster

19 February 2016

The war in Syria and Iraq has produced two new de facto states in the last five years and enabled a third quasi-state greatly to expand its territory and power. The two new states, though unrecognised internationally, are stronger militarily and politically than most members of the UN. One is Isis, which established its caliphate in eastern Syria and western Iraq in the summer of 2014 after capturing Mosul and defeating the Iraqi army. The second is Rojava, as the Syrian Kurds call the area they gained control of when the Syrian army largely withdrew in 2012, and which now, thanks to a series of victories over Isis, stretches across northern Syria between the Tigris and Euphrates. In Iraq, the Kurdistan Regional Government (KRG), already highly autonomous, took advantage of Isis's destruction of Baghdad's authority in northern Iraq to expand its territory by 40 percent, taking over areas long disputed between itself and Baghdad, including the Kirkuk oil fields and some mixed Kurdish-Arab districts.

The question is whether these radical changes in the political geography of the Middle East will persist—or to what extent they will persist—when the present conflict is over. Isis is likely to be destroyed eventually, such is the pressure from its disunited but numerous enemies, though its adherents will remain a force in Iraq, Syria, and the rest of the Islamic world. The Kurds are in a stronger position, benefiting as they do from US support, but that support exists only because they provide some 120,000 ground troops [35,000 each for two Peshmerga groups belonging to the Kurdistan

Democratic Party (KDP) and Patriotic Union of Kurdistan (PUK) in northern Iraq and 50,000 Kurdish led the Syrian Democratic Forces (SDF) forces in north-east Syria] which, in co-operation with the US-led coalition air forces, have proved an effective and politically acceptable counter to Isis. The Kurds fear that this support will evaporate if and when Isis is defeated and they will be left to the mercy of resurgent central governments in Iraq and Syria as well as Turkey and Saudi Arabia.

"We don't want to be used as cannon fodder to take Raqqa," a Syrian Kurdish leader in Rojava told me last year. I heard the same thing this month 500 miles to the east, in KRG territory near Halabja on the Iranian border, from Muhammad Haji Mahmud, a veteran Peshmerga commander and general secretary of the Socialist Party, who led 1,000 fighters to defend Kirkuk from Isis in 2014. His son Atta was killed in the battle. He said he worried that "once Mosul is liberated and Isis defeated, the Kurds won't have the same value internationally." Without this support, the KRG would be unable to hold onto its disputed territories.

The rise of the Kurdish states isn't welcomed by any country in the region, though some—including the governments in Baghdad and Damascus—have found the development to be temporarily in their interest and are in any case too weak to resist it. But Turkey has been appalled to find that the Syrian uprising of 2011, which it hoped would usher in an era of Turkish influence spreading across the Middle East, has instead produced a Kurdish state that controls half of the Syrian side of Turkey's 550-mile southern border. Worse, the ruling party in Rojava is the Democratic Union Party (PYD), which in all but name is the Syrian branch of the Kurdistan Workers' Party (PKK), against which Ankara has been fighting a guerrilla war since 1984. The PYD denies the link, but in every PYD office, there is a picture on the wall of the PKK's leader, Abdullah Ocalan, who has been in a Turkish prison since 1999.

In the year since Isis was finally defeated in the siege of the Syrian Kurdish city of Kobani, Rojava has expanded territorially in every direction as its leaders repeatedly ignore Turkish threats of military action against them. Last June, the Syrian Kurdish People's Protection Units (YPG) captured Tal Abyad, an important crossing point on the Turkish border north of Raqqa, allowing the PYD to link up two of its three main enclaves, around the cities of Kobani and Qamishli; it is now trying to reach the third enclave, further west, at Afrin. These swift advances are possible only because the Kurdish forces are operating under a US-led air umbrella that vastly multiplies their firepower. I was just east of Tal Abyad shortly before the final YPG attack and coalition aircraft roared continuously overhead. In both Syria and Iraq, the Kurds identify targets, call in air strikes, and then act as a mopping-up force. Where Isis stands and fights, it suffers heavy casualties. In the siege of Kobani, which lasted for four and a half months, 2,200 Isis fighters were killed, most of them by US air strikes.

Ankara has warned several times that if the Kurds move west towards Afrin, the Turkish army will intervene. In particular, it stipulated that the YPG must not cross the Euphrates: this was a "red line" for Turkey. But when in December the YPG sent its Arab proxy militia, the Syrian Democratic Forces, across the Euphrates at the Tishrin Dam, the Turks did nothing—partly because the advance was supported at different points by both American and Russian air strikes on Isis targets. Turkish objections have become increasingly frantic since the start of the year because the YPG and the Syrian army, though their active collaboration is unproven, have launched what amounts to a pincer movement on the most important supply lines of Isis and non-Isis opposition, which run down a narrow corridor between the Turkish border and Aleppo, once Syria's largest city.

On 2 February, the Syrian army, backed by Russian air strikes, cut the main road link towards Aleppo, and a week later, the SDF captured Menagh airbase from the al-Qaeda-affiliated al-Nusra Front, which Turkey has been accused of covertly supporting in the past. On 14 February, Turkish artillery started firing shells at the forces that had captured the base and demanded that they evacuate it. The complex combination of militias, armies, and ethnic groups struggling to control this small but vital area north of Aleppo makes the fighting there confusing even by Syrian standards. But if the opposition is cut off from Turkey for long, it will be seriously and perhaps fatally weakened. The Sunni states—notably Turkey, Saudi Arabia, and Qatar—will have failed in their long campaign to overthrow Bashar al-Assad. Turkey will be faced with the prospect of a hostile PKK-run statelet along its southern flank, making it much harder for it to quell the low-level but long-running PKK-led insurgency among its own seventeen million Kurdish minority.

Erdogan is said to have wanted Turkey to intervene militarily in Syria since May of last year, but until now, he has been restrained by his army commanders. They argued that Turkey would be entering a highly complicated war in which it would be opposed by the US, Russia, Iran, the Syrian army, the PYD, and Isis while its only allies would be Saudi Arabia and some of the Gulf monarchies. Entry into the Syrian war would certainly be a tremendous risk for Turkey, which, despite all its thunderous denunciations of the PYD and YPG as "terrorists," has largely confined itself to small acts of sometimes vindictive retaliation. Ersin Umut Güler, a Turkish Kurd actor and director in Istanbul, was refused permission to bring home for burial the body of his brother Aziz, who had been killed fighting Isis in Syria. Before he stepped on a landmine, Aziz had been with the YPG, but he was a Turkish citizen and belonged to a radical socialist Turkish party— not the PKK. "It's like something out of *Antigone*," Ersin said. His father had travelled to Syria and was refusing to return without the body, but the authorities weren't relenting.

The Turkish response to the rise of Rojava is belligerent in tone but ambivalent in practice. On one day, a minister threatens a full-scale ground invasion and on the next another official rules it out or makes it conditional on US participation, which is unlikely. Turkey blamed a car bomb in Ankara that killed twenty-eight people on 17 February on the YPG, which must increase the chances of intervention, but in the recent past, Turkish actions have been disjointed and counterproductive. When on 24 November, a Turkish F-16 shot down a Russian bomber in what appears to have been a carefully planned attack, the predictable result was that Russia sent sophisticated fighter aircraft and anti-aircraft missile systems to establish air supremacy over northern Syria. This means that if Turkey were to launch a ground invasion, it would have to do so without air cover and its troops would be exposed to bombing by Russian and Syrian planes.

Many Kurdish political leaders argue that a Turkish military invasion is unlikely: Fuad Hussein, the KRG's president's chief of staff, told me in Erbil last month that "if Turkey was going to intervene then it would have done so before shooting down the Russian jet"—though this assumes, of course, that Turkey knows how to act in its own best interests. He argued that the conflict would be decided by two factors: who is winning on the battlefield and the co-operation between the US and Russia. "If the crisis is to be solved," he said, "it will be solved by agreement between the superpowers"—and in the Middle East, at least Russia has regained superpower status. A new loose alliance between the US and Russia, though interrupted by bouts of Cold War-style rivalry, produced an agreement in Munich on 12 February for aid to be delivered to besieged Syrian towns and cities and a "cessation of hostilities" to be followed by a more formal ceasefire. A de-escalation of the crisis will be difficult to orchestrate, but the fact that the

US and Russia are co-chairing a taskforce overseeing it shows the extent to which they are displacing local and regional powers as the decision-makers in Syria.

For the Kurds in Rojava and KRG territory, this is a testing moment: if the war ends their newly won power could quickly slip away. They are, after all, only small states—the KRG has a population of about six million and Rojava 2.2 million—surrounded by much larger ones. And their economies are barely floating wrecks. Rojava is well organised but blockaded on all sides and unable to sell much of its oil. Seventy percent of the buildings in Kobani were pulverised by US bombing. People have fled from cities like Hasaka that are close to the front line. The KRG's economic problems are grave and probably insoluble unless there is an unexpected rise in the price of oil. Three years ago, it advertised itself as "the new Dubai," a trading hub and oil state with revenues sufficient to make it independent of Baghdad. When the oil boom peaked in 2013, the newly built luxury hotels in Erbil were packed with foreign trade delegations and businessmen. Today the hotels and malls are empty and Iraqi Kurdistan is full of half-built hotels and apartment buildings. The end of the KRG boom has been a devastating shock for the population, many of whom are trying to migrate to Western Europe. There are frequent memorial prayers in mosques for those who have drowned in the Aegean crossing from Turkey to the Greek islands. The state's oil revenues now stand at about $400 million a month; expenditure is $1.1 billion, so few of the 740,000 government employees are being paid. In desperation, the government has seized money from the banks. "My mother went to her bank where she thought she had $20,000," Nazdar Ibrahim, an economist at Salahaddin University in Erbil, told me. "They said: 'We don't have your money because the government has taken it.' Nobody is putting money in the banks and it is destroying the banking system."

The KRG promoted itself as a "different Iraq," and so, in some respects, it is: it's much safer to live in than Baghdad or Basra. Though Mosul isn't far away, there have been few bomb attacks or kidnappings in Iraqi Kurdistan compared to elsewhere in the country. But the KRG is an oil state that depends wholly on oil revenues. The region produces almost nothing else: even the vegetables in the markets are imported from Turkey and Iran and prices are high. Nazdar Ibrahim said that clothes she could buy in Turkey for ten dollars cost three times as much at home; Iraqi Kurdistan, she suggested, was as expensive to live in as Norway or Switzerland. The

KRG's president, Masoud Barzani, has declared he will hold a referendum on Kurdish independence, but this is not an attractive option at a time of general economic ruin. Asos Hardi, the editor of a newspaper in Sulaymaniyah, says protests are spreading and, in any case, "even at the height of the boom there was popular anger at the clientism and corruption." The Iraqi Kurdish state—far from becoming more independent—is being forced to look to outside powers, including Baghdad, to save it from further economic collapse.

Similar things are happening elsewhere in the region: people who have been smuggled out of Mosul say that the caliphate is buckling under military and economic pressure. Its enemies have captured Sinjar, Ramadi, and Tikrit in Iraq and the YPG and the Syrian army are driving it back in Syria and are closing in on Raqqa. The ground forces attacking Isis—the YPG, the Syrian army, Iraqi armed forces, and Peshmerga—are all short of manpower (in the struggle for Ramadi, the Iraqi military assault force numbered only 500 men), but they can call in devastating air strikes on any Isis position. Since it was defeated at Kobani, Isis has avoided set-piece battles and has not fought to the last man to defend any of its cities, though it has considered doing so in Raqqa and Mosul. The Pentagon, the Iraqi government, and the Kurds exaggerate the extent of their victories over Isis, but it is taking heavy losses and is isolated from the outside world with the loss of its last link to Turkey. The administrative and economic infrastructure of the caliphate is beginning to break under the strain of bombing and blockade. This is the impression given by people who left Mosul in early February and took refuge in Rojava.

Their journey wasn't easy since Isis prohibits people from leaving the caliphate—it doesn't want a mass exodus. Those who have got out report that Isis is becoming more violent in enforcing fatwas and religious regulations. Ahmad, a thirty-five-year-old trader from the al-Zuhour district of Mosul, where he owns a small shop, reported that "if somebody is caught who has shaved off his beard, he is given thirty lashes, while last year they would just arrest him for a few hours." The treatment of women in particular has got worse: "Isis insists on women wearing veils, socks, gloves, and loose or baggy clothes and, if she does not, the man with her will be lashed." Ahmad also said that living conditions have deteriorated sharply and the actions of Isis officials become more arbitrary: "They take food without paying and confiscated much of my stock under the pretence of supporting Isis militiamen. Everything is expensive and the stores are half-empty. The markets were crowded a year ago, but not for the last ten months because so many people have fled and those that have stayed are unemployed. There has been no mains electricity for seven months and everybody depends on private generators, which run on locally refined fuel. This is available everywhere but is expensive and of such poor quality that it works only for generators and not for cars—and the generators often break down. There is a shortage of drinking water." "Every ten days, we have water for two hours," Ahmad said. "The water we get from the tap is not clean, but we have to drink it." There is no mobile phone network and the internet is available only in internet cafés that are closely monitored by the authorities for sedition. There are signs of growing criminality and corruption, though this may mainly be evidence that Isis is in desperate need of money. When Ahmad decided to flee, he contacted one of many smugglers operating in the area between Mosul and the Syrian frontier. He said the cost for each individual smuggled into Rojava is between $400 and $500. "Many of the smugglers are Isis men," he said, but he didn't know whether the organisation's leaders knew what was happening. They certainly know that there are increasing complaints about living conditions because they have cited a hadith, a saying of the Prophet, against such complaints. Those who violate the hadith are arrested and sent for re-education. Ahmad's conclusion: "Dictators become very violent when they sense that their end is close."

How accurate is Ahmad's prediction that the caliphate is entering its final days? It is certainly weakening, but this is largely because the war has been internationalised since 2014 by US and Russian military intervention. Local and regional powers count for less than they did. The Iraqi and Syrian armies, the YPG, and the Peshmerga can win victories over Isis thanks to close and massive air support. They can defeat it in battle and can probably take the cities it still rules, but none of them will be able fully to achieve their war aims without the continued backing of a great power. Once the caliphate is gone, however, the central governments in Baghdad and Damascus may grow stronger again. The Kurds wonder if they will then be at risk of losing all the gains they have made in the war against Isis.

PART I. AN ISOLATIONIST IN THE AMERICAN TRADITION

I was in Erbil in northern Iraq in November 2016, covering the start of the siege of Mosul, when Donald Trump was elected US president. I had always taken his brand of American isolationism seriously during the campaign. I saw it as a very American type of populist nationalism that his multitude of critics in the US and the rest of the world found difficult to understand. Jingoistic in tone, laudatory of US military might, bursting with furious threats towards potential enemies—and frequently allies—it was also much against foreign wars and entanglements.

This bellicose bluster was to continue for the next three years, but at the time of writing, Trump has yet to start a war, though he has teetered on the edge of one with Iran. A hostile media and foreign policy establishment in Washington alternate between denouncing Trump as a warmonger, an appeaser—or a fool. Lost in this torrent of abuse is the fact that at the core of Trump's foreign policy is a brutal realpolitik and a realisation where power actually lies. His decision, for instance, in October 2019 to withdraw US troops from north-east Syria was a betrayal of the Syrian Kurds and was announced in a chaotic manner. But he was correct in recognising, as his critics often did not, that the US military position in this isolated corner of Syria was weak, risky, and unsustainable. In the event, thanks to push-back by the Pentagon, Republican hawks, and his own neoconservative-dominated cabinet, US troops withdrew from Syria and then half-returned in a messy compromise between different forces in Washington.

The assassination of Iranian General Qasem Soleimani at Baghdad airport on 3 January did not denote a real change in this strategy of avoiding all-out military conflicts. Trump said that he gave the order to kill Soleimani to prevent a war and not to start one, though it could have had that effect. It could also have worked to the advantage of the government in Tehran as millions of Iranians rallied to mourn Soleimani and revile the US. But, at that very moment, Iran shot down a Ukrainian airliner, killing 176 people, and lied about it for three days. The popular backlash was no longer against the US but against their own government. Lost in all this was the fact that the US had allowed Iran to fire ballistic missiles at US bases at Ain al-Asad in western Iraq and Erbil in Iraqi Kurdistan and had not retaliated, a remarkable degree of restraint in the face of an undoubted act of war, masked by Trump's belligerent rhetoric.

I had spoken to the leaders of pro-Iranian paramilitary groups in Baghdad in September 2019, and I could see that they believed that Trump would not act militarily against them or Iran. Their over-confidence stemmed from US lack of action over the previous summer, exemplified by Trump's last-minute change of mind over launching US air strikes against Iran, after it shot down an American drone on 20 June 2019. He showed equal restraint on 14 September when there was an Iran/Houthi drone and missile attack on Saudi oil facilities. In both cases, his instinct against retaliating directly against Iran was correct. Had strikes against Iranian radars and missile batteries gone ahead in either case, what exactly would he have achieved? This sort of limited military operation usually works better as a threat than in actuality. The US was never going to launch an all-out war against Iran in pursuit of a decisive victory, as in Iraq in 2003, and anything less than that would create more problems than it would solve.

This calculation still makes sense: Iran would inevitably retain the ability after the air strikes to launch pinprick attacks up and down the Gulf and, above all, in and around the thirty-five-mile wide Strait of Hormuz, through which passes 30 percent of the world's oil trade. Trump has chosen to rely on sanctions against Iran, re-imposed after he withdrew the US from the Iran nuclear deal in May 2018, that have devastated the Iranian economy. The US Treasury is a more lethal international power than the Pentagon, but what if the most rigorous sanctions do not force Iran to negotiate? Iran is likely to resume proxy attacks on US allies, because these are one of its few high-value cards in its con-frontation with the US. Each phase of the crisis sees an escalation that brings a shooting war closer, though neither side wants one. A rule of Middle East poli-tics is that every side overplays their hand at some point in the belief that they can win a complete victory. A compromise US-Iran deal is possible, but not if the US thinks it can force Iran to capitulate.

November 2016–June 2019

11 November 2016

"Make America Great Again" was the slogan of Donald Trump's election, but the immediate impact of his victory is to make the US less of a power in the world for two reasons: American prestige and influence will be damaged by a general belief internationally that the US has just elected a dangerous buffoon as its leader. The perception is pervasive but not very deeply rooted and likely to be temporary, stemming as it does from Trump's demagogic rants during the election campaign. Those about relations with foreign countries were particularly vague and least likely to provide a guide to future policy.

More damaging in the long term for America's status as a superpower is the likelihood that the US is now a more deeply divided society than ever. Trump won the election by demonising and threatening individuals and communities—Mexicans, Muslims, Latinos—and his confrontational style of politics is not going to disappear. Verbal violence produces a permanently over-heated political atmosphere in which physical violence becomes an option. At the same time, the election campaign was focused almost exclusively on American domestic politics with voters showing little interest in events abroad. This is unlikely to change.

Governments around the world can see this for themselves, though this will not stop them badgering their diplomats in Washington and New York for an inkling as to how far Trump's off-the-cuff remarks were more than outrageous attempts to dominate the news agenda for a few hours. Fortunately, his pronouncements were so woolly that they can be easily jettisoned between now and his inauguration. Real foreign policy positions will only emerge with the formation of a Trump cabinet when it becomes clear who will be in charge. But, if future policies remain unknowable, super-charged American nationalism combined with economic populism and isolationism are likely to set the general tone. Trump has invariably portrayed Americans as the victims of the foul machinations of foreign countries who previously faced no real resistance from an incompetent self-serving American elite.

This sort of aggressive nationalism is not unique to Trump. All over the world, nationalism is having a spectacular rebirth in countries from Turkey to the Philippines. It has become a successful vehicle for protest in Britain, France, Germany, Austria, and Eastern Europe. Though Trump is frequently portrayed as a peculiarly American phenomenon, his populist nationalism has a striking amount in common with that of the Brexit campaigners in Britain or even the chauvinism of Erdogan in Turkey. Much of this can be discounted as patriotic bombast, but in all cases, there is a menacing undercurrent of racism and demonisation, whether it is directed against illegal immigrants in the US, asylum seekers in Britain, or Kurds in south-east Turkey.

In reality, Trump made very few proposals for radical change in US foreign policy during the election campaign, aside from saying that he would throw out the agreement with Iran on its nuclear programme—though his staff is now being much less categorical about this, saying only that the deal must be properly enforced. Nobody really knows if Trump will deal any differently from Obama with the swathe of countries between Pakistan and Nigeria where there are at least seven wars raging—Afghanistan, Iraq, Syria, Yemen, Libya, Somalia, and South Sudan—as well as four serious insurgencies.

The most serious wars in which the US is already militarily involved are in Iraq and Syria and here Trump's comments during the campaign suggest that he will focus on destroying Isis, recognise the danger of becoming militarily overinvolved, and look for some sort of cooperation with Russia as the next biggest player in the conflict. This is similar to what is already happening. Hillary Clinton's intentions in Syria, though never fully formulated, always sounded more interventionist than Trump's. One of her senior advisers openly proposed giving less priority to the assault on Isis and more to getting rid of Assad. To this end, a third force of pro-US militant moderates was to be raised that would fight and ultimately defeat both Isis and Assad. Probably this fantasy would never have come to pass, but the fact that it was ever given currency underlines the extent to which Clinton was at one with the most dead-in-the-water conventional wisdom of the foreign policy establishment in Washington.

President Obama developed a much more acute sense of what the US could and could not do in the Middle East and beyond, without provoking crises exceeding its political and military strength. Its power may be less than before the failed US interventions in Iraq and Afghanistan following 9/11, but it is still far greater than any other country's. Currently, it is the US that is successfully coordinating the offensive against Isis's last strongholds in Mosul and Raqqa by a multitude of fractious parties in Iraq and Syria. It was never clear how seriously one should have taken Clinton's proposals for "safe zones" and trying to fight Isis and Assad at the same time, but her judgements on events in the Middle East since the Iraq invasion of 2003 all suggested a flawed idea of what was feasible.

Trump's instincts generally seem less well-informed but often shrewd, and his priorities have nothing to do with the Middle East. Past US leaders have felt the same way, but they usually end up being dragged into its crises one way or another, and how they perform then becomes the test of their real quality as a leader. The region has been the political graveyard for three of the last five US presidents: Jimmy Carter was destroyed by the consequences of the Iranian revolution, Ronald Reagan was gravely weakened by the Iran-Contra scandal, and George W Bush's years in office will be remembered chiefly for the calamities brought on by his invasion of Iraq. Barack Obama was luckier and more sensible, but he wholly underestimated the rise of Isis until it captured Mosul in 2014.

Obama resisted the temptation to fight new wars, but if Hillary Clinton had been in charge, her record suggests that she might well have done so. How would Donald Trump have responded? There is a bigger gap between his words and deeds than there are with most politicians. But words create their own momentum and his constant beating of the patriotic drum will make it difficult for him to exercise the degree of caution necessary to avoid ensnarement in the Middle East. Over-heated nationalism cannot be turned on and off like a tap. He may want to concentrate on radical change at home, but the vortex of crises in the Middle East will one day suck him in.

18 November 2016

Isis is under pressure in Mosul and Raqqa, but it is jubilant at the election of Donald Trump. Abu Omar Khorasani, an Isis leader in Afghanistan, is quoted as saying that "our leaders were closely following the US election, but it was unexpected that the Americans would dig their own graves." He added that what he termed Trump's "hatred" towards Muslims would enable Isis to recruit thousands of fighters. The calculation is that, as happened after 9/11, the demonisation and collective punishment of Muslims will propel a proportion of the Islamic community into its ranks. Given that there are 1.6 billion Muslims—about 23 percent of the world's population—Isis and al-Qaeda-type organisations need to win the loyalty of only a small proportion of the Islamic community to remain a powerful force.

Bloodcurdling proposals for the persecution of Muslims played a central role in Trump's election campaign. At one moment, he promised to stop all Muslims from entering the US, though this was later changed to "extreme vetting." The use of torture by waterboarding was approved and applauded, and Hillary Clinton was pilloried for not speaking of "radical Islamic terrorism." Trump and his aides may imagine that much of this can be discarded as the overblown rhetoric of the campaign, but Isis and al-Qaeda propagandists will make sure that Trump's words are endlessly repeated with all their original venom intact. Nor will this propaganda about the anti-Muslim bias of the new administration be so far from the truth, going by the track record of many of the people in its security and foreign policy team. Trump is reported to have offered the post of National Security Adviser to General Michael Flynn, who was sacked by President Obama as head of the Defence Intelligence Agency in 2014. Flynn notoriously sees Islamic militancy not only as a danger but as an existential threat to the US. He tweeted earlier this year that "fear of Muslims is RATIONAL."

There is an obsessive, self-righteous quality to Flynn's approach that led him to join chants of "lock her up" in reference to Hillary Clinton during election rallies. Former associates complain of Flynn's political tunnel vision that could wreak havoc in the Middle East. His consulting company, the Flynn Intel Group, appears to lobby for the Turkish government and Flynn recently wrote an article calling for all-out US support for Turkey, who Washington has been trying to stop launching a full-scale invasion of Syria and Iraq. Unsurprisingly, the Turkish president welcomed Trump's election with enthusiasm and sharply criticised protests against it in the US (something that would be swiftly dealt with by police water cannons in Turkey).

A striking feature of the aspirants for senior office under Trump is a level of personal greed high even by the usual standards of Washington. Trump famously campaigned under the slogan "Drain the Swamp" and castigated official corruption, but it is turning out that the outflow pipe from the swamp is the entry point of the new administration. One grotesque example of this is Rudy Giuliani, who exploited his fame as mayor of New York City at the time of 9/11 to earn millions in speaking fees and consultancy for foreign governments and companies. Apparently, none were too dubious for him to turn down. In 2011 and 2012, he reportedly made speeches defending the sinister Iranian cult-like movement, the Mujahideen e-Khalq (People's Mujahedin of Iran), that had been on the State Department's list of terrorist organisations. Giuliani is a swamp creature if ever there was one, yet this week he was publicly turning down the post of attorney general and was, at the time of writing, being considered for the post of secretary of state.

Isis and al-Qaeda may underestimate the degree to which they will benefit from Trump's election, which came at a bleak moment in their fortunes. He and his henchmen have already frightened and enraged hundreds of millions of Muslims and vastly expanded the constituency to which the jihadis can appeal. A clampdown against them that, in practice, targets all Muslims plays straight into their hands. What made 9/11 such a success for Osama bin Laden was not the destruction of the Twin Towers, but the US military reaction that produced the wars in Afghanistan and Iraq. This could happen again. There are other potential long-term gains for the beleaguered Isis leader Abu Bakr al-Baghdadi, whatever the outcome of the siege of Mosul. The Taliban, al-Qaeda, and Isis are all militarised fanatical movements born out of the chaos of war in Afghanistan and Iraq, and they are flourishing in similarly anarchic conditions in Syria, Libya, Yemen, Somalia, and beyond.

In theory, Trump is a non-interventionist; opposed to US military involvement in the Middle East and North Africa, he wants to bring the war in Syria to an end. But he has simultaneously opposed the agreement with Iran on its nuclear programme and criticised Barack Obama for pulling the last US troops out of Iraq in 2011 (though in fact this was under an agreement signed by George W. Bush). But Bush and Obama were both non-interventionists when first elected—until the course of events, and the enthusiasm of the Washington foreign policy establishment for foreign military ventures changed all that.

The US army and air force are today heavily engaged in Iraq and Syria and that is not going to end with Obama's departure. In contradiction to Trump's non-interventionism, leading members of his foreign policy team, such as John Bolton, the belligerent former US ambassador to the UN, has been advocating a war with Iran since 2003. Bolton proposes carving out a Sunni state in northern Iraq and eastern Syria, a plan in which every sentence betrays ignorance and misjudgements about the forces in play on the ground. As a recipe for deepening the conflict in the region, it could scarcely be bettered.

There have always been crackpots in Washington, sometimes in high office, but the number of dangerous people who have attached themselves to the incoming administration may be higher today than at any time in American history. For instance, one adviser to the Trump national security transition team is, according to Shane Harris and Nancy Youssef of *The Daily Beast*, one Clare Lopez, author of a book called *See No Sharia*, which says that Islamists and the Muslim Brotherhood in particular have infiltrated the White House and the FBI, as well as the US Departments of State, Justice, Defence, and Homeland Security. Lopez believes that terrorists caused the 2008 financial crash by short-selling stocks.

Optimists have been saying this week that Trump is less ideological than he sounds and, in any case, the US ship of state is more like an ocean liner than a speedboat, making it difficult to turn round. They add privately that not all the crooks and crazies will get the jobs they want. Unfortunately, much the same could have been said of George W. Bush when he came into office before 9/11. It is precisely such arrogant but ill-informed opportunists who can most easily be provoked by terrorism into a self-destructive overreaction. Isis is having a good week.

25 November 2016

Where does Donald Trump stand on the use of torture by US security agencies? During the presidential election campaign, he notoriously recommended a return to waterboarding, the repeated near-drowning of detainees that was banned by President Obama in 2009. But last week *The New York Times* reported that in an interview with its senior staff, he said that he had changed his mind after talking with retired Marine Corps General James Mattis, who is a leading candidate to be the next secretary of defence.

Trump quoted General Mattis as saying that "I've never found it [water-boarding] to be useful." He had found it more advantageous to gain the cooperation of terrorist suspects by other means: "Give me a pack of ciga-rettes and a couple of beers, and I'll do better." Trump recalled that he was very impressed by the answer, adding that torture is "not going to make the kind of difference that a lot of people are thinking." Trump's remarks were taken by *The New York Times* as a sign that the president-elect had changed his mind about waterboarding. Unfortunately, the full transcript of his talk, as pointed out by Fred Kaplan in *Slate*, shows exactly the opposite. Trump did indeed say that he was surprised by what Mattis said because the general was known for his toughness, but the president-elect went on to explain that "I'm not saying it changed my mind about torture." He added that "we have people that are chopping off heads and drowning people in steel cages and we're not allowed to waterboard." Though he had been given pause by what Mattis told him, he was convinced that "if it's so important to the American people, I would go for it. I would be guided by that."

The initial misreporting may have stemmed from wishful thinking by *Times* reporters—and American liberals in general—who hope that the most outrageous pieces of Trump demagoguery during the election were off-the-cuff campaign rhetoric which he is now abandoning. A pledge to prosecute Hillary Clinton is apparently being discarded, as is a plan for the immediate construction of a wall to seal off the Mexican border. The abandonment of agreements on climate change and on Iran's nuclear pro-gramme are becoming less categorical and more nuanced. But this is not so much a sign of a more moderate Trump emerging as it is fresh evidence of his shallowness and flippancy. He tells people whom he wants to influence exactly what they want to hear. Nothing is off-limits. He not only flatters his audience but does so in a way that is thrilling and attention-grabbing and sure to dominate the news agenda.

This sort of tough-guy talk is scarcely unique to Trump, but a common feature of American political leadership. Hillary Clinton frequently made distasteful boasts about her self-inflated role in the killing of Osama bin Laden and Muammar Gaddafi. Trump likewise uses and misuses macho slogans more than most politicians and then disowns them when they have served their purpose. But he does not disown all his election pledges and he has not disowned the one on waterboarding, banned by President Obama by means of an executive order, which is much more important than the prosecution of Clinton or building the Mexican wall. Ever since 9/11, and more particularly since the rise of Isis, there has been debate about the radicalisation of Muslims and how this might be prevented. Saudi-sponsored madrassas and imams have been blamed, with some reason, but a much simpler cause of radicalisation has nothing to do with the slow imbibing of extreme Islamist ideology. This is anger and a desire to retaliate provoked by specific injustices such as waterboarding, rendition of suspects to be tortured, and the abuses in Abu Ghraib and Guantanamo, which acted as powerful and persuasive recruiting sergeants for Isis and Islamic extremism.

Keeping this in mind, it is important to realise that the US now has a president-elect who has just restated that he believes in the value of waterboarding. His views will not pass unnoticed among the quarter of the world's population who are Muslims and know that they were the main victims of these abuses. Some members of the Trump administration, like General Mattis or General Flynn, the national security advisor, do not believe in torture, but others say that it works and that any criticism of it is unpatriotic.

Such senior figures include the newly appointed head of the CIA, Mike Pompeo, a Kansas congressman and a supporter of the Tea Party faction of the Republican Party. He has backed interrogation techniques amounting to torture and greater domestic surveillance by the NSA. He sees Christianity and Islam as engaged in a titanic struggle. Speaking in 2015 before a Christian flag at a church in his district that focuses on "Satanism and paranormal activity," he spoke of the "struggle against radical Islam, the kind of struggle this country has not faced since its great wars," and warned that "evil is all around us." He advised the congregation not to be put off by people who might call them "Islamophobes or bigots." On another occasion, he denounced a mosque in Kansas for holding a speaking event which coincided with Good Friday. As for Guantanamo, Pompeo described it as "a goldmine of intelligence about radical Islamic terrorism. I have travelled to GTMO and have seen the honourable and professional behaviour of the American men and women in uniform, who serve at the detention facility." He denounced the release of the revelatory 2014 Senate report on torture, saying that "these men and women [the interrogators] are not torturers, they are patriots. The programmes being used were within the law, within the constitution." It is worth recalling what waterboarding and other types of torture of which Trump and Pompeo approve really consist of.

The 2014 US Senate Report on torture by the CIA described water-boarding as a "series of near drownings," in addition to which detainees were subjected to sleep deprivation for up to a week and medically unnecessary "rectal feeding." One CIA officer described prisoners being held in a "dungeon" and interrogation leading to "hallucinations, paranoia, insomnia, and attempts at self-harm and self-mutilation." The report concludes that the CIA had lied about the number of detainees, their treatment, and had fed sympathetic journalists with false information about valuable intelligence acquired by means of torture. The "waterboarding" approved by Trump and Pompeo was only one in a range of torture techniques used by the CIA before they were banned, according to testimony in the case of Abd al-Rahim Hussein Muhammad al-Nashiri in a US appeals court hearing earlier this year. In addition to artificially induced suffocation, detainees "were kept naked, shackled to the wall, and given buckets for their waste. On one occasion, al-Nashiri was forced to keep his hands on the wall and not given food for three days. To induce sleep deprivation, detainees were shackled to a bar on the ceiling, forcing them to stand with their arms above their heads."

By such means, Trump intends to make America great again.

13 January 2017
As Trump prepares for his inauguration, he is struggling with opposition from the US media, intelligence agencies, government apparatus, parts of the Republican Party, and a significant portion of the American population. Impressive obstacles appear to prevent him from exercising arbitrary power.

He should take heart: much the same was said in Turkey about Erdogan in 2002 when he led his Justice and Development Party (AKP) to the first of four election victories. He faced an army that, through coups and the threat of coups, was the ultimate source of power in the country, and a secular establishment suspicious of his Islamist beliefs. But over the years he has outmanoeuvred or eliminated his enemies and—using a failed military coup on 15 July last year as an excuse—is suppressing and punishing all signs of dissent as "terrorism." As Trump enters the White House, the AKP and far-right nationalist supermajority in the Turkish parliament is this month stripping the assembly of its powers and transferring them wholesale to the presidency. President Erdogan will become an elected dictator able to dissolve parliament, veto legislation, decide the budget, and appoint ministers who do not have to be MPs.

All power will be concentrated in Erdogan's hands as the office of prime minister is abolished and the president, who can serve three five-year terms, takes direct control of the intelligence services. He will appoint senior judges and the head of state institutions, including the education system. These far-reaching constitutional changes are reinforcing an ever-expanding purge begun after the failed military coup last year, in which more than 100,000 civil servants have been detained or dismissed. This purge is now reaching into every walk of life, from liberal journalists to businessmen who have seen $10 billion in assets confiscated by the state.

The similarities between Erdogan and Trump are greater than they might seem, despite the very different political traditions in the US and Turkey. The parallel lies primarily in the methods by which both men have gained power and seek to enhance it. They are populists and nationalists who demonise their enemies and see themselves as surrounded by conspiracies. Success does not sate their pursuit of more authority. Hopes in the US that, after Trump's election in November, he would shift from aggressive campaign mode to a more conciliatory approach have dissipated over the last two months. Towards the media, his open hostility has escalated, as was shown by his abuse of reporters at his press conference this week.

Manic sensitivity to criticism is a hallmark of both men. In Trump's case, this is exemplified by his tweeted denunciation of critics such as Meryl Streep, while in Turkey, 2,000 people have been charged with insulting the president. One man was tried for posting on Facebook three pictures of Gollum, the character in *The Lord of the Rings*, with similar facial features to pictures of Erdogan posted alongside. Of the 259 journalists in jail around the world, no less than eighty-one are in Turkey. American reporters may not yet face similar penalties, but they can expect intense pressure on the institutions for which they work to mute their criticisms.

Turkey and the US may have very different political landscapes, but there is a surprising degree of uniformity in the behaviour of Trump and Erdogan. This type of political leadership is not new: the most compelling account of it was written seventy years ago in 1947 by the great British historian Sir Lewis Namier, in an essay reflecting on what he termed "Caesarian democracy," which over the previous century had produced Napoleon III in France, Mussolini in Italy, and Hitler in Germany. His list of the most important aspects of this toxic brand of politics is as relevant today as it was when first written since all the items apply to Trump, Erdogan, and their like. Namier described Caesarian democracy as typified by "its direct appeal to the masses: demagogical slogans; disregard of legality despite a professed guardianship of law and order; contempt of political parties and the parliamentary system, of the educated classes and their values; blandishments and vague, contradictory promises to all and sundry; militarism; gigantic blatant displays and shady corruption. *Panem et circenses* [bread and circuses] once more—and at the end of the road, disaster."

Disaster comes in different forms. One disability of elected dictators or strongmen is that, impelled by an exaggerated idea of their own capacity, they undertake foreign military adventures beyond their country's strength. The disaster that Namier predicted was the natural end of elected dictators has already begun to happen in Turkey. The Turkish leader may have succeeded in monopolising power at home, but at the price of provoking crises and deepening divisions within Turkish society. The country is embroiled in the war in Syria, thanks to Erdogan's ill-judged intervention there since 2011. This led to the PKK establishing a de facto state in northern Syria and Isis doing the same in Syria and Iraq. At home, Erdogan restarted the war with the Turkish Kurds for electoral reasons in 2015 and the conflict is now more intractable than ever. Every few weeks in Turkey, there is another terrorist attack, which is usually the work of Isis or a faction of the PKK—although the government sometimes blames atrocities on the followers of Fethullah Gulen, who are alleged to have carried out the attempted military coup last July. In addition to this, there is an escalating financial crisis, which has seen the Turkish lira lose 12 percent of its value over the last two weeks. Foreign and domestic investment is drying up as investors become increasingly convinced that Turkey has become chronically unstable.

Erdogan and Trump have a further point in common: both have an unquenchable appetite for power and achieve it by exploiting and exacerbating divisions within their own countries. They declare they will make their countries great again, but in practise make them weaker. They are forever sawing through the branch on which they—and everybody else—are sitting.

20 January 2017

Inequality has increased everywhere with politically momentous consequences, a development much discussed as a reason for the populist-nationalist upsurge in Western Europe and the US. But it has also had a significant destabilising impact in the wider Middle East. Impoverished Syrian villagers, who once looked to the state to provide jobs and meet their basic needs at low prices, found in the decade before 2011 that their government no longer cared what happened to them. They poured in their millions into gimcrack housing on the outskirts of Damascus and Aleppo, cities whose richer districts looked more like London or Paris. Unsurprisingly, it was these same people, formerly supporters of the ruling Baath Party, who became the backbone of the popular revolt. Their grievances were not dissimilar from those of unemployed coal miners in former Democratic Party strongholds in West Virginia who voted overwhelmingly for Donald Trump.

Neoliberal free-market economic reforms were even more destructive of political and social stability in the Middle East and North Africa than in Europe and the US. In dictatorships or arbitrary monarchies without political accountability or rule of law, such changes further crony capitalism: access to the narrow circle wielding political power becomes the essential key to riches. Governments turn into giant looting machines under the kleptocratic guidance of a few ruling families. In Baghdad a few years ago, heavier than usual winter showers flooded the streets to the depth of a foot or more with an evil-smelling grey mixture of water and sewage. I asked an advisor to the Ministry of Water Resources why this had happened and she explained, as if it was nothing out of the ordinary, that over the previous decade the Iraqi government had spent $7 billion on a new sewage system for the capital, but either it had never existed, or the sewers were too badly built to carry away rainwater.

In the US, Europe, and the Middle East, there were many who saw themselves as the losers from globalisation, but the ideological vehicle for protest differed markedly from region to region. In Europe and the US, it was right-wing nationalist populism which opposes free trade, mass immigration, and military intervention abroad. The latter theme is much more resonant in the US than in Europe because of Iraq and Afghanistan. Trump instinctively understood that he must keep pressing these three buttons, the importance of which Hillary Clinton and most of the Republican Party leaders, taking their cue from their donors rather than potential voters, never appreciated.

The vehicle for protest and opposition to the status quo in the Middle East and North Africa is, by way of contrast, almost entirely religious and is only seldom nationalist, the most important example being the Kurds. This is a big change from fifty years ago when revolutionaries in the region were usually nationalists or socialists, but both beliefs were discredited by corrupt and authoritarian nationalist dictators and by the collapse of the Soviet Union. Secular nationalism was, in any case, something of a middle-class creed in the Arab world, limited in its capacity to provide the glue to hold societies together in the face of crisis. When Isis forces were advancing on Baghdad after taking Mosul in June 2014, it was a fatwa from the Iraqi Shia religious leader Ali al-Sistani that rallied the resistance. No non-religious Iraqi leader could have successfully appealed to hundreds of thousands of people to volunteer to fight to the death against Isis.

The Middle East differs also from Europe and the US because states are more fragile than they look and once destroyed prove impossible to recreate. This was a lesson that the foreign policy establishments in Washington, London, and Paris failed to take on board after the invasion of Iraq, though the disastrous outcome of successful or attempted regime change has been bloodily demonstrated again and again. It was always absurdly simple-minded to blame all the troubles of Iraq, Syria, and Libya on Saddam Hussein, Bashar al-Assad, and Muammar Gaddafi, authoritarian leaders whose regimes were more the symptom than the cause of division. But it is not only in the Middle East that divisions are deepening. Whatever happens in Britain because of the Brexit vote or in the US because of the election of Trump as president, both countries will be more divided and therefore weaker than before. Political divisions in the US are probably greater now than at any time since the American Civil War 150 years ago. Repeated calls for unity in both countries betray a deepening disunity and alarm as people sense that they are moving in the dark and old norms and landmarks are no longer visible and may no longer exist.

The mainline mass media is finding it difficult to make sense of a new world order which may or may not be emerging. Journalists are generally more rooted in the established order of things than they pretend and are shocked by radical change. Only two big newspapers—the *Florida Times-Union* and the *Las Vegas Review-Journal* endorsed Trump before the election and few of the American commentariat expected him to win, though this has not dented their confidence in their own judgement. Criticism of Trump in the media has lost all regard for truth and falsehood with the publication of patently concocted reports of his antics in Russia, but there is also genuine uncertainty about whether he will be a real force for change, be it good or ill.

Crises in different parts of the world are beginning to cross-infect and exacerbate each other. Prior to 2014, European leaders, whatever their humanitarian protestations, did not care much about what happened in Iraq and Syria. But the rise of Isis, the mass influx of Syrian refugees heading for Central Europe, and the terror attacks in Paris and Brussels showed that the crises in the Middle East could not be contained. They helped give a powerful impulse to the anti-immigrant authoritarian nationalist right and made them real contenders for power.

The Middle East is always a source of instability in the world and never more so than over the last six years. But winners and losers are emerging in Syria where Assad is succeeding with Russian and Iranian help, while in Iraq, the Baghdad government backed by US airpower is slowly fighting its way into Mosul. Isis probably has more fight in it than its many enemies want to believe but is surely on the road to ultimate defeat. One of the first real tests for Trump will be how far he succeeds in closing down these wars, something that is now at last becoming feasible.

10 February 2017

President Trump made a great play when he came into office with his return of a bust of Winston Churchill to the Oval Office, presenting the move as a symbol of his admiration for adamantine patriotic resolve in pursuit of patriotic ends. Presumably, Trump was thinking of Churchill in 1940, not Churchill in 1915–16 when he was the leading advocate of the disastrous Gallipoli campaign in which the Turks decisively defeated the British army with great slaughter.

Trump is reputed to seldom read books or show much interest in history other than that of his own life and times, but it would be worth his while reflecting on Gallipoli because Churchill was only the first of six British and American leaders to have suffered political shipwreck in the Middle East over the last century. The prime reason for these successive disasters is that the region has always been more unstable and prone to wars than anywhere else in the world. Mistakes made on its battlefields tend to be calamitous and irretrievable. Avoiding this fate is not easy: the six British and American leaders who came a serious cropper in the Middle East were generally abler, more experienced, and better-advised than Trump. It is therefore worthwhile asking, at the beginning of his administration, what are the chances of him becoming the next victim of the permanent state of crisis in the wider Middle East. He campaigned as an isolationist who would avoid being sucked into armed conflicts abroad, but his first weeks in office and his senior appointments suggest that he will try to take a central role in the politics of the region.

These failings unite with a crippling ignorance on the part of foreign powers about the complexity and dangers of the political and military terrain in which they are operating. This was true of Churchill, who wrongly assessed likely Turkish military resistance in 1915. Lloyd George, one of the most astute of British prime ministers, made the same mistake in 1922 when his government destroyed itself by threatening to go to war with Turkey. Anthony Eden lost office after the Suez Crisis in 1956 when he failed to overthrow Nasser in Egypt. Tony Blair's reputation was forever blasted for leading Britain into war in Iraq in 2003.

Of the three US presidents badly or terminally damaged by crisis in the Middle East, Jimmy Carter was the most unlucky, as there was nothing much he could do to stop the Iranian Revolution in 1979 or the seizure of diplomats in the US embassy in Tehran as hostages. Ronald Reagan's presidency saw military intervention in Lebanon where 241 US Marines were blown up in 1983, and the Iran-Contra scandal that permanently weakened the administration. Significant though these disasters and misadventures seemed at the time, none had the impact of George W Bush's invasion of Iraq in 2003, which led to the regeneration of al-Qaeda and the spread of chaos through the region.

In retrospect, these leaders may look foolhardy as they plunged into bottomless quagmires or fought unwinnable wars. Some, like Carter, were victims of circumstances, but entanglements were not inevitable, as was shown by President Obama, who did read books, knew his history, and was acutely aware of the pitfalls the US needed to skirt in Afghanistan, Iraq, Syria, and beyond. Avoiding disaster that nobody else knew existed will seldom win a politician much credit, but Obama deserves credit for escaping being sucked into the civil war in Syria or into a broader conflict against Iran as the leader of the Shia axis.

Trump continually promised during the presidential election that he would focus exclusively in the Middle East on destroying Isis, but one of the first moves of his administration has been to shift the US closer to Saudi Arabia by backing its war in Yemen. In almost his first statement of policy, Secretary of Defence James Mattis said that Iran is "the single biggest state sponsor of terrorism in the world." One of the dangers of Trump's demagogic rants and open mendacity is that they tend to give the impression that less theatrical members of his team, especially former generals like Mattis or Michael Flynn, are monuments of good sense and moderation. Yet both men are set on threat inflation when it comes to Iran, though without providing any evidence for its terrorist actions, just as their predecessors inflated the threat supposedly posed by Saddam Hussein's non-existent WMD and fictional support for al-Qaeda.

Given the high decibel level of the Trump administration's threats and warnings, it is impossible to distinguish bellicose rhetoric from real operational planning. A confrontation with Iran will probably not come soon; but in a year or two, when previous policies conceived under Obama have run their course, Trump may well feel that he has to show how much tougher and more effective he is than his predecessor, whom he has denounced as weak and incompetent. In four years' time, the select club of American and British leaders who failed in the Middle East, with disastrous consequences for everybody, may have a voluble seventh member.

3 November 2017

In his jeremiad against Iran on 13 October, Trump justified his refusal to certify the Iran nuclear deal with gobbets of propaganda, one-sided history, and straight lies. He proposed a new US policy towards Iran based "on a clear-eyed assessment of the Iranian dictatorship, its sponsorship of terrorism, and its continuing aggression in the Middle East and all around the world." The speech sounded like the opening volley in a new campaign against Iran, to be fought out on multiple fronts.

Some sort of collision between the US and Iran looks possible or even likely, a battle which will probably be carried out by proxies and will not be fought to a finish. It may not come to that: such is the intensity of political strife in the US that new foreign policy ventures do not look very feasible. But any sensible leader in the Middle East always looks at the worst-case scenario first. The wars in Syria and Iraq are either coming to an end or their present phase is ending, but in both cases, the situation is fragile.

It is doubtful if either the US or Iran would come out the winner in any new confrontation, but Iraqis would certainly come out the losers. The best policy for the US in Iraq, Syria, and elsewhere is to do nothing very new. But this may be difficult for Trump. It is not just him who has wrongheaded ideas about the Middle East. There has recently been a stronger than usual surge of apocalyptic commentary about how Iran is winning victory after victory over the US in the region. Washington think-tankers, retired generals, and journalists warn of Iran opening up "a land corridor" to the Mediterranean as if the Iranians travel only by chariot and could spread their influence by no other means. It could be that Trump's menaces really are serious, in which case the Iranians are understandably going to react. But even if they are largely rhetorical, they might trigger an Iranian overreaction.

"The Iranians are under the impression that others want to topple their regime," an Iraqi politician told me. "The Iranians are very smart. They do not send their armies abroad. Once you do that, you are lost. They fight by proxy on many fronts outside their borders, but this destabilises everybody else." Once again, Iraq would find itself in the front line. Curiously, Iran owes much of its expanded influence not to its own machinations but to the US itself. It has been the collateral beneficiary of US-led regime change in two of its neighbours, Afghanistan and Iraq, both of which had been viscerally anti-Iranian.

The sheer ignorance of Trump and his administration about the Middle East is dangerous. It is usual, particularly in liberal circles, to see people in the Middle East as passive victims of foreign intervention. This is largely true, but it masks the fact that at any one time, there are several governments and opposition movements trying to lure the US into a war with its enemies by demonising them as a threat to the world. Trump may speak of confronting Iran, but there is no sign that he has a coherent plan to do so. Much of what is happening in the region is beyond his control and US influence is going down, but for reasons that have nothing to do with him.

26 January 2018
Seldom has an important new US foreign policy crashed in flames so quickly and so spectacularly, achieving the very opposite results to those intended.

It was only ten days ago that Rex Tillerson unexpectedly announced that American military forces would remain in Syria after the defeat of Isis. Their agenda was nothing if not ambitious: it included the stabilisation of the country, getting rid of Bashar al-Assad, rolling back Iranian influence, preventing the resurgence of Isis, and bringing an end to the seven-year Syrian war. Tillerson did not seem to care that this new departure was sure to offend a lot of powerful players in and around Syria and was quite contrary to past US pledges that it was only fighting in Syria to defeat Isis and had no other aims. In effect, the US was reversing its old policy of trying to keep its distance from the Syrian quagmire and was blithely plunging into one of the messiest civil wars in history.

The first sign of this radical new development came early last week with an announcement that the US was going to train a 30,000-strong border force that, though this was not stated, would be predominantly Kurdish. This was furiously denounced by Turkey and Tillerson appeared to disavow it. But his speech spelling out the new interventionist American policy on 17 January was just as explosive and was the reason why, five days later, Turkish tanks were rumbling across the Turkish-Syrian border into the Kurdish enclave of Afrin. A fertile and heavily populated pocket of territory, this is one of the few parts of Syria that had not been devastated by the war. But this is changing fast as Turkish bombers and artillery pound the town of Afrin and the 350 villages around it. The YPG have been fighting back hard, but unless there is some diplomatic solution to the crisis, the enclave will end up looking like much of the rest of Syria with whole streets reduced to mounds of smashed masonry.

The fighting over the last five days has exposed as a dangerous fantasy; the US hopes that its new interventionist policy would stabilise northern Syria. Instead of weakening Assad and Iran, it will benefit them, showing the Kurds that they badly need a protector other than the US. The Kurds are now demanding that the Syrian army go to Afrin to defend it against the Turks because it is an integral part of Syria. A military confrontation between Turkey and the US would be much in the interests of Tehran and Damascus. The Iranians, denounced by the US as the source of all evil, will be glad to see America in lots of trouble in Syria without them having to stir a finger.

The post-Isis US policy in Syria and Iraq coming out of the Trump administration has more far-reaching goals than before but is vague on how they should be achieved. The US may want to get rid of Assad and weaken Iran across the region, but it is too late. Pro-Iranian governments in Iraq and Syria are in power and Hezbollah is the most powerful single force in Lebanon. This is not going to change any time soon and, if the Americans want to weaken Assad by keeping a low-level war going, then this will make him even more reliant on Iran. The US obsession with an exaggerated Iranian threat—about which, in any case, it cannot do much—makes it difficult for Washington to mediate and cool down the situation. Trump and his chaotic administration have not yet had to deal with a real Middle East crisis yet and the events of the last week suggest that they will not be able to do so.

14 September 2018

Before his election as president, it was understandable that Trump's critics should have vastly underestimated his ability as a politician. It is much less excusable—and self-destructive to effective opposition to Trump—that they should go on underestimating him almost two years after his victory. Every week there are more revelations showing the Trump administration to be chaotic, incompetent, and corrupt. The latest are the anonymous op-ed in *The New York Times* in which one of his own senior officials claims to be working against him and Bob Woodward's book portraying the White House as a sort of human zoo.

The media gleefully reports these bombshells in the hope that they will finally sink, or at least inflict serious damage, on the Good Ship Trump. This has been the pattern since he announced his presidential candidacy, but it never happens. Political commentators, overwhelmingly anti-Trump, express bafflement at his survival, but such is their loathing and contempt for him that they do not see that they are dealing with an exceptionally skilled politician. His abilities may be instinctive or drawn from his vast experience as a showman on television. Priority goes to dominating the news agenda regardless of whether the publicity is good or bad. Day after day, hostile news outlets like *The New York Times* and CNN lead on stories about Trump to the exclusion of all else.

The media does not do this unless they know their customers want it: Trump is an American obsession, even greater than Brexit in Britain. A friend of mine recently met a group of American folk singers touring the south coast of Ireland, who told him that they had often pledged to each other that they would get through the day without mentioning Trump, but so far, they had failed to do so. This tactic of dominating the news by deliberately headline-grabbing behaviour, regardless of the criticism it provokes, is not new but is much more difficult to carry out than it looks. Boris Johnson is currently trying to pull the same trick with outrageous references to "suicide vests," but his over-heated rhetoric feels contrived. MP David Lammy's jibe about Johnson as "a pound-shop Donald Trump" is apt.

Trump is never boring: it is a simple point and central to his success but is seldom given sufficient weight. During the presidential campaign, Hillary Clinton's supporters complained that Trump got excessive amounts of free television time, while her speeches were ignored or were given inadequate attention. The reason was not any pro-Trump bias—quite the contrary given the political sympathies of most people in the media—but because her speeches were boring and his were not. He has the well-developed knack of always saying something the media cannot leave alone. An example of this is his tweeted retort this week to a claim by JPMorgan Chase CEO Jamie Dimon that he could "beat" Trump in a presidential election and is tough and smarter than him. This silly boast was not much of a news story, until Trump tweeted: "The problem with banker Jamie Dimon running for president is that he doesn't have the aptitude or 'smarts' and is a poor public speaker and nervous mess—otherwise he is wonderful." Not many politicians or journalists could put so much punching power into a single sentence.

Trump is regarded with a peculiar mixture of fear and underestimation by opponents across the board from the Democratic Party leaders to the EU heads of state. They believe—rightly—that Trump is a monster and hope—wrongly—that this means he will one day implode. This would be deeply convenient for them all because, until this happens, they do not have to act themselves. Trump will hopefully pass away like a bad dream. There is no need for the EU leaders or prominent Democrats to devise and explain policies that would divide them. Sometimes this policy of sitting on your hands and doing nothing until your opponent makes a mistake is the correct one. But it carries the grave risk of creating a vacuum of information that will be filled by your enemies. During the presidential election, it was easy to deride Trump's vague promises to bring factory jobs back to the US, but he did not have to say much about this because Hillary usually said nothing at all.

Trump is at war with the institutions of the US government. This is unsurprising: US presidents have invariably been frustrated by the sense that they reign but do not rule. A convincing explanation for the fall of Richard Nixon is that different branches of the bureaucracy used Watergate to frustrate his grab for power and get rid of him. They may yet succeed in Trump's case. Many Americans want to witness a sequel to Watergate with Trump in the starring role. But this is almost impossible to do without control of Congress and the ganging-up of bureaucrats against an elected president will not be palatable to a lot of voters.

The anonymous senior White House official of the *New York Times* op-ed says that he is part of a group within the administration pledged to thwart "Mr. Trump's more misguided impulses." This is the latest emergence of "adults in the room" who are going to prevent the US government abandoning policies essential to its existence. The problem is that these "adults" are promoting policies that are often just as dangerous as anything Trump has in mind, if not more so. For instance, Trump has periodically said that the US ought to pull its 2,000 troops, which are backed by the US Air Force, out of north-east Syria. This would be a sensible move to negoti-ate because the US has a weak hand in Syria and could not determine the course of events without a full-scale war.

Trump is not "an isolationist" in the classic sense, but his instinct is to avoid wars or situations that might lead to one. Talking to Kim Jong-un and Vladimir Putin may not produce anything very substantial, but it does make war less, rather than more, likely. Yet, such is the bitterness of divisions in the US, that liberal commentators were furiously denouncing Trump as a traitor for meeting either man in terms that Senator McCarthy would have recognised seventy years ago. It is easy to sympathise with their rage. Trump is the worst thing to happen to the US since the Civil War, but miscalculating his strengths and weaknesses is not the way to deal with him. His near-miraculous ability to survive repeated scandals reminds me of what the diplomat, politician, and writer Conor Cruise O'Brien wrote about Charlie Haughey, the Irish political leader, who was notorious for surviving against the odds in similar challenging circumstances: "If I saw Mr. Haughey buried at midnight at a crossroads with a stake driven through his heart," wrote O'Brien, "I should continue to wear a clove of garlic around my neck, just in case."

21 December 2018
President Trump's decision to withdraw US troops from Syria is being denounced by an impressive range of critics claiming that it is a surrender to Turkey, Russia, Syria, and Iran—as well as a betrayal of the Kurds and a victory for Isis. The pull-out may be one or all of these things, but above all, it is a recognition of what is really happening on the ground in Syria and the Middle East in general. This point has not come across clearly enough because of the undiluted loathing for Trump among most of the American and British media. They act as a conduit for the views of diverse figures who condemn the withdrawal and include members of the imperially-minded foreign policy establishment in Washington and terrified Kurds living in north-east Syria who fear ethnic cleansing by an invading Turkish army.

Opposition to Trump's decision was supercharged by the resigna-tion of Secretary of Defence James Mattis, which came after he failed to persuade the president to rescind his order. Mattis does not mention Syria or Afghanistan in his letter of resignation, but he makes clear his disagreement with the general direction of Trump's foreign policy in not confronting Russia and China and ignoring traditional allies and alliances. The resignation of Mattis has elicited predictable lamentations from commentators who treat his departure as if it was the equivalent of the Kaiser getting rid of Bismarck. The over-used description of Mattis as "the last of the adults in the room" is once again trotted out, though few examples of his adult behaviour are given aside from his wish—along with other supposed "adults"—to stay in Syria until various unobtainable objectives were achieved: the extinction of Iranian influence; the displacement of Assad; and the categorical defeat of Isis (are they really likely to sign surrender terms?).

In other words, there was to be an open-ended US commitment with no attainable goals in an isolated and dangerous part of the world where it was already playing a losing game.

It is worth spelling out the state of play in Syria because this is being masked by anti-Trump rhetoric, recommending policies that may sound benign but are far detached from political reality. This reality may be very nasty: it is right to be appalled by the prospects for the Syrian Kurds who are terrified of a Turkish army that is already massing to the north of the Turkish-Syrian frontier. There is a horrible inevitability about all this because neither Turkey nor Syria were ever going to allow a Kurdish ministate to take permanent root in north-east Syria.

This is a good moment to make a point about this commentary: it is an explanation, not a justification for the dreadful things that may soon happen. I have visited the Kurdish controlled part of Syria several times and felt that it was the only part of Syria where the uprising of 2011 had produced a society that was better than what had gone before, bearing in mind the constraints of fighting a war. I met the men and women of the People's Protection Units (YPG and YPJ) who fought heroically against Isis, suffering thousands of dead and wounded. But I always had a doomed feeling when talking to them as I could not see how their statelet, which had been brought into existence by temporary circumstances, was going to last beyond the end of the Syrian civil war and the defeat of Isis. One day the Americans would have to choose between two million embattled Kurds in Syria and eighty million Turks in Turkey and it did not take much political acumen to foresee what they would decide.

Turkey had escalated its pressure on the US to end its protection of the Kurds and this finally paid off. A telephone conversation with Erdogan a week ago reportedly convinced Trump that he had to get US soldiers and airpower out of Syria. Keep in mind that Trump needs—though he may not get as much as he wants—Turkey as an ally in the Middle East more than ever before. His bet on Crown Prince Mohammad bin Salman and Saudi Arabia as the leader of a pro-American and anti-Iranian Sunni coalition in the Middle East has visibly and embarrassingly failed. The bizarre killing of Jamal Khashoggi by a Saudi team in Istanbul was only the latest in a series of Saudi pratfalls showing comical ineptitude as well as excessive and mindless violence.

Critics of Trump raise several other important questions in opposing his withdrawal decision: is he not letting Isis off the hook by prematurely announcing their defeat and thereby enabling them to make a comeback? There is something in this, but not a lot. Isis is no more and cannot be resurrected because the circumstances that led to its spectacular growth between 2013 and 2015 are no longer there. Trump is right to assume in a tweet that "Russia, Iran, Syria & many others…will have to fight ISIS and others, who they hate, without us." Isis may seek to take advantage of chaos in eastern Syria in the coming months, but there will be no power vacuum for them to exploit. The vacuum will be filled by Turkey or Syria or a combination of the two.

A further criticism of the US withdrawal is that it unnecessarily hands a victory to Vladimir Putin and Assad. But here again, Trump's manoeuvre is more of a recognition of the fact that both men are already winners in the Syrian war. Nor is it entirely clear that Russia and Iran will have greater influence in Syria and the region after the US withdrawal. True they have come out on the winning side, but as the Syrian state becomes more powerful, it will have less need for foreign allies. The close cooperation between Russia and Turkey was glued together by US cooperation with the Kurds and once that ends, then Turkey may shift—though not all the way—back towards the US.

By denouncing Trump's decision to withdraw from Syria, his opponents are once again making the mistake of underestimating his instinctive political skills.

13 May 2019

Saudi Arabia's claim that two of its oil tankers have been sabotaged off the coast of the UAE is vague in detail—but could create a crisis that spins out of control and into military action. Any attack on shipping in or close to the Strait of Hormuz, the thirty-mile wide channel at the entrance to the Gulf, is always serious because it is the most important choke point for the international oil trade.

A significant armed action by the US or its allies against Iran would likely provoke Iranian retaliation in the Gulf and elsewhere in the region. Although the US is militarily superior to Iran by a wide margin, the Iranians as a last resort could fire rockets or otherwise attack Saudi and UAE oil facilities. Such apocalyptic events are unlikely—but powerful figures in Washington, such as the National Security Adviser John Bolton and Secretary of State Mike Pompeo, appear prepared to take the risk of a war breaking out. Bolton has long publicly demanded the overthrow of the Iranian government. "The declared policy of the United States should be the overthrow of the mullahs' regime in Tehran," he said last year before taking office. "The behaviour and the objectives of the regime are not going to change and, therefore, the only solution is to change the regime itself."

Bolton and Pompeo are reported to have used some mortar rounds landing near the US embassy in Baghdad in February as an excuse to get a reluctant Pentagon to prepare a list of military options against Iran. These would include missile and air strikes, but it is unclear what these would achieve from the US point of view. Paradoxically, the US and Saudi Arabia have been talking up war against Iran just as economic sanctions are seriously biting. Iranian oil exports have dropped from 2.8 to 1.3 million barrels a day over the last year and are likely to fall further. Inflation in Iran is at 40 percent and promises by the EU, UK, France, and Germany to enable the Islamic republic to avoid sanctions on its oil trade and banking have not been fulfilled. Commercial enterprises are too frightened of being targeted by the US Treasury to risk breaching sanctions.

Iran is becoming economically—though not politically—isolated. This is in contrast to previous rounds of sanctions on Iran under President Obama prior to the nuclear deal when the reverse was true. One reason why it is unlikely that Iran would carry out sabotage attacks on Saudi oil tankers is that its strategy has been to play a long game and out-wait the Trump administration. Though the Iranian economy may be badly battered, it will probably be able to sustain the pressure. Much tighter sanctions against Saddam Hussein after his invasion of Kuwait in 1990 did not lead to the fall of his regime.

The circumstance of the alleged sabotage at 6 a.m. on Sunday remain mysterious. Saudi Arabia's Energy Minister Khalid al-Falih says the attack "didn't lead to any casualties or oil-spill" but did cause damage to the structure of the vessels. The incident has the potential to lead to conflict in the context of an escalating confrontation between the US and Iran. The rise in temperature reached particularly menacing levels this month as the US sent an aircraft carrier to the Gulf and Iran suspended in part its compliance with the 2015 nuclear deal after President Trump withdrew last year. However, Iran has made serious efforts to show moderation and cultivate support from the EU, Russia, and China. For this reason, it appears unlikely that it has had a hand in attacking the Saudi oil tankers. Iranian foreign ministry spokesperson Abbas Mousavi asked for more information about what had really happened to the tankers. He warned against any "conspiracy orchestrated by ill-wishers" and "adventurism" by foreigners.

In this febrile atmosphere, almost any incident, true or false—such as the unconfirmed sabotage of tankers or a few mortar rounds fired towards the US embassy in Baghdad—might provide the spark to ignite a wider conflict.

17 May 2019

In its escalating confrontation with Iran, the US is making the same mistake it has made again and again since the fall of the Shah forty years ago: it is ignoring the danger of plugging into what is in large part a religious conflict between Sunni and Shia Muslims.

I have spent much of my career as a correspondent in the Middle East, since the Iranian revolution in 1979, reporting crises and wars in which the US and its allies fatally underestimated the religious motivation of their adversaries. This has meant they have come out the loser, or simply failed to win, in conflicts in which the balance of forces appeared to them to be very much in their favour. It has happened at least four times. Now the same process is underway yet again, and likely to fail for the same reasons as before: the US, along with its local allies, will be fighting not only Iran but whole Shia communities in different countries, mostly in the northern tier of the Middle East between Afghanistan and the Mediterranean. Trump looks to sanctions to squeeze Iran while National Security Adviser John Bolton and Secretary of State Mike Pompeo promote war as a desirable option. But all three denounce Hezbollah in Lebanon or the Popular Mobilisation Units in Iraq as Iranian proxies, though they are primarily the military and political arm of the indigenous Shia, which are a plurality in Lebanon, a majority in Iraq, and a controlling minority in Syria. The Iranians may be able to strongly influence these groups, but they are not Iranian puppets, which would wither and disappear once Iranian backing is removed.

Allegiance to nation-states in the Middle East is generally weaker than loyalty to communities defined by religion, such as the Alawites, the two-million-strong ruling Shia sect in Syria to which Bashar al-Assad and his closest lieutenants belong. This is not what Trump's allies in Saudi Arabia, UAE, and Israel want Washington to believe; for them, the Shia are all Iranian stooges. For the Saudis, every rocket fired by the Houthis in Yemen into Saudi Arabia—though minimal in destructive power compared to the four-year Saudi bombing campaign in Yemen—can only have happened because of a direct instruction from Tehran. On Thursday, for instance, Prince Khalid Bin Salman, the vice minister for defence and the brother of Saudi Arabia's de facto ruler Crown Prince Mohammed Bin Salman, claimed on Twitter that drone attacks on Saudi oil pumping stations were "ordered" by Iran. He said that "the terrorist acts, ordered by the regime in Tehran, and carried out by the Houthis, are tightening the noose around the ongoing political efforts." He added: "These militias are merely a tool that Iran's regime uses to implement its expansionist agenda in the region."

There is nothing new in this paranoid reaction by Sunni rulers to actions by distinct Shia communities (in this case the Houthis) attributing everything without exception to the guiding hand of Iran. I was in Bahrain in 2011, where the minority Sunni monarchy had just brutally crushed protests by the Shia majority with Saudi military support. Among those tortured were Shia doctors in a hospital who had treated injured demonstrators. Part of the evidence against them was a piece of technologically advanced medical equipment—I cannot remember if it was used for monitoring the heart or the brain or some other condition—which the doctors were accused of using to receive instructions from Iran about how to promote a revolution.

This type of absurd conspiracy theory used not to get much of a hearing in Washington, but Trump and his acolytes are on record as saying that nearly all acts of "terrorism" can be traced to Iran. This conviction risks sparking a war between the US and Iran because there are plenty of angry Shia in the Middle East who might well attack some US facility on their own accord.

It might also lead to somebody in one of those states eager for a US-Iran armed conflict to stage a provocative incident that could be blamed on Iran.

But what would such a war achieve? The military invasion of Iran is not militarily or politically feasible, so there would be no decisive victory. An air campaign and a close naval blockade of Iran might be possible, but there are plenty of pressure points through which Iran could retaliate, from mines in the Strait of Hormuz to rockets fired at the Saudi oil facilities on the western side of Gulf. A little-noticed feature of the US denunciations of Iranian interference using local proxies in Iraq, Syria, and Lebanon is not just that they are exaggerated but, even if they were true, they come far too late. Iran is already on the winning side in all three countries.

If war does come, it will be hard-fought. Shia communities throughout the region will feel under threat. As for the US, the first day is usually the best for whoever starts a war in the Middle East, and after that, their plans unravel as they become entangled in a spider's web of dangers they failed to foresee.

7 June 2019

Is Donald Trump a fascist? The question is usually posed as an insult rather than as a serious inquiry. A common response is that "he is not as bad as Hitler," but this rather dodges the issue. Hitler was one hideous exponent of fascism, which comes in different flavours, but he was by no means the only one.

The answer is that fascist leaders and fascism in the 1920s and 1930s were similar in many respects to Trump and Trumpism. But they had additional toxic characteristics, born out of a different era and a historic experience different from the United States. What are the most important features of fascism? They include ultra-nationalism and authoritarianism; the demon-isation and persecution of minorities; a cult of the leader; a demagogic appeal to the "ignored" masses and against a "treacherous" establishment; contempt for parliamentary institutions; disregard for the law while stand-ing on a law and order platform; control of the media and the crushing of criticism; slogans promising everything to everybody; a promotion of force as a means to an end leading to violence, militarism, and war.

The list could go on to include less significant traits such as a liking for public displays of strength and popularity at rallies and parades; a liking also for gigantic building projects as the physical embodiment of power.

Hitler and Mussolini ticked all these boxes and Trump ticks most of them, though with some important exceptions. German and Italian fascism was characterised above all else by aggressive and ultimately disastrous wars. Trump, on the contrary, is a genuine "isolationist" who has not started a single war in the two-and-a-half years he has been in the White House.

It is not that Trump abjures force, but he prefers it to be commercial and economic rather than military, and he is deploying it against numerous countries from China to Mexico and Iran. As a strategy, this is astute, avoiding the bear traps that American military intervention fell into in Iraq and Afghanistan. It is an approach which weakens the targeted state economically, but it does not produce decisive victories or unconditional surrenders. It is a policy more dangerous than it looks: Trump may not want a war, but the same is not true of Mike Pompeo, or John Bolton. And it is even less true of US allies like Saudi Arabia and the United Arab Emirates.

Trump's aversion to military intervention jibes with these other influences, but it is erratic because it depends on the latest tweet from the White House. A weakness, not just of fascist leaders but of all dictatorial regimes, is their exaggerated dependence on the decisions of a single individual with God-like confidence in their own judgement. Nothing can be decided without their fiat and they must never be proved wrong or be seen to fail. Trump has modes of operating rather than sustained policies that are consequently shallow and confused. One ambassador in Washington confides privately that he has successfully engaged with the most senior officials in the administration, but this was not doing him a lot of good because they had no idea of what was happening.

The result of this Louis XIV approach to government is institutionalised muddle: Trump may not want a war in the Middle East, but he could very easily blunder into one.

PART II. THE BATTLE FOR MOSUL

American commanders expected the battle for Mosul to last for two months, but Isis held out for almost nine months of ferocious fighting. The Iraqi government offensive began on 16 October 2016 and went on until 10 July 2017, by which time large parts of the city were in ruins. It was the biggest military operation in the world since the US and UK invaded Iraq in 2003 and lasted longer than the battle of Stalingrad.

I was based for much of this time in the Kurdish capital Erbil which is only fifty miles from Mosul. The long straight road between the two cities passes through territory which is inhabited by a medley of rival ethnic and religious groups, most of which had their own fighting forces manning checkpoints and regarded foreign journalists with a mixture of indifference and suspicion. Any one of them could stop a reporter from getting to the front line or keep them waiting for hours while they sought authority to let them through.

The Kurdish Peshmerga soldiers had advanced to what they considered to be the limit of Kurdish territory on the Nineveh Plain east of Mosul. They would generally let journalists pass, but soldiers at the first Iraqi army checkpoint a few miles down the road looked askance at anybody coming from the direction of Kurdistan and might refuse entry. If they stopped me and it became clear that they were not going to change their minds, I would turn south down a side road with burnt-out villages, from which Isis had recently withdrawn, on either side of it. The checkpoints became more dilapidated the further I went and were guarded by Shia militiamen, often recruited from the Shia part of the Kurdish-speaking Shabak minority or from the Shia heartlands of central and southern Iraq. My aim was to reach a pontoon bridge over the Tigris River south of Mosul and cross it in order to approach the city from the south. This became easier to do after Iraqi government forces over-ran the last Isis positions in east Mosul in January and started their attack on west Mosul on 19 February 2017.

I met refugees from Mosul on the road, dazed and frightened people conscious that the Iraqi army saw them as likely Isis sympathisers. Sectarian differences ran deep: Sunni Arab escapees, particularly young men of military age, looked terrified as they queued up to be interrogated by the overwhelmingly Shia Iraqi army security men. The refugees told me what was happening behind Isis lines, but what they said was dubiously reliable because they were desperate to show that they were hostile to Isis and always had been. Most came from the suburbs of Mosul and few had succeeded in making it from the more isolated Old City, the main Isis stronghold where snipers shot anybody trying to escape.

I only began to understand the terrible fate of the hundreds of thousands of people trapped behind Isis lines after the fall of east Mosul. I had gone to the top of a mound by the Nabi Yunus shrine (Jonah's Tomb) that had been blown up by Isis, and which was the highest point in the entire city, from which one could look down on the other side of the Tigris where Isis was still in control. I saw that the Iraqi army had erected mobile phone masts on top of Nabi Yunus, which was an important development because it meant that people inside the Isis enclave would be able to use their phone again. Isis had blown up the original mobile masts soon after capturing Mosul in June 2014 and said they would hang anybody trying to use their phone, something they did on many occasions.

I thought that in the middle of the siege, Isis would have things on its mind other than enforcing its mobile phone ban. I was to speak by phone over the following weeks to many desperate people crammed together inside the shrinking Isis enclave: Jasim (not his real name) described to me how civilians in the Old City were searching the garbage to find something to eat. He was trying to get his mother to safety across the river, but Isis was shooting at them, as were Iraqi army soldiers from the other side of the Tigris, suspecting escapees of being suicide bombers.

Soon Jasim's house was hit by a bomb launched by an American drone and he was wounded in the leg. He crawled to a first-aid post, but they could do nothing for him. Later, his neighbours were to tell me, an Isis sniper shot Jasim dead as he tried to cross the Tigris with his mother and ten others using rubber tyres. The neighbours said his mother sat by his body for three days and then disappeared. They believed she had also been shot and her body had been carried away by the river water. I was in touch by phone with others in the Old City who still survived but, gradually, they all fell silent and, when the siege ended in July and I searched for them, not a single one was still alive.

October 2016–August 2017

17 October 2016

The Iraqi government and its allies may eventually capture Mosul from Isis, but this could be just a new chapter in the war. It will only win because of the devastating firepower of the US-led air forces and sheer weight of numbers. But the fight for the city is militarily and politically complex. The Iraqi army, Kurdish Peshmerga, the Hashd al-Shaabi (the Shia paramilitary forces Popular Mobilisation Units), and Sunni fighters from Mosul and Nineveh province, which make up the anti-Isis forces, suspect and fear each other almost as much as they hate Isis.

The Western media is portraying the first advances towards Mosul as if it is as orderly and well-planned as the D-Day landings in Normandy in 1944. But in private, Iraqis, who have seen many decisive victories turn out to be no such thing, are more sceptical about what they are seeing. One Iraqi observer in Baghdad told me that "the whole Mosul offensive seems to be a ramshackle affair held together by the expected high level of support from the US air force and special forces." At least twelve US generals and 5,000 US troops are reportedly in Iraq and they will play a crucial role in the coming struggle. The observer I spoke to added: "I don't think that the Iraqi forces, Peshmerga, Hashd, and Sunni volunteers can singly or jointly take back the city without the physical and psychological props provided by the US." The US participation is crucial because although the Iraqi army and the Kurdish Peshmerga have been successful in driving back

Isis since it won a succession of blitzkrieg victories in 2014, they have relied on US-led air support. The US has carried out 12,129 air strikes against Isis in the past two years, enabling Iraqi government forces and their allies to recapture cities like Ramadi, Fallujah, Baiji, and Tikrit while the Peshmerga captured Sinjar.

There are now about 25,000 Iraqi army, Hashd, and other volunteers in and around the Qayara area forty miles south of Mosul, while some 4,000 Peshmerga are advancing from the east. The earliest part of the campaign in the open countryside should be the easiest because airpower and artillery can be most easily deployed. Villages and towns, many of them formerly inhabited by Christians or the Shabak minority, on the Nineveh Plain east of Mosul are empty and can be bombarded without risk of civilian casualties. But military and political calculations will change when the Kurds reach the built-up outskirts of Mosul, which may still have a million people in it. They are pledged not to enter the city, which is the biggest Sunni Arab urban centre in Iraq, though it used to have a substantial Kurdish minority. The Hashd are also not supposed to enter Mosul because of Sunni sensitivities, but they can besiege it.

The Iraqi army has some experienced combat units such as the Golden Division, but these are limited in number and have complained in the past of being all fought out because they are too frequently deployed. The nature of the fighting in Mosul will differ from and be more difficult than in Ramadi and Fallujah, both of which were surrounded. In Mosul, Isis has not been yet been encircled and cut off from the rest of Iraq. The US will probably be inhibited in employing its airpower in Mosul, so the Iraqi army and its elite counterterrorism units might suffer heavy casualties in street fighting with the 4,000 to 8,000 Isis fighters believed to be in the city. This supposes that Isis will want to stand and fight for Mosul in a way that it did not in other Iraqi cities. Ever since it lost some 2,000 fighters, mostly to US air strikes, in its abortive four-and-a-half month siege of the Syrian Kurdish city of Kobani in 2014–15, its commanders have been reluctant to let their forces, which are overwhelmingly light infantry, fight from fixed positions that can be precisely targeted and obliterated by shelling and bombing. They might do better in Mosul, but the end result would likely be the same.

But not to fight for Mosul would be a bad blow to Isis. It contains one-third of the population under its control in Iraq. It is the heart of the "caliphate" that was declared here just over two years ago. It was the capture of Mosul by an Isis force of a few thousand defeating a garrison numbering at least 20,000 that astonished the world in June 2014. Isis leaders themselves saw their victory as miraculous and a sign of divine assistance. The loss of the city would, on the contrary, be evidence that the caliphate has no miraculous formula for victory and has gone into irreversible decline. Yet if Isis is going to fight anywhere, it would be best to do so in Mosul where it has been long entrenched. If the Iraqi army counterterrorist forces get bogged down in street fighting, Baghdad might face a number of unpalatable choices. It could ask the US-led coalition to escalate the bombing, but this might be embarrassing and lead to comparisons with the Russian and Syrian bombardment of east Aleppo over which the Western powers frequently express their revulsion.

Another alternative would be for Baghdad to use the primarily Shia, government-sponsored Hashd paramilitaries, but this would be seen as an anti-Sunni move. Meanwhile, Turkey is struggling to be a player in deciding the fate of Mosul and maintaining its Sunni Arab character. Its local proxy is the former governor at the time of Isis's capture of the city, Atheel al-Nujaifi, who has 5,000 militiamen trained by the Turks, many of them former policemen in Mosul. The Iraqi Prime Minister Haider al-Abadi has furiously demanded that a Turkish force of 1,500 soldiers at Bashiqa close to the front line return to Turkey and has exchanged abuse with Turkish President Erdogan. Isis has always benefited from the divisions of its opponents and nowhere are these more glaring than in and around Mosul where so many sectarian and ethnic fault lines meet. These divisions have helped Isis survive for so long, but its savagery has also united leaders and parties who otherwise might fight each other. This is true of the Baghdad government and the Iraqi Kurds.

This shifting mosaic of different parties and interests makes the course, intensity, and outcome of the battle for Mosul highly unpredictable. One way or another, it looks likely that Isis will lose, but it is less certain who will win and fill the vacuum left by the overthrow of the caliphate. There are many contenders for this role, making it possible that the present battle for Mosul will not be the last.

18 October 2016

Mosul has been a dangerous place since the US-led invasion of 2003. It is the greatest Sunni Arab city of Iraq during an era in which the Sunni had lost their old predominance and have struggled against Shia-dominated governments in Baghdad and Kurdish rulers next door in Iraqi Kurdistan.

If the anti-Isis forces ultimately succeed in recapturing Mosul, it will be the fifth time the city has changed hands in the course of thirteen years of war. The first time was in April 2003 when the Iraqi army was breaking up and surrendering and the Kurdish Peshmerga burst into the city. There was looting on a mass scale which the Arabs blamed on the Kurds and vice versa, but in fact, both took part. I saw crowds ransack the governor's mansion, the Central Bank, and the university.

The Arabs, three-quarters of the city's population of two million, were appalled by the Kurdish incursion. I visited the biggest hospital in Mosul, where the director Dr. Ayad Ramadani told me that "the Kurdish militias are looting the city. Today the main protection is from civilians organised by the mosques." By the entrance to the hospital, a family was loading the body of a deceased relative into the back of a truck when there was a burst of machine gun fire. This frightened the truck driver who sped away, leaving the body behind and the family angrily waving their fists after him.

Relations between Arabs and Kurds did not get much better over the following years. The KRG claimed parts of Nineveh province around Mosul, which it said had a Kurdish majority or had historically belonged to the Kurds. Mosul sits at the heart of a fascinating but confusing ethnic and sectarian mosaic made up of Arabs, Kurds, Shabak, Yazidis, and Christians of different denominations. Few of these communities had any liking for the others.

The Kurdish takeover was followed by the Americans and for the rest of 2003, General David Petraeus commanded the 101st Airborne Division in the city. He could see how the "de-Baathification" campaign mandated by the US authorities in Baghdad was alienating former Iraqi army officers and officials who were now out of a job. A high proportion of the army officer corps had always come from Mosul and, in keeping with this military tradition, the defence minister under Saddam Hussein was from the city. Petraeus issued de-Baathification certificates on his own authority, so these unemployed officers were at least eligible for a job. It was not enough. The Americans over-confidently thinned out their troops and then withdrew the remainder to take part in the recapture of Fallujah. In November 2004, Iraqi armed opposition fighters raced into the city, the newly reformed Iraqi army fled, and the rebels captured government weapons stores. They withdrew after a few days and Baghdad, backed by the US, regained a shaky control. But Baghdad's rule was always contested between 2004 and 2014. There were repeated guerrilla attacks. I would travel from Erbil in KRG to visit the Kurdish deputy governor whose well-fortified office was on the far side of the Tigris River. But we either had to drive very fast or go more slowly in convoys defended by troops and armoured vehicles. Al-Qaeda in Iraq never entirely lost its grip on Mosul even when it was at its lowest ebb before 2011. Local businesses had to pay it protection money, close down, or risk assassination. A Turkish businessman with several big construction contracts there recalled later that he had to pay $500,000 (£400,000) a month and, when this was increased and he refused to pay up, one of his employees was killed. He stopped work, withdrew his staff to Turkey and complained to the government in Baghdad. But their only proposal was that he pay the protection money and add the sum to his contract price. The government was much disliked in Mosul, but even so, the Isis capture of the city was a staggering victory of a few thousand fighters against a garrison that was meant to total 60,000 and may have had as many as 20,000 soldiers and police. The difference between the two figures was made up of "ghost soldiers." Many other soldiers had simply gone on leave to Baghdad and never come back as the security situation deteriorated. When Isis attacked the army and police dissolved.

Isis was never popular in Mosul, but they ferociously suppressed all dissent. They drove out the Christians and murdered and enslaved the Yazidis. They blew up iconic monuments like Jonah's Tomb. People may have disliked them, but there was not much they could do about it. Isis also benefited from fear among Sunni in the city about what would happen if the Iraqi army and Shia paramilitary militias came back. They know that the whole five or six million Sunni Arab population of Iraq, a fifth of the thirty-three million population, are under threat and as many as a third have been displaced. In the sectarian war in Baghdad in 2006-7, the Sunni in Iraq had been driven into several enclaves, mostly in the west side of the city, which US diplomats described as "islands of fear." This is now happening in the rest of Iraq. Other Iraqis may see them as complicit in Isis's crimes and seek vengeance. Whatever conciliatory statements come from Iraqi leaders, sectarian and ethnic hatreds are running deep and people in Mosul face a frightening and uncertain future.

1 November 2016

The Iraqi army has entered Mosul for the first time in over two years. The significance of the fight for Mosul will be all the greater for Isis because its self-declared caliph, Abu Bakr al-Baghdadi, is believed to be still inside the city, according to a senior Kurdish official I spoke to.

Fuad Hussein, chief of staff to Kurdish President Masoud Barzani, told me that his government had information from multiple sources that "Baghdadi is there and, if he is killed, it will mean the collapse of the whole [Isis] system." Isis would have to choose a new caliph in the middle of a battle, but no successor would have the authority and prestige of Baghdadi, the leader who surprised the world by establishing the caliphate after capturing Mosul. Baghdadi has kept himself concealed for the last eight or nine months, according to Mr. Hussein, who added that the caliph had become very dependent on Isis commanders from Mosul and Tal Afar, a city just to the west of Mosul. Other senior and better-known figures in Isis, particularly those from Syria and other countries, have been killed since their initial triumphs in the summer of 2014.

The presence of Baghdadi in Mosul may complicate and prolong the battle for Mosul as his surviving adherents fight to the death to defend him. Mr. Hussein said that "it is obvious that they will lose, but not how long this will take to happen." He said that Kurdish Peshmerga forces had been impressed by the extraordinary number of tunnels that Isis had dug in order to provide hiding places in the villages around Mosul.

Iraqi Special Forces advanced into Mosul on Tuesday, seizing the state television on the east bank of the Tigris River that divides the city in half. Mr. Hussein said that the speed of the fall of Mosul would depend on many factors, especially whether or not Isis "is going to destroy the five bridges over the river." Iraqi army units backed by US-led air strikes have been attacking across the Nineveh Plain to the east of Mosul, capturing empty towns and villages from which the inhabitants have almost entirely fled. Where Christians and other minorities have tried to return to their old homes in towns like Bartella and Qaraqosh, they have found them looted and often burned by retreating Isis fighters. Iraqi troops entered Gogjali, a district inside Mosul's city limits, and later the borders of the more built-up Karama district, according to Major General Sami al-Aridi of the Iraqi special forces.

As night fell a sandstorm blew up cutting visibility to only 100 yards, making air support for Iraqi forces more difficult and bringing the fighting to an end. "Daesh is fighting back and have set up concrete blast walls to block off the Karama neighbourhood and [stop] our troops' advance," General Aridi said. He added later that the troops had taken the nearby state television building, the only one in Nineveh province, but there had been heavy fighting when they tried to move further into built-up areas.

They are still some six miles from the city centre. "I assure you that the Iraqi army and the Peshmerga do not move one millimetre forward without American permission and coordination," said one Kurdish observer. He did not think that the battle for Mosul would necessarily go on a long time. But it is increasingly difficult for the 3,000 to 5,000 Isis fighters in Mosul and the 1,500 to 2,500 on the outskirts to escape, even if they wanted to. The Iraqi army and the Peshmerga encircle the city to the north, east, and west and the Hashd are moving in from the west, cutting the last routes to Syria.

US spokesman Colonel John Dorrian said that the US-led airpowers had noticed that Isis forces could no longer move in large numbers. "And when we see them come together where there are significant numbers, we will strike them and kill them," he said during a televised press conference. Some 1,792 Iraqis of whom 1,120 were civilians were killed in October according to the UN, though the total probably does not include Isis fighters. Eyewitnesses inside Mosul, where Isis is reported to have killed forty Iraqi prisoners at the weekend and thrown their bodies into the Tigris, say there are few fighters to be seen in the streets. "There are mostly just teenagers with guns," said one Mosul resident reached by telephone. Part of the city is shrouded in smoke because of air strikes and artillery fire, but also because Isis fighters are lighting fires to produce a smokescreen, which will make observation from the air more difficult.

Isis has never been popular in Mosul according to local residents who detest its extreme violence, religious bigotry, and subjugation of women. But it found more support in Sunni Arab villages around the city and among the Sunni Turkman of the nearby city of Tal Afar, who have always been notorious for their religious extremism and hatred for Shia and Kurds. Some observers believe that Isis might want to fight here against the Shia paramilitaries of the Hashd because the US-led air coalition has not been providing air cover for the Hashd on the grounds that they are sectarian and under Iranian influence. The fighting is so far on the eastern side of Mosul that traditionally had a Kurdish and Christian population while, if Isis has local support, it will be in the overwhelmingly Sunni Arab west of the city. Life here is said to be still relatively normal, with markets open and people in the streets. In addition to the indigenous population of Mosul, there are believed to be several hundred thousand Sunni Arabs, many of them Isis supporters, who fled there from Iraqi provinces such as Anbar, Diyala, and Salahuddin, where Isis has already been defeated.

3 November 2016

Foreign fighters for Isis are choosing to stand and fight the Iraqi army in east Mosul, while the group's local militants are crossing the Tigris River with their families to the more defensible western side of the city, according to a former jihadi I spoke to. The fighter, who calls himself Faraj, described scenes of growing chaos and an apparent breakdown of discipline among Isis forces in Mosul. He said that local fighters seeking to leave the east of the city were being stopped at checkpoints and cross-questioned by Isis security officers, whom he said were mostly Libyans and much-feared for inflicting severe punishments. On this occasion, he said that "fighters accompanied by families are being allowed to cross the bridges to the west bank, while individuals are being sent back to the front line."

Faraj said he had a cousin who left Raqqa, the de facto Isis capital in Syria, four months ago, had gone with his family to live in east Mosul. His cousin was not fighting on the front line, but was manning checkpoints and carrying out other activities for Isis. Nevertheless, when the Iraqi army entered Gogjali district on the extreme east side of Mosul, he found himself at the front with fifteen other fighters, but they later retreated over the Tigris and took up positions in the Yarmouk neighbourhood on the west bank. He said that imams in the mosques were calling over loudspeakers for people "to stay and resist the apostates and unbelievers." But their pleas were being ignored by many. Faraj quotes his cousin as saying that that "thousands of civilians on the eastern bank were fleeing and seeking safety with the Iraqi forces without our men [Isis] preventing them because some of them were also running away though others continued to fight."

Faraj's account of the confusion inside Mosul confirms reports from other eyewitnesses of a partial breakdown of order, particularly in the east of the city. He adds that "most local fighters who had families have withdrawn from the eastern bank, but most of the foreign fighters have stayed." There are signs that Isis's iron control of Mosul may be eroding, but it is still a force to be feared as it seeks to eliminate anybody who might oppose it. Some ninety former police officers have been detained and confined in a school in central Mosul. There are reports of local resistance units ambushing and assassinating Isis officials and small groups of fighters. Heavy weapons have been evacuated from east Mosul to the west and defensive positions by the bridges over the Tigris abandoned, suggesting that Isis intends to blow them up. Residents speak of little movement on the streets of Mosul with people keeping to their houses. Markets are still operating in the west, but there is a shortage of petrol, food, and medicine and no public supply of electricity and drinking water (though many people have generators and others have dug wells).

As the struggle for Mosul reaches a crisis point, Baghdadi has emerged for the first time in almost a year to issue a call to arms. The tape of his speech was released late on Wednesday night, but it is not known when or where it was recorded. He calls on his followers to obey orders and to remain resilient and aggressive: "Oh you who seek martyrdom! Start your actions! Turn the night of the disbelievers into day." He calls for a general attack on the territories of the enemy so their blood will "flow like rivers." He calls in particular for attacks on Turkey and Saudi Arabia. Though Baghdadi has called for all-out resistance, there is an air of desperation to his defiance as if he knows that defeat is unavoidable.

4 November 2016

As the Iraqi army advanced further into east Mosul today, Isis fighters responded by firing mortar shells into the Gogjali district that had been freed earlier in the week. We met the families fleeing the mortar barrage crammed into their battered cars and pick-ups at an army checkpoint at Bartella a dozen miles down the road. We had been told we could not go any further because it was too dangerous and Isis fighters were firing at the road not far ahead between Bartella and Mosul.

"We thought we had got rid of Daesh and then they started firing mortars at us," said one middle-aged woman in black robes. She added that a rocket had landed on her neighbour's house in the morning and killed him and three women. She expressed hatred for Isis and said that when Iraqi soldiers had knocked at her door and asked for information about Isis positions, her small son Yusuf, who looked about eight, had gone to show them the nearest Isis headquarters. The people escaping from the eastern side of Mosul give a convincing picture of what is happening there as the army moves forward. Mehdi, a former metalworker but jobless since Isis captured Mosul, said that the shelling had started at 8 a.m. and had gone on for an hour. He had put his wife and seven children into their car and driven out of the city without much idea of where they were going, so long as it was safe. Mehdi confirmed reports that Isis were withdrawing from the eastern side of Mosul. "They are leaving some two or three fighting positions behind in every district and the fighters there are being killed," he said. Those who stayed behind were foreign members of Isis. Asked about their nationality, Mehdi said he did not know because he never went near them. He pointed to a cigarette packet in his shirt pocket and said: "We cannot talk to the foreigners because as soon as they smell cigarette smoke from you, they send you off to be whipped.

There is no doubt that the great majority of people in Mosul will be glad to get rid of Isis, but it is not at all clear what comes next. It is already resorting to guerrilla raids such as one today when a group of Isis fighters took over a mosque and part of the town of Shirqat, sixty miles south of Mosul, and were resisting counter-attack. But the effect of the recapture of Mosul, the second-largest city in Iraq, on the morale and war-making capacity of Isis should be great. Isis will no longer have the human and financial resources of the self-declared caliphate, at its peak a powerful administrative machine, to support its campaign of slaughter at home and abroad. The very fact of defeat is likely to be damaging for a movement that claimed its victories were divinely inspired. Another point seldom noticed will make it difficult for Isis to revert to guerrilla warfare of the type that it has waged in the past. The secret network of supporters and helpers that once sustained al-Qaeda in Iraq, and Isis in its early days, no longer exists. When Isis became the ruler of the area where it had previously had a hidden presence, its local activists came out of hiding and became the new rulers. But with Isis on the retreat and losing its territory, its old guerrilla networks are paying a price for becoming too visible during their day of triumph.

Isis may be weaker, but this does not mean that it is no longer to be feared. Security may be greater for the minorities living in the Nineveh Plain, but only by comparison with what went before when they were persecuted and driven out by Isis.

The television pictures since the anti-Isis offensive began on 17 October are deceptively similar to newsreels of French villagers greeting allied armies in France in 1944. "The media is full of talk of the 'liberation' of Mosul and the surrounding Nineveh villages," comments one expert on the area. "I will not speak about 'liberation' until the displaced civilians, and especially the powerless minorities, are able to go back to their homes and live in peace and dignity, with a credible guarantee of security." There were no signs of any such guarantee being given anywhere on the Nineveh Plain today. People who wanted to go back to Bartella, for the first time in two years, were being held back at army checkpoints and those who were hoping to welcome relatives trapped in Mosul for two years were left staring at an empty road. There were only a few vehicles with frightened drivers and poles bearing ragged white flags sticking out of the windows.

Not far from Bartella, there is the empty Syriac Catholic town of Qaraqosh. Yohanna Towara, a local community leader, explains that when they come back after having fled in 2014, they will find that their homes have been destroyed. He says that "my brother's house was destroyed by an air strike [by the US-led coalition] and my house was damaged. Daesh burned the other houses before they left and they have all been looted a long time ago." Even where houses are still standing, there is no water or electricity or likelihood of it being restored any time soon. The chances of restoring any form of security to the Nineveh Plain depends on first of all capturing Mosul from which Isis has destabilised the whole of northern Iraq. It will take time to discover if Mosul is going to be destroyed as well as "liberated."

It was difficult not to wonder today how soon the Sunni Arabs, who were fleeing Mosul because of a mortar barrage, would be able to go back. It may be that the conflict in Iraq is not going to end with any form of power-sharing, as so often recommended by foreign powers, but because the war has finally produced winners and losers—and the people of Mosul will be among the latter.

7 November 2016

In the half-burned church of St Mary al-Tahira in Qaraqosh, twenty miles from Mosul, several dozen Syriac Catholics are holding a mass in Aramaic amid the wreckage left by Isis. The upper part of the stone columns and the nave are scorched black by fire and the only artificial light comes from three or four candles flickering on an improvised altar. Isis fighters used the courtyard outside as a firing range and metal targets set at one end of it are riddled with bullets. In his sermon, the Syriac Catholic Bishop of Baghdad Yusuf Abba calls for the congregation to show cooperation and goodwill to all. But the people of Qaraqosh wonder just how much goodwill and cooperation they can expect in return.

The Christians are still traumatised by the disasters of the last two-and-a-half years. When Isis took Qaraqosh on 8 August 2014, it had a population of 44,000, almost all Syriac Catholics, who fled for their lives to Erbil. Some 40 percent of these have since migrated further to countries like Australia and France or, within the Middle East, to Istanbul and Lebanon. But the 28,000 people from Qaraqosh who stayed inside Iraq have understandable doubts about going home, even if Isis is fully defeated and loses Mosul. "There is no security while Isis is still in Mosul," says Yohanna Towara, but even when Isis is gone, the Christians will be vulnerable. He says that "the priority is for us to control our local affairs and to know who will rule the area in which we live." He adds that the need for permanent security outweighs the need to repair the destruction wrought primarily by Isis but also by US-led air strikes.

This destruction is bad enough, though it is not total. Isis fighters set fire to many ordinary houses in addition to the churches in the days before they left, but—possibly because there was no furniture left to burn since it all had been looted—most of these houses look as if they could be made habitable after extensive repairs. It will take time because not only has the furniture gone, but cookers and fridges so, even if light fittings or taps are still in place, there is no water or electricity. Isis did not fight for Qaraqosh and there are no booby traps or improvised explosive devices. But they must at one time have thought of doing so because they dug networks of tunnels in the nearby Christian village of Karemlash as if they intended to wage an underground guerrilla war against the Iraqi army. In the event, there are few signs of Isis resistance, except the rather pathetic remains of burned-out tyres used to impede aircraft visibility. There were not many air strikes, but where they did take place, the results devastated whole buildings, reducing them to heaps of rubble.

Visiting Qaraqosh from Erbil forty miles away, it is easy to understand why people displaced from Qaraqosh and in the rest of the Nineveh Plain feel insecure and dubious about returning to their old homes, even where they are still standing. They know that if they do, they will be at the mercy of Arab and Kurdish authorities eager to fill the vacuum left by the fall of Isis and wishing to stake new claims to territory and power. Arriving at a Kurdish Peshmerga checkpoint on the main road from the Kurdish region to Mosul at 9 a.m., we make our way through crowds of people originally from Qaraqosh waiting to pass through. "See how they are treating people," says a critical Christian observer. "People have been waiting here since 5 or 6 a.m., but the Peshmerga say they need a senior officer to give permission for them to pass."

After another two Peshmerga checkpoints, we reach an Iraqi army checkpoint with whom the Christians have better relations. Closer to Qaraqosh, the checkpoints are manned by soldiers of the Iraqi army and local Christian members of the Nineveh Protection Units (NPU) with their multi-coloured red, white, and blue flags. Relations between the NPU and the army appear good, but the soldiers are Shia and at one checkpoint, they had laid out a table and were serving sweet tea and biscuits as part of the Shia Arbaeen commemoration. The diversity of officially-sanctioned armed groups appears never-ending: at some checkpoints, there were also visible the dark uniforms of federal police, whom locals say are recruited from the Shabak and Turkmen communities. Fear of Isis had united diverse groupings and communities, but that unity is showing signs of fraying. The outcome of the war all over Iraq and Syria has ensured that minorities that were once spread throughout the two countries, now only feel secure if they can rule their own territory. But in Iraq, the Christians do not have the numbers to defend themselves.

13 November 2016
The Iraqi armed forces are becoming bogged down in the battle for Mosul. Its elite special forces and an armoured division are fighting to hold districts in the eastern outskirts of the city against counter-attacks by Isis fighters using networks of tunnels to move about unseen. "In one day we lost thirty-seven dead and seventy wounded," said a former senior Iraqi official, adding that the Iraqi forces had been caught by surprise by the extent of the tunnel system built by Isis, said to be forty-five miles long.

The Iraqi Counter-Terrorism Service (CTS) and the Ninth Armoured Division have been trying for two weeks to fight their way into that part of Mosul city. Isis is sending waves of suicide bombers either as individuals who blow themselves up or in vehicles packed with explosives, snipers, and mortar teams, to restart the fighting in a dozen districts that the Iraqi army had said were already captured. "At first, I was optimistic that we might capture Mosul in two or three weeks, but I now believe it will take months," Khasro Goran, a senior Kurdish leader familiar with conditions in Mosul told me. He said he had changed his mind about the likely length of the siege when he witnessed the ferocity of the fighting in the outer defences of Mosul. He added that "if they [Isis] continue fighting like this, then a lot of Mosul will be destroyed. I hope it will not be like Aleppo."

A prolonged siege of Mosul with heavy civilian casualties and the possibility of Turkish military intervention is likely to be the first international crisis to be faced by the incoming administration of President-elect Donald Trump. The slow and heavily-contested advance of the Iraqi armed forces into the city means that the attack will still be going on when he is inaugurated in Washington on 20 January. Mr. Trump will have to decide if he is willing to sanction an escalation in US-led air strikes to destroy Isis defences, though this would inevitably lead to heavy loss of life. A threatened military intervention by Turkey will also become more likely if the best Iraqi combat units suffer heavy losses and look for reinforcements from the Shia paramilitary Hashd al-Shaabi forces and the Kurdish Peshmerga. In the battle for Ramadi in 2015, some 70 percent of the city was destroyed, but almost all of the 350,000 population had fled and Isis did not fight to the last man. The same was true of the outer ring of towns around Mosul like Bartella and Qaraqosh a dozen more miles from the city.

The Baghdad government offensive that began on 17 October went well until it reached Mosul's outskirts two weeks ago. Since then, the fighting has swung backwards and forwards with districts being captured or recaptured three or four times. In al-Qadisiyah al-Thaniya district, which the CTS had entered on Friday, the elite soldiers later retreated and Isis fighters returned. A local resident told a news agency that "they came back to us again, and this is what we feared. At night there were fierce clashes and we heard powerful explosions." In Intisar, another embattled east Mosul district, the Iraqi army's Ninth Armoured Division has found that its tanks are vulnerable in street fighting for which its soldiers have neither experience nor training. Last Tuesday, it lost two T-72 tanks. There were some signs of Isis disarray at the start of the siege. Hoshyar Zebari, the former Iraqi finance and foreign minister says that by far, "the biggest surprise for Isis was some months back when the Iraqi government and the leaders of the KRG agreed on a joint offensive against Isis in Mosul." Isis did not expect this—Baghdad and the KRG had previously been barely on speaking terms because of economic and territorial disputes.

When Iraqi forces first attacked east Mosul, there were reports of wavering morale among some Isis fighters, but the Isis leadership has mercilessly enforced its control. The UN says that it has executed some seventy civilians in Mosul accused of collaboration with Iraqi forces over the last week. Last Tuesday alone, forty people were dressed in orange jumpsuits and shot for "treason and collaboration" before being hanged from electricity poles. Another 20 civilians have been shot for using mobile phones to leak information to the Iraqi army and their bodies were hanged at traffic lights. The real level of support for Isis in Mosul is unclear. The 54,000 people who have fled the city and sought refuge behind Peshmerga or Iraqi army lands all express their hatred of the movement and deplore its atrocities. But local

Christians and Kurds view the displaced civilians from Isis with suspicion as possible covert Isis supporters. "I see that Isis are getting their families to safety," said one Christian driving past a camp of white tents occupied by Internally Displaced People (IDPs) at Khazar, east of Mosul.

Mr. Goran is an expert on the internal politics of Mosul, where he was deputy governor between 2003 and 2009, and leader of the KDP in the city until 2011. Speaking of the political sympathies of its people, he said that "a third of the population supports Isis, much of the rest is passive, and only a small percentage actively resisted them." He believes that reports of extensive anti-Isis armed resistance inside the city was largely propaganda designed for the media. He pointed out that there might be a lot of foreign fighters in Mosul, but "the majority of fighters are Iraqis." During the almost two-and-a-half years in which Isis has ruled Mosul since it captured it in June 2014, it has concentrated on recruiting young adolescents and teenagers to its cause. These are given extensive ideological and technical training to turn them into fanatical fighters or suicide bombers.

15 February 2017

The Iraqi armed forces will eventually capture west Mosul, which is still held by Isis fighters, but the city itself will be destroyed in the fighting, a senior Iraqi politician has told me. Hoshyar Zebari says that Isis will fight to the last man in the densely-packed urban districts it still holds.

"I think west Mosul will be destroyed," says Mr. Zebari, pointing to the high level of destruction in east Mosul just taken by government forces. He adds that no date has yet been set for the resumption of the Iraqi government offensive into west Mosul, but he expects the fighting to be even tougher than before. A further reason for fanatical resistance by Isis is that Mr. Zebari is certain that Baghdadi is still in west Mosul and reports of him being killed or injured in an air strike elsewhere in Iraq are incorrect. He says that Isis sector commanders in the city are experienced professional soldiers, all of whom were once officers in Saddam Hussein's Republican Guard or Special Forces, and will fight effectively to defend their remaining stronghold in the larger part of the city to the west of the Tigris River.

The elite CTS had expected to take the whole of Mosul by the end of 2016. But ferocious resistance by some 3,000 Isis fighters on the east bank of the Tigris meant that this part of the city was only captured after three months of fighting with heavy loss of life on all sides, especially among civilians. Mr. Zebari, who originally comes from Mosul, describes the present situation in the city as "horrible" and "a shambles," even in those parts of it that Iraqi government forces have captured, though not fully occupied and secured. "There are Isis 'sleeper cells' with maybe sixteen to twenty-four men in each district which come out of hiding and kill people who are cooperating with the government," he says. "They target restaurants which have reopened and serve soldiers." There has also been a complete failure by the government to restore basic services like electricity and water supply. Asked about casualties, Mr. Zebari said those on the Iraqi security forces side had been heavy, but the government in Baghdad has refused to produce exact figures. US reports say that some units of the Golden Division, which is a sort of highly trained army within the army, had suffered up to 50 percent losses. He discounts official Iraqi claims that 16,000 Isis fighters had been killed, saying that the real figure was probably between 1,500 and 2,000 Isis dead out of a total of 6,000 in Mosul. He thought that they had brought in reinforcements and there were probably 4,000 Isis fighters left who would defend west Mosul, which is home to about 750,000 people.

This account is borne out by other reports from in and around east Mosul where this week two suicide bombers attacked a market, killing twelve and wounding thirty-three people. Mortars and rockets fired by Isis are still exploding and the main water system was destroyed in fighting in January. Pictures show cavernous craters reportedly caused by bombs dropped by US Air Force B-52s to aid the Iraqi army advance. People who fled Mosul at the height of the fighting and have been returning to it are often leaving again. The UN says that it is worried by arbitrary arrests of displaced people as possible Isis sympathisers and records that on 8 and 9 February some 1,442 came back to east Mosul, but 791 left for displacement camps. Despite the Iraqi security forces' focus on weeding out Isis supporters and "sleeper cells," Mr. Zebari says that this does not provide real security because travel documents can be bought from corrupt security officers for 25,000 Iraqi dinars (£17). Drivers on Iraqi roads have told me that the main concern of checkpoints is not security, but to extract bribes from passing vehicles. This would explain how Isis suicide bombers driving vehicles packed with explosives are able to pass through multiple checkpoints before detonating explosives in civilian areas in Baghdad or other cities.

Mr. Zebari notes that rivalry between the US and Iran in Iraq is increasing under President Donald Trump, with the latter slow to call the Iraqi

Prime Minister Abadi and making US help conditional on a reduction in Iranian influence. During the US presidential election campaign, Mr. Trump claimed that Iran had taken over Iraq. There is also growing friction between the different Shia parties and movements that Mr. Zebari says makes "inter-Shia fighting imminent."

There is an ominous precedent for what may happen in Mosul because other Sunni cities and towns up and down Iraq have been wrecked or rendered uninhabitable by government counter-offensives since 2014. In practice, the Shia-dominated Iraqi government wants to break the back of Sunni resistance to its rule so it will never be capable of rising again.

27 March 2017
Civilians trying to flee the besieged Isis-held enclave in west Mosul are being shot dead by Isis and Iraqi army snipers as they try to cross the Tigris River, says an eyewitness trapped inside the city with his family. Jasim, a thirty-three-year-old Iraqi Sunni living in west Mosul near the Fifth Bridge, told me: "I want to rescue my mother and take her to the eastern part, but it is dangerous. Three people were killed in our neighbourhood trying to cross the river to the eastern side. They were shot dead by the snipers." Jasim explained that "Daesh have snipers who cover the riverbank between the Fifth and Sixth Bridges."

"The problem is that even at night, things are not that easy," he said. "The Iraqi army, the federal police, and counter-terror forces shoot anyone coming from the western side as there is curfew at night and they believe anyone coming from the western side must be a Daesh fighter." As a result, civilians are being killed by both Iraqi army mortars and Isis snipers when they try to escape. On several occasions in the past, the Iraqi security forces have announced that they have killed Isis infiltrators seeking to cross the Tigris from the west and these may have been civilians trying to escape. Speaking about civilian casualties inside his neighbourhood, Jasim says that "dozens of civilians are killed every day, including children. Yesterday, two children were killed by a mortar shell of the Iraqi army coming from the eastern part." He says that Iraqi government media claims that they have "smart artillery" is quite untrue. This is confirmed privately by senior Iraqi officers, one saying that many of the civilian casualties are not being caused by air strikes, but by "Tuz" Russian-made rockets mounted on the back of vehicles, which have no guidance systems. In a grim demonstration of the danger from air attack facing anybody living in west Mosul, Jasim was himself injured in a drone attack hours after he spoke to me. He has been removed to hospital, but the extent of his injuries is not known.

Jasim gives one of the few accounts from inside the closely besieged western part of Mosul still held by Isis, describing the increasingly desperate living conditions of at least 300,000 people trying to survive there. I spoke to him by mobile phone late at night from inside the western part of Mosul. Though the signal was weak, messages can be passed to east Mosul. Referring to the growing shortage of food, Jasim says that "people in our neighbourhood are searching in the garbage to find something that can be eaten to take it to their children." There have been no vegetables or fruit available for over a month. He and his family have a little flour and rice stored, but they want to keep it as a last resort to feed their children. He says they roam other neighbourhoods to see if they can find food there so as not to use up these last reserves before they have to.

Where food is available, it is often too expensive for most people to buy. Jasim says that "where bakeries work, many women beg and ask those who have money to buy some bread for their children. Most of my neighbours eat bread only; they live on bread and water." Even water can be difficult to obtain because the only source is neighbourhood wells from which it is pumped. But those who get water here need to provide petrol, which costs the Iraqi dinar equivalent of fifteen dollars a litre, to run the pump. Surprisingly, there is a limited supply of electricity, though not in all areas, according to Jasim. He says that "we have electricity for about two hours every three days, though in some areas they haven't had electricity since last month. People move during the day into other neighbourhoods to charge their phones." The mobile network is available only at night because it is then that there is electricity in the eastern government-held part of Mosul where there are mobile phone towers mounted on trucks.

The Isis-held enclave in Mosul, centred on the impenetrable warren of streets and alleys so narrow that two people cannot walk abreast, is being heavily bombarded and is very dangerous. But people are still dying even in districts in east Mosul where fighting is supposed to have ended. An example of this happened on Monday in the east of the city in Nabi Yunus covered market, which is full of tiny booths and small shops, and which was crowded with shoppers when it was hit by the first of three Isis mortar bombs at 10 a.m. It struck a shop selling perfumes, which burst into flames, killing eleven adults and a child who were caught by the blast or burned to death by the fire which followed. Two more mortar bombs fired by Isis from the other side of the Tigris fell in the same area over the next hour, killing another child and two adults. A small crowd was looking at the blackened burned out little shops when we arrived as a soldier in a red cap and a policeman tried with limited success to disperse them. "Go home and don't stand here because Daesh might send a suicide bomber!" shouted the soldier angrily and some in the crowd looked worried, recalling that this is a favourite Isis tactic, and quickly walked away. The policemen said that many of the injured had been badly burned by the blazing perfume shop and were unlikely to survive. The mortar attack on Nabi Yunus market is only one incident out of dozens that are killing people every day in Mosul.

Controversy continues to rage over the death of as many as 240 civilians, many hiding in cellars, killed during an air strike by the US-led air coalition on the Jadida district on 17 March, which reduced three buildings to heaps of rubble. The coalition says it did carry out air strikes called in by Iraqi ground forces on this area at that time, but the Iraqi Defence Ministry claims that only sixty-one civilians were killed and these died because Isis had booby-trapped the walls of the buildings in which they had taken shelter. Since Saturday, it has banned journalists from entering those parts of west Mosul that it holds, making it difficult to verify how many bodies have been taken from the rubble. The online newsletter *Shaafaq News*, which first broke the story of the Jadida air strike, says that it has been told by a security source that the true figure for casualties in west Mosul since the start of the offensive is 3,864 dead and 22,759 injured.

30 March 2017

People trapped in the Old City of Mosul are dying of hunger because they have not received any food for almost three weeks, according to a resident. Karim, a twenty-eight-year-old taxi driver who lives in the ancient centre of Mosul, tells me that many people, including several he knows, one of them a friend, have already died of malnutrition. "Some areas of the Old City have not had any food delivered for twenty days and most people have spent all their savings," says Karim. He adds that during this period, there has been no water and no electricity and nobody can leave the area because Isis shoots them if they try to do so. "We cannot get out of our houses," he says, "it is not safe at all."

Karim's account, given over a weak mobile telephone link to east Mosul, throws light on what is happening in the Old City. Aid agencies estimate that there are 400,000 people living here and a further 200,000 on the

outer periphery whose status in terms of food and safety has hitherto been
unknown. People are unable to escape to areas already captured by Iraqi
government forces and join the tens of thousands fleeing south away from
the fighting. These board blue and white buses that take them to camps
at Hamam Alil where they are vetted to detect Isis members, fed, receive
medical attention, and housed in tents.

Karim gives a vivid picture of the confusion and terror in Old City.
Isis squads of half a dozen or more fighters, including highly experienced
snipers and bomb makers, slip from house to house through holes in the
walls. Surprisingly, Karim says there are not many Isis fighters in the southern part of the Old City, but the army has not yet entered the area. Though
Karim is still in an Isis-held neighbourhood, the Iraqi security forces or the
Hashd al-Shaabi are not far away. He says that "Yesterday, I heard some
Shia songs. When we hear such songs, we realize that the Hashd or the
army are close to the area. The Hashd usually raises the volume of their
songs, which can be heard clearly at night."

Karim believes that Isis is moving its wounded to the north part of the
Old City away from the front line in the south. He says that "I talked to
my cousin who lives in Az Zanjili neighbourhood. He said his son was with
dozens of people in al-Jumhuri Hospital [where they had gone to escape air
strikes in the belief that it would not be hit] and they could see the Daesh
wounded were being transported to other areas to the north of the city.
People who live near the hospital said that the Daesh vehicles transported
the wounded to Hay 17 Tamouz neighbourhood."

Isis fighters are under intense pressure from air attack and ground forces
that far outnumber them. They have managed to hold back Iraqi Federal
Police and other units on the southern periphery of the Old City, inflicting heavy casualties. The Iraqi government does not reveal its losses, but
US General Joseph Votel says that Iraqi forces have lost 284 killed and
1,600 wounded so far in their bid to capture west Mosul that started on
19 February, compared to 490 killed and 3,000 wounded in its successful
battle for east Mosul. Civilian loss of life is not known. Iraqi government
forces have changed their tactics and Isis is now being attacked by the so-
called Golden Division. The plan is evidently to make multiple attacks on
Isis to spread them out and make it easier for assault teams to penetrate into
the Old City.

Everywhere in and around those parts of west Mosul held by Isis, perhaps
a quarter of the city as a whole, remain highly dangerous where a simple

mistake can have lethal consequences. Earlier this week, the thirty-three-year-old taxi driver called Jasim made just such a mistake, which almost cost him his life as it led to his house being targeted by a drone. By his account, three weeks ago, the Iraqi military had told people in Mosul not to cover their car or property with canvas or any other material, or they would be targeted by drones or aircraft. The reason apparently was that Iraqi officers, or American special forces that are also calling in air strikes, believed that Isis was using these materials to hide weapons and munitions. People in government-held east Mosul were told about this and asked to inform their relatives and friends in the west if they could reach them by phone. Unfortunately for Jasim, he misunderstood the point and thought the warning only applied to canvas covering cars and also forgot that there was a piece of canvas covering one part of the roof of his house.

Jasim, whose house is close to the Tigris River, had other worries last Sunday because he was trying to find a way of getting his mother safely across the river to the government-held east of the city without her being killed by Isis or government snipers. What happened on the following day is best described in his own words as they give a graphic sense of the perils facing people trying to survive in Mosul today. He says:

> We see small jet aircraft every day and when they get close, we see that they are a drone flying without a pilot. There is a small lobby in my house that opens on one side onto a small square. The drone threw a bomb which fell on the corner of the house near the water tank. When it exploded, I didn't lose consciousness. Everything in front of me had become all dusty as part of the wall collapsed. After a while, I felt a severe pain on my leg, and after a few moments, I realised I was injured. I partly walked and partly crawled to a small temporary clinic nearby, but they could not treat my leg properly. They said it needed surgery, but they do not have the equipment. They gave me some bandages to help ease the pain.

Jasim went back to his house, which he shares with his mother and three sisters. When I spoke to him again, he was in bed and crying because of the pain of his injury and complaining that the sound of explosions and aircraft overhead prevented him from sleeping. He explained that many people in west Mosul like himself did not know they should not use canvas to cover cars or other property if they wanted to avoid being targeted by drones. He says that his ignorance of this was scarcely surprising because in west Mosul mobiles can seldom be used, "and people cannot visit each other [to exchange information] even in daytime in some places because of the air strikes and Daesh."

People in Mosul, once a city of two million, are desperate to escape by any means. Isis fighters demand a bribe of $2,000 to let a person escape according to one source, though this is difficult to verify. One man with his wife and two children who tried to cross the Tigris at a place called Dawasa was shot dead by a sniper earlier this week.

31 March 2017

Standing high above Mosul beside the ruins of the Nabi Yunus shrine, destroyed by Isis as idolatrous in 2014, one can see the west of the city on the far side of the Tigris River. There the Iraqi security forces and Isis are engaged in the fiercest and longest battle of the Iraq conflict. Like many battlefields, the scene is eerily pretty as spring rains turn the trees and grass a fresh green colour, and buildings are too distant to tell if they have been damaged or destroyed. A single large column of black smoke and three smaller plumes of white smoke rise over west Mosul but do not look very menacing. There is the crash of an artillery piece firing close by and, a few seconds later, another wisp of smoke or dust appears on the other side of the city.

In modern war, every bombardment of a city from ground and air is different, but the justification by politicians and military commanders is usually much the same. Those ordering the air, missile, or artillery attacks emphasise the meticulous care they take to avoid civilian casualties and, if these inadvertently occur, it is only because of the devilish practices of the other side who are using ordinary folk as human shields. Much the same lies were used to justify the Israeli bombardment of Lebanon in 1982, 1996, and 2006 and of Gaza in 2008, 2009, and 2014; the American bombing of Iraq in 1991 and 2003; the Syrian government levelling of whole towns since 2011, and the Russians doing much the same since they intervened in Syria in 2015.

In all cases, if you bomb an area containing both combatants and civilians you will kill many of the latter because you can never distinguish sufficiently between the two, even if that was not your original intention. The grisly tradition of trying to explain away heavy civilian loss of life caused by aerial and artillery bombardment of cities is being maintained by the US-led air coalition and Iraqi government during the siege of Mosul. Once again, the propaganda myth that "surgical strikes" can distinguish the innocent from the guilty has been pumped out. But what counts is the accuracy not only of the weapons but of the information about who is going to be on the receiving end—something which, in the chaos of war, is always inadequate. People in flight from Mosul are caustic about Iraqi and US claims about the accuracy of their weapons. Mohammed Ali Suleiman, a sixty-six-year-old shopkeeper, said: "they talk about 'smart bombs' but my neighbourhood is 90 percent destroyed by them."

Isis snipers are killing anybody who tries to leave west Mosul because they do not want to lose their "human shields," but even if they did not do so, a proportion of the civilian population would stay behind and be targeted along with Isis fighters. Unexplained is why the Baghdad government at first urged civilians in Mosul to stay in their homes, though this played into the hands of Isis. Somebody grossly underestimated the strength of Isis resistance, or did not want to cope with a million displaced people, or had foolish and romantic ideas about a popular uprising against Isis.

The obvious falsehood that a bombardment can be conducted in a confined area where civilians are present without killing a lot of them has a quite limited sell-by date. Israelis, Americans, Syrians, Russians, and Iraqis have all, at different times, responded to mass killings for which they are being blamed by a flat denial that it happened at all, by stating that it was not as large as reported or that somebody else is responsible. Where the evidence is incontrovertible, the aim is to muddy the waters until the news agenda has moved on. An old PR adage about how to deal with damaging news advises those rebutting it "first to say 'no story' and then say 'old story'"; this works well in most cases. The problem is that, in the case of bombing campaigns, disaster is always just around the corner. A sympathetic media generally goes along with the pretence that bombing and shelling is more discriminating than it really is and plays down evidence to the contrary. But this just stores up trouble for the future when calamity finally strikes—as it always does—and denials and evasions simply underline the guilt of the perpetrator.

2 April 2017

Omar, a thirty-nine-year-old resident of the Old City, told me that the last lights were going out in houses on his street because they had no fuel left for the neighbourhood generator, even if they could get to it. "This is the last call I can make because nobody can go out to turn on the generator and there is no petrol, so there is no way of charging my mobile after this call," Omar shouted over a feeble phone link to east Mosul in an appeal for help. He said that nobody had any idea what was happening in their neighbourhood because of the proximity of the fighting. "I am with my family in my neighbour's house, which is fairly big and contains about thirty-five people," says Omar. "Children are crying from hunger and we have run out of the flour. We have only wheat and bran that we put some in water to become soft and give it to the children."

Omar describes what life is like for many of the people who are not able to escape the Old City and cannot find out what is happening around them. "We hear explosions and shooting from outside. but nobody knows who is fighting," he says. "An old woman joined us in the house yesterday and said that nobody is fighting [nearby] and the army has stopped advancing in the Old City." This may well be true of the Federal Police who are stalled in the south, but the elite Golden Division has begun an attack from the west. "We have been stranded for four days," says Omar. "We know from the people in Yarmuk district that the army is fighting there, but in our district, which is surrounded by the Federal Police, no advances have happened for more than a week. The closest street to the house where we are sitting is Faruk Street. We can hear the sounds of the explosions and air strikes and yesterday we felt as if it were an earthquake. The explosion was huge and we could hear the screaming of people outside, but no one could go out to see what is happening."

"The Old City is like an underground prison," concludes Omar. "Anyone who enters it will be lost, and the one who escapes from it is a newborn baby."

As well as their houses, people are faced with the likely loss of any vehicles they may own. Omar says that "my cousin Adnan lives in Hay 17 Tamouz district, but people there are suffering from Daesh who take their cars by force or pay little money for them, even if the car is expensive. He says that Daesh took many cars from their district and they are turned into car bombs and sent to destroy the tanks and vehicles of the Iraqi army in Yarmouk and al-Zinjili districts." Adnan said that when Daesh took his neighbour's car, they told him that "when we [Isis] conquer Baghdad, we will pay you or, if the infidels win the battle, they will compensate you."

Nobody knows how long the battle for Mosul will go on for now, with many Iraqi soldiers saying that it will be at least a month and possibly much longer. With each passing week, more and more of west Mosul is being destroyed.

6 July 2017

The voice of Abdulkareem, forty-three, a former construction worker trapped inside the fast-shrinking Isis enclave in Mosul, trembles with fear as he describes the battle raging around him. He knows that it would be dangerous to try to escape, but it may be even more risky to stay where he is. He told me in a phone interview: "I cannot speak more loudly because they [Isis] will shoot me if they catch me talking on the phone."

Abdulkareem lives in the Dachat Barga neighbourhood near the al-Maydan district, which is being heavily fought over as the Iraqi security forces pin Isis fighters, who may number only 300 combatants, in a small part of the Old City of Mosul with their backs to the Tigris River. "It is a small area, but it is like Stalingrad in that the buildings wrecked by bombs and shells provide good defensive positions," says one observer, who wished to remain anonymous. Abdulkareem can hear the sounds of fighting all around him, but he dare not go out and see exactly what is happening. "We can hear the roar of the bombing and the mortar fire," he says. "But we don't know whether it is the Iraqi army, the coalition air strikes, or Daesh." A week ago, his sister and her husband were injured. A mortar shell hit their house, though nobody knew who fired it. He heard later that they were safe in the al-Farouq neighbourhood which had been overrun by Iraqi forces.

Nobody knows how many people are dying in the last stages of the siege, as the last resistance of Isis is extinguished. Iraqi military commanders prematurely announce the capture of a neighbourhood long before it is secured. Hasan, who is working with a medical team searching the rubble for bodies, says that people are flooding out of the ruins when they think it safe to do so. "We are receiving hundreds of civilians from al-Farouq and al-Maydan and the other surrounding areas of the Old City," he says. "Most of the victims are women and children. Yesterday three women dressed in black were wearing explosive belts. They blew themselves up and killed dozens of civilians and wounded many others."

Some people have kept the dead bodies of their children and family members in their houses, because they will be shot if they try to go outside to bury them. "A woman was trying to flee with her three children," says Hasan. "The children were shot and the Isis militants let the woman go.

This happened two days ago in a small neighbourhood in the old city called Dachat Barga."

The level of destruction in Mosul is worse than in any previous battle in Iraq, say senior UN officials. Some 900,000 people have fled the city and over a third of them are in camps. Lise Grande, the UN coordinator for humanitarian affairs in Iraq, is quoted as saying that "the level of damage is far higher than we expected." Six districts, including most of the ancient Old City, have been totally destroyed while all the others have been damaged to a greater or lesser degree. Basic repairs to water, electricity, and health care facilities will be costly, far greater than the UN had predicted. There are no precise figures for civilian casualties since the start of the siege, but the UN says there have been 15,000 trauma injuries sent for treatment.

Fearful that government forces suspect that groups escaping include Isis fighters and suicide bombers in disguise, displaced people try to establish their credentials as opponents of Isis by denouncing each other as Isis "sleepers." The dilemmas facing people within the last Isis strongholds in Mosul are explained by Abu Mohammed, fifty-three, who last week fled the Old City with a group of civilians. Isis had, in fact, retreated from their neighbourhood, but they were not sure of this. The decision that they must all flee was taken by "a man whom the people of our neighbourhood all respect. He was rich and helped people a lot until he had become bankrupt. This man asked us to move out of our houses and rush towards the Iraqi army." When they reached Iraqi forces, they told them "about some Daesh men with us. I know a teenager who was with our group. He was later arrested and turned out to be Daesh. He was Iraqi but not from Mosul." Abu Mohammed says that they suspected the teenager because he was looking healthy and well-fed and "not suffering from starvation like the other civilians."

Iraqi government forces on the ground have never believed the propaganda line that Isis had no popular support among the Sunni Arab population of Mosul. They suspect that many refugees come from the families of Isis fighters or at least supported them. A UN aid worker said that she had "never seen such terrified people as a group of young men of military age just before they were vetted by the Iraqi forces as possible Isis fighters."

9 July 2017

Iraq is declaring victory over Isis in Mosul as Prime Minister Abadi, wearing a black military uniform, arrived in the city to congratulate his soldiers.

Elite Iraqi government forces raised the country's flag on the banks of the Tigris River this morning, though Isis snipers are still shooting from the last buildings they hold in the Old City.

The devastation in the city is huge: the closer one gets to the fighting in the centre, the greater the signs of destruction from air strikes. A volunteer medical worker, who wished to remain anonymous, said that on bad days "some 200 to 300 people with injuries had turned up at my medical centre. I hear stories of many families dying, trapped in basements where they had been sheltering from the bombs." Away from the present battle zone in Mosul, many districts are deserted and only passable because bulldozers have cut a path through the debris.

In a side street in the al-Thawra district, where some buildings were destroyed, a crowd of people, mostly women in black robes which covered their faces as well their bodies, were this weekend frantically trying to obtain food baskets donated by an Iraqi charity. "These women are from Daesh families, so I don't have much sympathy for them," said Saad Amr, a volunteer worker from Mosul who had once been jailed by Isis for six months in 2014.

"I suffered every torture aside from rape," he recalled, adding that men from Isis families had been taken to Baghdad for investigation, but evidence of their crimes is difficult to obtain so most would be freed. The prospect made him edgy. Asked about popular attitudes in Mosul towards Isis, Saad, who works part-time for an Iraqi radio station, said that three years ago, when Isis captured Mosul, "some 85 percent of people supported them because the Iraqi government forces had mistreated us so badly. The figure later fell to 50 percent because of Isis atrocities and is now about 15 per cent." Ahmed, Saad's brother, who lives in east Mosul, said later that he was nervous because so many former Isis militants were walking about the city after shaving off their beards.

In a medical facility in a converted shop in al-Thawra, a wounded Isis fighter who had been hit in the face by shrapnel from a mortar round, was lying in a bed attached to a drip feed. "You cannot talk to him because he is still under investigation," warned a uniformed guard. A further thirty Isis suspects were being held in a mosque nearby, though these are more likely to have been administrative staff rather than fighters.

Saad said that the behaviour of Iraqi combat troops, particularly the Golden Division, towards civilians was excellent and "the soldiers often give their rations to hungry people." He was more dubious about how incoming Iraqi army troops and police would act towards local people.

The Iraqi government victory is very real, but it also has its limitations. The weakness of the Iraqi forces is that they depend on three elite units, notably the Counter-Terrorism Service, the Emergency Response Division, and the Federal Police, backed up by the devastating air power of the US-led coalition. The CTS combat units, perhaps less than 3,000 men, have been the cutting edge of the military offensive in Mosul and have suffered some 40 percent casualties.

This shortage of effective military units may make it difficult for Baghdad to consolidate its victory. This became clear during our five-hour drive to Mosul from the Kurdish capital of Erbil sixty miles away to the east, as we tried to find a road where the innumerable checkpoints would let us get through.

Driving across the Nineveh Plain east of Mosul, a land of ruined and abandoned towns and villages, most of the checkpoints were manned by Hashd al-Shaabi. We crossed the Tigris by a pontoon bridge near Hamam al-Alil. Here there are camps for some 100,000 displaced people from Mosul. A few days earlier some 160 Isis fighters had staged a surprise counter-attack in Qayara district, killing soldiers and police along with two Iraqi journalists.

Travelling north towards Mosul, the police posts would not at first permit us to pass, so we circled around the city to the west travelling on a winding track through rocky scrubland where there were a few impoverished hamlets in which the houses were little more than huts and from which their inhabitants had fled. For half a dozen miles not far from Mosul, there were no Iraqi security forces and we became nervous that US planes or drones might mistake our two vehicles for an Isis suicide bombing mission and attack us. We turned back to the main road and finally persuaded a police post to let us use the road running past Mosul airport and a row of bombed-out factories.

Our journey showed that the Iraqi government may have won the nine-month struggle for Mosul, but the war is not quite over. Isis may be able to regroup as it did before in 2007–11. Out in the vast desolate deserts of western Iraq and eastern Syria, its fighters can still hide and plan their revenge.

11 July 2017

"There were very few Daesh in our neighbourhood, but they dropped a lot of bombs on them," says Qais, forty-seven, a resident of the al-Jadida district of Mosul. "We reckon that the air strikes here killed between 600 and 1,000 people." He shows pictures on his phone of a house that had stood beside his own before it was hit by a bomb or missile that had reduced it to a heap of smashed-up bricks. "There were no Daesh in the house," says Qais. But there were seven members of the Abu Imad family living there, of whom five were killed along with two passers-by.

People in west Mosul say that the intensity of the bombardment from the air was out of all proportion to the number of Isis fighters on the ground. Saad Amr, a volunteer medic, worked in both east and west Mosul during the nine-month siege. He says that "the air strikes on east Mosul were fewer but more accurate, while on the west there were far more of them, but they were haphazard."

Nobody knows how many civilians died in Mosul because many of the bodies are still buried under the rubble in forty-seven degrees heat. Asked to estimate how many people had been killed in his home district of al-Thawra, Saad Amr said: "we don't know because houses were often full of an unknown number of displaced people from other parts of the city." Some districts are so badly damaged that it is impossible to reach them. We heard that there had been heavy air strikes on the districts of Zanjili and Sahba, and from a distance, we could see broken roofs with floors hanging down like concrete flaps. But we could not get there in a car because the streets leading to them were choked with broken masonry and burned-out cars.

Local people accuse the US-led coalition of massive overuse of force. The sighting of a single sniper on a roof would lead to a whole building being destroyed along with the families inside them. A sign that Isis was not present in any numbers is that, while there are bombed out buildings in every street, there are surprisingly few bullet holes in the walls from automatic rifles or machine guns. In cities like Homs in Syria today or Beirut during the civil war, wherever there had been street fighting of any intensity, walls were always pock-marked with bullet holes.

Isis will be even further weakened after the loss of Mosul if fresh reports turn out to be true that its leader al-Baghdadi was killed earlier in the year. The Syrian Observatory for Human Rights says that it has "confirmed information" that he is dead as Russia's Defence Ministry had claimed in June. It said that it might have killed him when one of its air strikes hit a gathering of Isis commanders on the outskirts of the Syrian city of Raqqa. "We have confirmed information from leaders, including one of the first rank who is Syrian, in Isis in the eastern countryside of Deir Ezzor," said

Rami Abdulrahman, the director of the British-based group. The source did not say when or how Baghdadi had died.

13 July 2017

"The people of Mosul will receive their salaries, while the people of Basra will receive the bodies of their martyrs," runs a bitter comment on Iraqi social media. Many Iraqis see the inhabitants of Mosul as willing collaborators with Isis during its three years in power in the city. In particular, there are calls for the punishment of "Daesh families" whose male members had become Isis fighters or officials.

The desire for revenge runs deep among the victims of Isis in the wake of the fall of Mosul, which is scarcely surprising given the cruelty and violence of Isis rule. Grounds for suspicion that a person was associated with Isis may be flimsy, but they are deeply held. "When women and children appear without any male relatives with them, it is assumed that the men were with Isis and have been killed, arrested, or have fled," says Belkis Wille, the senior researcher in Iraq for Human Rights Watch. "They may say that the men were killed in the bombing, but nobody knows what the truth is." Young men from Mosul and Nineveh province, of which it is the capital, find it difficult to persuade the victorious Iraqi security forces that they spent years under Isis without doing some form of military service.

Revenge killings of suspected Isis activists and collaborators are still limited in number away from the battlefield, where few prisoners are taken. There have been some abductions and killings in the Sunni Arab villages south of Mosul, but no mass killings along the lines frequently carried out by Isis in Iraq and Syria. As many as 1,700 air force cadets, singled out because they were Shia, were massacred by Isis in June 2014, leading to the execution of thirty-six convicted perpetrators by the Iraqi government last year.

Yazidis who once lived to the west of Mosul, and Christians, are convinced that their Sunni Arab neighbours, with whom they had previously lived peacefully, were complicit with Isis in murdering, raping, and stealing. They say they cannot return to their villages and towns if Isis collaborators are allowed to live there. In addition, the Shia-dominated Iraqi government and the Kurdish authorities have an interest in rounding off or expanding the territory occupied by their communities at the expense of the Sunni Arabs whose fortunes, willingly or unwillingly, have become linked to Isis and the foundering caliphate.

Communal punishment in the shape of the forced expulsion of "Daesh families," which may mean sanctions against whole villages, is taking place in different parts of northern and central Iraq. Ms. Wille says that at the IDP camps in Khazar and Hassan Shami in Kurdish controlled territory east of Mosul, Sunni Arabs in the camps can "see their former villages, but are not being allowed to return there. On the other hand, they are being told that they are free to take the bus to east Mosul any time they want to go." She adds that Sunni Arab tribal authorities are often taking the lead in expelling Isis families from their villages and sending them to IDP camps because they want revenge, saying they cannot protect them, or see them as tainted. She believes that a further motive is that "the Sunni community wants to show Baghdad and the world that they are not all Isis."

Sectarian and ethnic cleansing by state authorities or militia groups in Iraq may have long-term political objectives, but they also fulfil popular wishes. For instance, in the aftermath of the recapture of Mosul earlier this week, two hashtags in Arabic went viral on Facebook, Twitter, and Instagram. The first one was a variant of either "Mosul is ours" or "Mosul is ours and we took it." The second hashtag read, "People of Mosul Deserve," accompanied by photos of the destruction in Mosul. There are hundreds of social media accounts evidently from Iraqi Shias, accusing the people of Mosul of supporting Isis. One post has two photographs, one showing people celebrating in the streets as Isis seized Mosul in 2014 and similar scenes of celebration when the Iraqi armed forces retook it this month. The writer comments: "This is ridiculous."

Since the US invasion of 2003, Iraq has witnessed politically significant demographic change. The Shia-Sunni sectarian war in and around Baghdad in 2006–7 saw the Sunni compressed into smaller enclaves and mixed areas become wholly Shia. Since the counter-offensive against Isis began in 2014, Sunni Arabs have been forced to leave villages and towns in strategic areas south of Baghdad and in northern Hilla province. They are unlikely to be allowed to return because they could attack the roads between the capital and the Shia holy cities of Najaf and Karbala.

There are still some 500,000 Sunni Arab IDPs in Kirkuk province, who are being allowed to return to wholly Sunni centres but not to those where Shia also live. In both Iraqi and Kurdish controlled areas, there are camps that are little better than "open prisons," says Ms. Wille, where IDPs cannot come and go from the camp freely, receive visitors, or even own a mobile phone. Enforced demographic change may be one motive for this, but there is also genuine, though probably exaggerated, fear of Isis "sleeper cells" waiting to strike. An Isis raid on Kirkuk in 2016 led to the destruction of villages from which the raiders were believed to have come.

19 July 2017

More than 40,000 civilians were killed in the devastating battle to retake Mosul from Isis, according to intelligence reports, a death toll far higher than previous estimates. Hoshyar Zebari, until recently a senior minister in Baghdad, told me that many bodies "are still buried under the rubble." "The level of human suffering is immense," he said. "Kurdish intelligence believes that over 40,000 civilians have been killed as a result of massive firepower used against them, especially by the federal police, air strikes, and Isis itself."

Mr. Zebari emphasised in an exclusive interview that the unrelenting artillery bombardment by units of the Iraqi federal police, in practice a heavily armed military unit, had caused immense destruction and loss of life in west Mosul. The figure given by Mr. Zebari for the number of civilians killed in the nine-month siege is far higher than those previously reported, but the intelligence service of the KRG has a reputation for being extremely accurate and well-informed. Isis prevented any monitoring of casualties, while outside groups have largely focused on air strikes rather than artillery and rocket fire as a cause of civilian deaths.

Mr. Zebari accuses the government in Baghdad of not doing enough to relieve the suffering. "Sometimes you might think the government is indifferent to what has happened," he said. He doubts if Christians, Yazidis, Kurds, and other minorities, who have lived in and around Mosul for centuries, will be able to reconcile with the Sunni Arab majority whom they blame for killing and raping them. He says some form of federal solution for future governance would be best.

Reading from Kurdish intelligence reports, Mr. Zebari says that a high level of corruption among the Iraqi military forces occupying Mosul is undermining security measures to suppress Isis in the aftermath of its defeat. He says that suspect individuals are able to pass through military checkpoints by paying $1,000 (£770) and can bring a vehicle by paying $1,500. He says corruption of this type is particularly rife in the Sixteenth and Ninth Iraqi army divisions and the Tribal Volunteers (Hashd al-Ashairi), drawn in part from the Shabak minority in the Nineveh Plain.

The ability of Isis militants to remain free or be released from detention by paying bribes has led to a change in attitude among people in Mosul whom Mr. Zebari says "were previously willing to give information about Isis members to the Iraqi security forces." They are now way of doing so because they see members of Isis, whom they had identified and who had been arrested, returning to the streets capable of exacting revenge on those who informed against them. Several anti-Isis people in Mosul have confirmed to me that this is indeed the case.

Corruption by the occupying military forces takes different forms, according to Kurdish intelligence information cited by Mr. Zebari. Some people are "being charged $100 for removing a body from the rubble and others $500 to reoccupy their house," where it is still standing. Iraqi army and militia units have always been notorious for exacting fees and protection money from civilians, with trucks moving goods on the roads being a particularly profitable target when they pass through military checkpoints.

Mr. Zebari says that he is disappointed by the lack of Iraqi government plans to reconstruct Mosul. As finance minister in Baghdad until late last year, he had made provision for $500 million in the budget for rebuilding Mosul. He says: "I wanted $500 million upfront to encourage other donors, but now the government has withdrawn from the fund and used the money elsewhere. This was not an encouraging sign." Even if there is reconstruction, Mr. Zebari, who grew up in Mosul and still has a house in the east of the city (though long confiscated, first by Saddam Hussein and later by Isis), laments that "the soul of Mosul has gone and its iconic buildings are destroyed." He says he cannot imagine Mosul without the Nabi Yunus mosque (the tomb of Jonah) that Isis blew up in 2014 and the al-Nuri mosque, with its twelfth century leaning minaret, which Isis destroyed in the last stage of the battle for the Old City.

Asked if Baghdadi is alive or dead, Mr. Zebari said he did not know. But he added that, if Baghdadi was dead, it was strange that no new caliph or Isis leader had been declared since part of the ideology of such movements is that they do not rely on a single human being. Successors had been quickly announced when Abu Musab al-Zarqawi, the leader of al-Qaeda in Iraq, was killed in a US air strike in 2006 and Osama bin Laden was shot dead by US special forces in Pakistan in 2011. Moreover, he says that there "has been no sign of a change in the Isis command and control structure."

17 August 2017

On 22 May, Ahmed Mohsen, an unemployed taxi driver, left his house in the Isis-controlled western part of Mosul to try to escape across the

Tigris to the government-held eastern side of the city. He and his mother, along with ten other people, carried rubber tyres down to the river: most of them couldn't swim, and they planned to tie them together to make a raft. The siege of Mosul was in its seventh month and Ahmed was both desperate and starving: he and his mother were living on handfuls of wheat they cooked, though he said it made him feel sick. His friends believe that lack of food made him light-headed and led him to risk crossing the river. "Even if I die in the river," he told them, "it will be better than living here."

When I wrote about Ahmed for a newspaper report, I changed his name (to Jasim) and age and avoided any detail that might identify him to Isis, of whom he was terrified. I hoped to meet him when the siege was over, though I could see from his own account that there was a good chance he wouldn't survive. In 2014, Ahmed, who came from a poor family, was driving his taxi between Mosul and Baghdad, a journey of about four hours. His friends say he was a friendly and generous man, who liked talking to passengers and who took great care of his car, of which he was proud. He didn't own it outright, but had bought a share in it and was saving up to buy the rest. When Isis overran Mosul, travel to government-held areas was still just about possible and Ahmed went on driving to Baghdad. But a few months later, he was arrested by Isis, accused of helping members of the Iraqi police and army to escape the city. As a friend of his put it, "he stayed in prison for three months and was badly tortured. He would talk a lot about that." He was released but could no longer work, and then he was jailed again for a month and a half. He worried about his mother: his brother in Germany was able to send back small amounts to support her but wasn't officially allowed to work. "When Ahmed was freed for the second time," his friend said, "he sold his share in his taxi and spent the money over the remaining two years of Isis rule. Recently, he went bankrupt."

Despite these disasters, Ahmed and his mother remained optimistic well into the siege that Isis rule wouldn't last much longer and that things would improve. They planned to travel to Turkey, where Ahmed's brother would meet them. This brother now appears to be the only surviving member of the family; he is trying to get a death certificate issued for Ahmed, which would entitle him to asylum in Germany and allow him to get a job. His married sister has disappeared: she is believed to have been killed in an air strike, though her body hasn't been found. This is far from unusual: at one stage, the Civil Defence Corps in west Mosul had just twenty-five men, one bulldozer, and a forklift truck to search for bodies, estimated to number in the thousands, buried under the ruins. They haven't been paid their salaries by the central government and won't search for a body unless a relative can give them a clear idea of where it is.

All the people I was in contact with inside the Isis-held part of the Old City are dead. Ahmed Mohsen was wounded by a drone and then killed by an Isis sniper; his mother and sister have disappeared and are presumably dead. I was also in touch with Rayan Mawloud, a thirty-eight-year-old businessman with a wife and two children who had a trading company based in a shop in one of Mosul's markets. He came from a well-off family and his father had a fleet of trucks that used to carry goods to and from Basra and Jordan. When the attack on Mosul began, a friend of Rayan's says that he spent his savings buying food to give not just to his relatives "but also to many people whom he did not know." Rayan, knowing that his family would probably be shot by Isis snipers if they tried to escape, took the opposite decision to Ahmed Mohsen and stayed with his family in their house. It was hit in an air strike on 23 June, killing his wife and five-year-old son. He remained in the part of the house that was still habitable, but it was hit by another air strike on 9 July. He was severely injured and died three days later.

PART III. THE IRAQI KURDS: AN UNNECESSARY DEFEAT

The reasons why able, experienced leaders make gargantuan errors of judgement is mysterious, but it can be highly revealing about their strengths and weaknesses. A striking example of this is what occurred in Iraqi Kurdistan on 25 September 2017 when President Masoud Barzani held a referendum for or against Kurdish independence.

I was surprised because Barzani, a veteran survivor of many crises, seemed to have chosen the worst possible moment for the poll. For the first time in decades, there was a powerful and victorious Iraqi government army, which had just captured Mosul after a nine-month siege, close to Kurdish-held territory. All the Kurds' usual allies, above all the US, opposed the referendum as did neighbouring states such as Turkey, Iran, and Syria, which had their own disaffected Kurdish minorities. I half-suspected that Kurdish leaders, normally so adept at weaving their way through the minefields of Iraqi politics, must have a good reason to believe that Baghdad did not have a military option, but the reason for their belief was elusive.

The penalty for getting this one wrong was going to be very high: it would set back by decades the heroic struggle of the Iraqi Kurds for self-determination and perhaps stifle it forever. Some experienced leaders, such as my friend Omar Sheikhmous, had premonitions of disaster, telling me that he feared that calling the referendum might be one of the classic miscalculations of Iraqi history, resembling, in its disastrous potential, Saddam Hussein's decision to invade Iran in 1980 and Kuwait in 1990.

He turned out to be all too correct: Kurdish voters overwhelmingly endorsed independence, which was scarcely a surprise. But the poll did not bring independence closer, though it did provoke the government in Baghdad which, to its own surprise, found that it held all the political and military cards in its hands: the Kurds were divided among themselves, without supportive foreign allies, and an Iraqi army was nearby capable of enforcing Baghdad's will. On 16 October, Iraqi tanks and troops swept into Kirkuk city, meeting little *resistance and, in a few days, reversed all the territorial gains made by the Kurds since the US invasion in 2003.*

I visited Kirkuk at the end of October and asked a Kurdish leader who was still in the city if they could have resisted the Iraqi government forces if their own side had been united. "Of course not," he replied. The Iraqi forces had tanks and planes and we had no chance. Maybe we could have lasted a day if we had fought, but the only result would have been bloodshed." This was a fair assessment of the balance of forces.

Many Kurds and their foreign supporters took refuge in conspiracy theories to explain away this defeat: it was all the fault of an Iranian plot and the treachery of the leaders of the rival Kurdish party, the Patriotic Union of Kurdistan.

I thought that what had happened had its roots in the weaknesses of Kurdish nationalism and perhaps nationalism everywhere (I was thinking of Brexit). The strength of nationalist movements is their communal solidarity against oppression, but this is frequently accompanied by exaggerated ideas of ethnic superiority and political strength. Ever since the fall of Saddam Hussein, Kurdish leaders had become increasingly contemptuous of Iraqi governments in Baghdad. They had not noticed that the siege of Mosul—in which the Kurds had not participated—marked a turn of the tide. If the US and Iran, the crucial foreign players, had to choose between the Iraqi government and the Kurds, they would choose Baghdad. At one time, Kurdish leaders had understood the real balance of forces, but years of success had eroded their understanding.

September–November 2017

22 September 2017

On 10 April 2003, I was driving on a road west of Kirkuk, waiting for the city to be captured by the Kurdish Peshmerga and worried that we might arrive there before the Iraqi army had withdrawn or broken up. We could see no cars from Kirkuk coming towards us, which might mean that there was fighting still going on. We could see abandoned Iraqi army camps beside the road but no looters, a bad sign in Iraq in wartime where only extreme danger will deter looters from trying to grab the richest pickings. We were havering about what to do when a car appeared from the direction of Kirkuk, whose driver leaned out the window to shout: "It is finished—the way to Kirkuk is open."

An orgy of looting was going on inside the city, with the theft of everything from mattresses to fire engines. I saw two looters drive away a large yellow bulldozer they had just stolen. The Kurdish Peshmerga had taken over the city a few hours earlier, saying that they were there to fill the vacuum left by the disintegration of the Iraqi army and to restore order, though they did little to stop the looters.

They had repeatedly promised the Americans that they had no plans to seize Kirkuk and, even now, were insisting that their occupation was only temporary. A senior Kurdish officer standing in the wreckage of the governor's office told me that "we're expecting to withdraw some of our men within forty-five minutes."

Fourteen years later, the Kurds still control Kirkuk, the oil capital of northern Iraq with a mixed population of Kurds, Arabs, and Turkmen, as well as much of the surrounding province. The leaders of the US-led coalition during the invasion had feared that, if the Kurds captured the city, they would provoke a Turkish invasion, since Turkey had declared that it would not tolerate such a thing. I wrote an article describing the Kurdish takeover with the headline "Kurdish victory provokes fears of Turkish invasion."

It never happened: in the years following 2003, Iraqi Kurdistan has been like the eye at the centre of a hurricane, always brushed by disastrous winds but avoiding complete catastrophe. Journalists reporting on Kirkuk frequently referred to it as a "powder keg" because of its ethnic and sectarian divisions along with its oil wealth, which so many different parties would like to control. The cliché is a useful one for reporters in Iraqi Kurdistan in general, because it suggests that an explosion will happen without saying when. Again and again, predictions of Turkish invasions or war between the Peshmerga and Iraqi central government forces over disputed territories have proved false or premature.

The referendum on independence for the Kurdish controlled territory, due to take place on 25 September, is the latest event billed as threatening the stability of Iraq and a good chunk of the Middle East. Seldom has a democratic poll in such a small place been so universally denounced by so many international powers, including the US, UK, Germany, and France. A White House statement emphasises "to the leaders of the Kurdistan Regional Government (KRG) that the referendum is distracting from efforts to defeat Isis and stabilise the liberated areas. Holding the referendum in disputed areas is particularly provocative and destabilising."

Regional powers like Turkey and Iran have likewise demanded that the referendum be cancelled and threatened retaliation if it is not. In Baghdad, Abadi has denounced it and the Supreme Court ruled that it was "unconstitutional." But for all the sound and fury, it looks as if the vote is going ahead. A peculiarity of this hysterical reaction is that the referendum is non-binding and does not commit KRG President Masoud Barzani to do anything concrete to achieve self-determination. He himself says that the purpose of the poll "is to tell the world that we want independence," adding that outside powers had believed that the calling of the referendum was merely "a pressure card," a ploy to extract concessions from Baghdad. By pressing ahead with it, he believes he has put Kurdish independence firmly on the agenda. If nothing else, he has demonstrated that the international community is terrified by anything that destabilises Iraq and that the coop-eration of the Kurds cannot be taken for granted.

Among the Iraqi Kurds, Barzani has already re-established his creden-tials as the standard-bearer of Kurdish nationalism, defying threats and pleas for postponement or cancellation of the vote. Even Kurdish leaders opposed to it as too risky are calling for as large a "yes" vote as possible, so as not to undermine the demand for a Kurdish state. The national issue also diverts attention from the corruption and incompetence of the KRG gov-ernment and the dreadful condition of its economy. Barzani has scheduled presidential and parliamentary elections for 1 November, when he and his Kurdistan Democratic Party should benefit from an overwhelmingly posi-tive referendum result thirty-five days earlier.

The political landscape of northern Iraq is changing in other ways. Isis is on the run and on Thursday, the Iraqi army started an offensive against one of its last substantial enclaves at Hawijah west of Kirkuk. As always, calcu-lating the political and military balance of power in Iraq is difficult because so many players are involved and the way they come together is unpredicta-ble. How, for instance, will Abadi react to being treated so contemptuously by the KRG? His forces have just won a historic victory over Isis by recap-turing Mosul. He will not want to lose the credit won then by being faced down by Barzani. On the other hand, Baghdad's hard-fought success at Mosul depends on the air support of the US-led coalition. Without it, the central government's military strength is, for the moment, too modest to give it a military option against the Kurds.

There is another reason why the Kurdish leadership may show caution after the referendum, assuming there is no last-minute postponement: they have a lot to lose. The Kurdish demand for self-determination is not like that of the Algerians or Vietnamese after the Second World War because, in many respects, the KRG is already highly independent and has been so since 2003. Its government is stronger politically and militarily than many members of the UN. But it is also true that the Kurds' real share of power within the nominally power-sharing government in Baghdad has been shrinking. For practical purposes, Iraq is already two countries, despite the pretence that it is a unitary state.

The real constraint on self-determination for Iraqi Kurdistan is that, referen-dum or no referendum, it remains a minnow in shark-infested waters. The US and its allies will no longer need the Kurds to the degree they do today once Isis is defeated. The Iraqi central government will get stronger rather than weaker.

The safest course for the Kurds is still a confederal power-sharing agreement with Baghdad, but so far, neither side has had the will to make this happen.

25 September 2017

Iraqi Kurds go to the polls today to cast their votes in the non-binding referendum on Kurdish independence. The vote is taking place not only in the territory of the KRG but in areas in dispute—including Kirkuk. President Masoud Barzani says holding the referendum is "risky," but "we are ready to pay any price for our independence."

An overwhelming "yes" vote is forecast, but there are signs in the last few days of Kurdish leaders playing down nationalist rhetoric. Kurdish Prime Minister Nechirvan Barzani, nephew of the president, said at a press conference that there would be no immediate independence or "redrawing of borders" between Kurdish- and central government-controlled zones, and that the Kurdish regional leadership would resolve its differences peacefully with the central government in Baghdad.

Haider al-Abadi has condemned the poll in a television address to the nation, saying that it "threatens Iraq, peaceful coexistence among Iraqis, and is a danger to the region." He said that his government would take measures to secure the unity of the nation and protect all Iraqis, but did not spell out what those might be. International powers like the US, UK, France, and Germany—as well as Iraq's neighbours, Turkey and Iran—have all denounced the referendum, with only Israel supporting it.

It will take time to emerge how far the Kurdish demand for self-determination expressed during the referendum campaign, and the vague threats made by Mr. Abadi to prevent it, carry any real weight. The surge in Kurdish nationalism has generated its own momentum, and relations between Kurdish leaders and their counterparts in Baghdad have deteriorated. Clashes in disputed areas—a vast swathe of territory stretching across northern Iraq from Syria to Iran—are possible. In addition, the Iraqi government will be even less willing than previously to share power, oil, and money with the Kurds.

The Kurds have been in de facto control of Kirkuk and the surrounding province since they captured it during the US-led overthrow of Saddam Hussein. During that time, there has been continual friction and occasional confrontation between the Kurdish Peshmerga and the Iraqi government forces, but these have never led to full-scale warfare.

The US and its allies fear the break-up of Iraq, which might lead to the fall of Mr. Abadi and his replacement with a more pro-Iranian leader.

Turkey, for its part, has been rattling sabres, calling on the Kurds to abandon "utopic goals." Much of this is shadowboxing, because the referendum, unlike the Brexit vote in Britain in 2016, does not oblige the Kurdish leadership to move towards independence. If it turns out that it is more in the nature of a glorified opinion poll and an attempt to put Kurdish self-determination back on the international agenda, but without any follow-through, then the long-term effect of the poll could be limited.

26 September 2017

Iraq's Kurds have voted overwhelmingly for independence. The referendum in northern Iraq is re-energising Kurdish nationalism and the demand for a separate Kurdish state. "Bye-bye, Iraq! Bye-bye, Iraq!" chanted demonstrators in Erbil as they danced in the streets after the polls closed.

The impact of the referendum is not confined to Iraq but is producing outbursts of nationalist enthusiasm in Iran, where thousands of Iranian Kurds marched through the streets of their cities to show their support for the vote. Many wore masks to hide their faces from the Iranian security forces observing the demonstrations.

The angry and threatening response to the referendum by government leaders in states surrounding Iraqi Kurdistan underlines how difficult it will be for any of the thirty million Kurds in the region to win independence. Turkish President Erdogan has warned that he can close the oil pipeline carrying crude from the KRG to the Mediterranean, demanding that the Iraqi Kurdish leadership "abandons this adventure with a dark ending." The Defence Ministry in Baghdad has announced wide-scale joint military manoeuvres with the Turkish army.

These menaces need not be taken too seriously for the moment. Mr. Erodgan often issues apocalyptic warnings directed against his enemies but is usually more cautious in acting against them. The condemnation of the Kurdish referendum, however, by everybody from Washington to Tehran does show the degree to which the Kurds in Iraq are isolated and without allies if they do opt for independence. Only Israel has given them full support, something that will hardly win them friends in the region. Critics in Baghdad often accuse the Kurds of wishing to establish "a second Israel" in the Arab world.

Did President Masoud Barzani make a mistake in holding the referendum, as so many foreign powers now contend? The answer to this depends on whether any of the threats now being made against the Kurds turn out to be more than words. If they remain rhetorical, however belligerent in tone, Mr. Barzani can claim that he has successfully put the national aspirations of the Kurds back on the international agenda, even if Kurdish statehood remains a long way off.

29 September 2017

The Iraqi government has banned international flights to the Kurdish capital Erbil from 6 p.m. this Friday, isolating the Kurds in Iraq to a degree they have not experienced since the overthrow of Saddam Hussein. The isolation is political as well as geographical as traditional Kurdish allies have opposed the referendum on Kurdish independence while near neighbours in Turkey, Iran, and Baghdad are moving to squeeze the Kurds into submission.

The referendum succeeded in showing that the Kurds, not just in Iraq but in Turkey, Iran, and Syria, still yearn for their own state. Paradoxically, the outcome of the poll has demonstrated both the strength of their demand for self-determination and the weakness of their ability to obtain it. The KRG is revealed as a minnow whose freedom of action—and even its survival—depends on playing off one foreign state against the other and keeping tolerable relations with all of them, even when they detested each other. In the past, an American envoy would go out one door just as the head of the Iranian Revolutionary Guards came in the other.

The referendum has ended, perhaps only temporarily, these delicate balancing acts at which the Kurdish leadership was very skilled. The poll was always a dangerous gamble, but it is too early to say that it has entirely failed: minority communities and small nations must occasionally kick their big power allies in the teeth. Otherwise, they will become permanent proxies whose agreement with what their big power ally wants can be taken for granted. The skill for the smaller player is not to pay too high a price for going their own way.

Barzani will benefit from his decision to defy the world and press ahead with the vote when it comes to the presidential and parliamentary elections in KRG on 1 November. But the price of this could be high. It is not only Barzani who is facing an election in which national self-assertion is an issue in the coming months. Iraqi Prime Minister Abadi has a parliamentary election in 2018 and does not want to be accused of being insufficiently tough on the Kurds. Banning of international flights to Erbil is far less than many Iraqi MPs say they want.

By holding a referendum in the disputed territories, Barzani promoted this issue to the top of the Iraqi political agenda. It might have been in the interests of the Kurds to let it lie since the contending claims for land are deeply felt and irreconcilable. But by putting the future status of the KRG and the territories in play, Barzani has presented the Iraqi government, Turkey, and Iran with a threat and an opportunity. The four countries with Kurdish minorities fear that secessionism might spread, but a further problem is that they do not believe that an Iraqi Kurdish state would be truly independent, but would shift into the orbit of another power. The Iranians are paranoid about the possibility that such a state would be an American base threatening Iran. Politicians in Baghdad say that, if the Kurds are serious about self-determination, they would cling onto the oil fields of Kirkuk and be dependent on Turkey through which to export their crude.

Once the KRG dreamed of becoming a new Dubai with gleaming malls and hotels, but since 2014 it has looked more like Pompeii. The skyline is punctured by dozens of half-completed tower blocks beside rusting cranes and abandoned machinery. The boom town atmosphere disappeared in 2014 when the price of oil went down, money stopped coming from Baghdad, and Isis seized Mosul two hours' drive away. The state is impoverished and salaries paid late, if at all. This will now all get a lot worse with airports and border crossings closed and 35,000 federal employees no longer being paid.

At all events, the political landscape in Iraq and Syria is changing: we are at the beginning of a new political phase in which the battle to defeat Isis is being replaced by a power struggle between Arabs and Kurds.

16 October 2017

Elite Iraqi security forces have captured the Kurdish government headquarters buildings in the centre of Kirkuk with the Iraqi Prime Minister Abadi ordering the Iraqi flag to be raised over Kirkuk and other disputed territories. An Iraqi Oil Ministry official said that it would be "a very short time" before the Iraqi military seized all the oil fields in Kirkuk province.

The century-old movement for Kurdish independence has suffered a calamitous defeat as Iraqi military forces retake Kirkuk, facing little resistance so far from the Peshmerga fighters. Kurdish officials accuse part of the forces belonging to the Patriotic Union of Kurdistan of "treason" in not resisting the Iraqi assault. Iraqi Kurdish dreams of achieving real independence depended on controlling the oil wealth of Kirkuk, which is now lost to them, probably forever. Such autonomy as they did have will be curtailed, with Turkey announcing that it will hand over control of the border gate between Turkey and Iraqi Kurdistan to the central government in Baghdad.

The Iraqi government operation began early on Monday morning as troops swiftly seized two major oil fields and the headquarters of the North Oil Company. A convoy of armoured vehicles from Baghdad's CTS drove unopposed to the quarter of Kirkuk occupied by the governor's office and other administration buildings. Iraqi oil officials in Baghdad say that the Kurdish authorities of the KRG had tried to close down oil production by evacuating oil workers, but that output would soon be resumed.

The streets in Kirkuk city were deserted in the morning as people stayed in their houses or fled to KRG territory further north. So far, there has been little shooting as the Peshmerga abandoned their positions in what appears to have been a prearranged withdrawal. The city has a population of one million made up of Kurds, Arabs, and Turkmen, the latter two communities hostile to Kurdish rule. A resident of Kirkuk said today that ethnic Turkmen were firing guns into the air in celebration of the takeover by government forces.

Mr. Abadi told his security forces in a statement read on state television "to impose security in Kirkuk in cooperation with the population of the city and the Peshmerga." He called on the Peshmerga to serve under federal authority as part of the Iraqi armed forces. Coming after the recapture of Mosul from Isis, Mr. Abadi will be politically strengthened by his victory over the Kurds, whose commanders had promised to defend Kirkuk to the end.

The referendum is seen, even by many of those who originally supported it, as a disastrous miscalculation by Mr. Barzani. Kamran Kardaghi, a Kurdish commentator and former chief of staff to Iraqi President Jalal Talabani who died last week, says that "the Kurdish leadership never expected that there would be such consequences to the referendum."

The withdrawal of part of the Kurdish forces is ultimately a reflection of deep divisions between the Kurdish leaders and their parties, whose rivalry has always been intense. The two main political parties, the KDP led by Masoud Barzani and the PUK, founded and led for decades by Jalal Talabani, have always had separate armed forces, intelligence, and political management. The KDP, strongest in west Kurdistan, fought a savage civil war with the PUK, based in the east, in the 1990s. Kirkuk was always considered PUK territory, though its PUK governor, Najmaldin Karim, has recently inclined towards support for Mr. Barzani's policies.

Part of the PUK, much divided since its leader Jalal Talabani suffered a stroke and sank into a coma, opposed the independence referendum as a manoeuvre by Mr. Barzani to present himself as the great Kurdish nationalist leader. Ala Talabani, leader of the PUK parliamentary delegation in Baghdad, was shocked at the funeral of her uncle Jalal last Friday to find that the Iraqi flag had been removed from the coffin and there was only a Kurdish flag.

President Trump's denunciation of Iran when he decertified the deal over its nuclear programme last Friday could have energised Iran, traditionally a supporter of the PUK, to back an Iraqi government offensive in Kirkuk. The Iranians have always been worried about Iraqi Kurdistan becoming a base for US forces that could be used against them. A simpler explanation for what happened is that the Kurdish leadership was more divided than expected and the Iraqi armed forces stronger, while Mr. Barzani had alienated his traditional allies. A meeting of Kurdish leaders on Sunday called for mediation and a non-military solution to the crisis, but by then it was too late.

17 October 2017

The Kurds may have lost 40 percent of the territory they previously controlled over the last two days as they withdraw from areas long disputed with Baghdad. Kurdish Peshmerga fighters are pulling back from a great swathe of land in northern Iraq.

It is becoming clear that the KDP and PUK both agreed at a meeting on Sunday that they had no choice but to withdraw from Kirkuk and other disputed territories. They knew that they were too weak to fight the Iraqi security forces and they had no allies to whom they could appeal for help. Kurdish leaders are now blaming each other for the debacle, which will go down as one of the great disasters in Kurdish history.

The political geography of northern Iraq is to be transformed, much to the disadvantage of the Kurds. Kurdish military units have retreated from the Sinjar region close to the Syrian border, which is home to the Yazidis, who were massacred and enslaved by Isis when they advanced in August 2014. A paramilitary force made up of Yazidis, but owing allegiance to Baghdad has taken over. At the other end of the dividing line between Kurd and non-Kurd, Peshmerga have left the towns of Khanaqin, Jaloula, and Mandali close to the Iranian border north-east of Baghdad. These are all places where the Kurdish parties had exerted themselves to firmly establish their rule in the last few years and are now most likely lost forever. Peshmerga have also abandoned the last two oil fields they held near Kirkuk city.

Celebrations are widespread in Baghdad at what is seen as a second great victory for Iraq and the Prime Minister Haider al-Abadi this year, the first being the recapture of Mosul. "What I fear now is triumphalism in Baghdad, where there is talk about enforcing central government authority everywhere in Iraq," said one Kurdish commentator who did not want his name published. This might mean Baghdad putting heavy political and military pressure on the three Kurdish provinces that make up the KRG and which now look vulnerable.

The Iraqi President Fuad Masum, himself a Kurd, has called for dialogue between the central government and the Kurdish leaders to resolve the crisis sparked by the referendum. Mr. Abadi referred to the referendum as "finished and a thing of the past" but also called for dialogue "under the constitution," which would rule out Kurdish independence. There is no doubt that the balance of power has swung dramatically towards Baghdad and away from the Kurdish capital Erbil.

Mr. Barzani and his KDP Party sought on Monday to blame the PUK Peshmerga for the unopposed advance of the Iraqi security forces, accusing them of betraying the Kurds by reaching a separate deal with Baghdad. But Kurdish sources say that both the KDP and the PUK have agreed that they were too weak to fight for Kirkuk, though orders did not reach all Peshmerga commanders in time. A hospital in the Kurdish city of Sulaimaniyah says that it has received the bodies of twenty-five dead fighters and treated forty-four wounded. Overall, casualties on both sides have been slight, which is evidence that a deal on withdrawal had been struck before the Iraqi government advance.

Many Kurds will see the hand of Iran and the Islamic Revolutionary Guard Corps (IRGC) as manipulating the Baghdad government and the Kurdish parties to produce the present outcome. Iran will be pleased that the Baghdad government has been strengthened and Mr. Barzani, who is traditionally close to the US, has been weakened, but there is no need for conspiracy theories to explain what happened. Essentially, Mr. Barzani started a confrontation which he could not win.

30 October 2017

Iraqi Prime Minister Abadi is triumphant as he describes his country's security forces driving out Isis from its last strongholds in western Iraq. "Our advances have been fantastic," he said in an interview with me in Baghdad. "We are clearing the deserts of them right up to the border with Syria." Isis is being eradicated in Iraq three years after its columns were threatening to capture Baghdad. Once criticised as vacillating and weak, Mr. Abadi—who became Prime Minister in August 2014—is now lauded in Baghdad for leading the Iraqi state to two great successes in the past four months.

The son of a neurosurgeon in Baghdad, Mr. Abadi, sixty-five, spent more than twenty years of his life in exile in Britain before the fall of Saddam Hussein. Trained as an electrical engineer, he gained a PhD from the University of Manchester, before working in different branches of industry. A member of the Shia opposition Dawa Party from a young age, two of his brothers were killed by Saddam Hussein's regime and a third imprisoned. He returned to Iraq in 2003, where he became an MP and a leading figure in the ruling Dawa Party.

As the man with the strongest claim to be the architect of the two biggest victories ever won by the Iraqi state, Mr. Abadi's reputation has soared at home and abroad. He is particularly pleased that there were so few casualties when Iraqi forces retook the great swath of territory disputed with the Kurds. "I gave orders to our security forces that there should be no bloodshed," he says, explaining that fighting the Peshmerga would make reconciliation difficult between the Kurds and the government.

Soft-spoken and conciliatory, Mr. Abadi is determined to end the quasi-independence of the KRG. He says: "All border crossings in and out of Iraq must be under the exclusive control of the federal state." This includes the Kurdish oil pipeline to Turkey at Faysh Khabour, by which they once hoped would assure their economic independence, as well as the main Turkish-Iraqi land route at Ibrahim Khalil in the north-west KRG. This crossing has been Iraqi Kurdistan's lifeline to the rest of the world for a quarter of a century. Iraqi officials will likewise take over the international side of the airports in the Kurdish cities of Erbil and Sulaimaniyah. These administrative changes do not sound dramatic, but they effectively end the semi-independence of the Iraqi Kurds, which they had built up over the past twenty-six years.

Mr. Abadi is in a strong position because the KRG's two biggest neighbours, Turkey and Iran, agree with him on re-establishing federal control of the border and Kurdish oil exports. Mr. Abadi says the Turks admit that "they made a mistake" in the past in dealing directly with the KRG and not with the central government in Baghdad. He emphasises that he will not be satisfied with Iraq government officials having a symbolic "spot" at different crossing points on the border, but they must have exclusive control of borders and international flights. Asked if this would include visas, Mr. Abadi says: "This is a must."

He wants the Peshmerga either to become part of the Iraqi government security forces or a small local force. He is curious to know how many Peshmerga there really are, expressing scepticism that there are really 300,000 men under arms as claimed by the Kurdish authorities. He says: "I have been told by many leaders in Kurdistan that there is a small fighting force and the rest stay at home."

He recalls that after Isis unexpectedly captured Mosul, he made inquiries as to why five Iraq divisions had collapsed. He found that the main reason was corruption and in many units, half the soldiers were drawing their salaries but were not there. He suspects the Peshmerga operate the same corrupt system, which he says would explain "why they failed to defend the borders of KRG [against Isis] in 2014 and had to seek the help of the US and Iran." The number of the Peshmerga may be in dispute, but Mr. Abadi is adamant that "I am prepared to pay those Peshmerga under the control of the federal state. If they want to have their local small force—it must not be that large—then they must pay for it." He says that the KRG must not become "a bottomless well" for federal payments. He would also expect Kurdish government expenditure to be audited in the same way as spending in Baghdad.

If all these changes are implemented, then Kurdish autonomy will be much diminished. It is easy to see why Mr. Barzani is stepping down to avoid the humiliation of giving up so much of his authority. Resistance by the Kurdish leadership will be difficult since they are divided and discredited by the Kirkuk debacle. But Mr. Abadi's strength is that for the first time since 1980, the Kurds do not have any backers in neighbouring states and the US has done little during the crisis except wring its hands at the sight of its Kurdish and Iraqi government allies falling out. When Mr. Barzani unwisely forced Washington to choose between Baghdad and Erbil, the Americans were always going to choose the Iraqi state.

Queried about Iranian influence on the Iraqi government. Mr. Abadi is exasperated and derisive by turns, particularly about Qasem Soleimani, the director of foreign operations of the IRGC whose negotiations with the Kurdish leadership have been reported as playing a decisive role in the retreat of the Peshmerga from Kirkuk. "He definitely didn't have any military role on the ground in the crisis [over Kirkuk]," says Mr. Abadi. "I can assure you that he had zero impact on what happened in Kirkuk." Mr. Abadi says that it was he himself who called the Kurdish leadership and persuaded them not to fight and to withdraw the Peshmerga from the disputed territories.

A more substantive allegation is that the Hashd al-Shaabi are sectarian and under Iranian influence or control. Asked about his recent meeting with Rex Tillerson who said the Hashd should "go home" or be dismantled, Mr. Abadi said that there was either "a misquotation or misinformation" and Mr. Tillerson seemed to be under the impression that the IRGC was fighting in Iraq and did not know that the Hashd were all Iraqis.

He said that Iraq had plenty of foreign advisers from the US, UK, France, and elsewhere, including Iran, but the number of Iranian advisers was only thirty, well down from 110 a few years ago. As for the Hashd, he said they had to be under government control, well-disciplined, and to have no political role, particularly not in the Iraqi general election on 12 May 2018, which he pledged not to postpone.

Mr. Abadi is in a strong position because he is one of the first Iraqi leaders whose government has good relations with all Iraq's neighbours: Turkey, Iran, Kuwait, Saudi Arabia, Jordan, and Syria. "We got the international community on our side," says Mr. Abadi, reflecting on the course of the Kirkuk crisis. "We made it very simple: we said the unity of Iraq is very important for combating terrorism." The division of Iraq, through the prospect of Kurdish independence, would open up cracks which Isis would exploit. Mr. Abadi certainly knew what buttons to press when it came to getting neighbouring states on his side. He is patient and strong-minded and the tides that once tore Iraq apart may now be running in his favour.

31 October 2017

The defeat of the Kurds in Kirkuk is devastatingly complete. "We used to be in control here and now we are not," says Aso Mamand, the Kurdish leader in the city, summing up the situation in a helpless and embittered tone as he describes the fall of Kirkuk and the nearby oil fields to the Iraqi government forces. He would like some new power-sharing arrangements and warns of dire consequences if this does not happen, but he does not sound very hopeful.

Many Kurds fled at the time and not all have returned, but there is no sign of damage from the fighting and shops and markets are open. A thunderstorm briefly emptied the streets when we were there, but otherwise traffic was heavy and there are few soldiers or checkpoints. "Do you see anything out of the ordinary?" asks the acting governor, Rakan Saeed Ali al-Jubouri, the Arab former deputy governor, whose office looks little changed from when it was occupied by the Kurdish governor Najmaldin Karim who was forced to flee to Erbil. Mr. Jubouri says that "the local police are the same and there are just two battalions of the counterterrorism forces in Kirkuk." Iraqi battalions are small, so this probably means only a few hundred soldiers.

Mr. Mamand insists that things aren't quite what they look like. He says that "the government needs to do something to calm down the Kurdish street." He suggests the appointment of a Kurdish governor or some arrangement to share power. Asked if there had been any significant security incidents, he cited only some shots fired by a former KDP security police officer at an army checkpoint. But, around about the time he was speaking, there was, in fact, a savage murder in a town called Duquq just south of Kirkuk city, which might give substance to Mr. Mamand's fear that the potential for violence is just below the surface.

The victim was Arkan Sharifi, fifty, a Kurdish cameraman working for Kurdistan TV, who was knifed to death by four or five men who broke into his house and locked his wife and children in a separate room. When they got out five hours later, they found him lying in a pool of blood, his body mutilated and with a knife stuck in his mouth, evidence that he been killed because of something he had said or reported. His family says that the killers spoke the Turkmen language, suggesting that what happened may be the outcome of the ongoing feud between the Kurds and the Shia Turkmen that is particularly fierce south of Kirkuk.

I drove through the area where the murder took place earlier in the day and there was no sign of violence there or anywhere else on the closely guarded road from Baghdad. But the murder is a reminder that at all times, Iraq is a very violent country. I spoke to a Turkmen member of the Hashd al-Shaabi called Jawdat Assaf, who explained that he came from a village called Tisin Khadim, which had been destroyed by Saddam Hussein in 1980. "I survived because I was under fifteen, but they killed 353 people—everybody over that age, including my father and two brothers," he recalled. "They accused us of supporting the [Shia revolutionary] Dawa Party, though we had hardly heard of it."

The murder of Arkan Sharifi is striking in its brutality, but no fewer than 465 Iraqi journalists have been killed in the last fourteen years. Otherwise, the takeover of Kirkuk was unexpectedly pacific. Iraqi government troops on Tuesday set up a checkpoint at the most important border crossing at Ibrahim Khalil between Turkey and Iraqi Kurdistan. Vehicles crossing the border must now be checked three times—by Turks, Iraqi forces, and the Kurds. "Habur border gate has been handed over to the central government as of this morning," said Turkish Prime Minister Binali Yildirim. With Turkey and Iran cooperating with Baghdad, the Iraqi Kurdish authorities are in no position to resist the central government's takeover of their main powers.

Yet the quiet takeover of Kirkuk could be a little deceptive. Weak though the Kurds may now be, political circumstances may not always be so wholly against them or in favour of the Iraqi state. The Kurds looked utterly defeated in 1975 when Saddam Hussein signed the Algiers Agreement with the Shah, who abandoned his previous alliance with the Kurds. But the start of the Iran-Iraq War in 1980 forced the withdrawal of much of the Iraqi army from Iraqi Kurdistan, which was then taken over by Kurdish nationalist forces. Defeated again through savage repression, Saddam's overthrow by the US-led coalition in 1991 enabled the Kurds to start building a statelet, which became a powerful player when the US invaded in 2003.

If the central government in Baghdad exploits its present superiority over the Kurds too greedily, then it could provoke a powerful communal counter-reaction by the Kurdish population. This approach is likely to be opposed by Mr. Abadi but approved by his predecessor as prime minister, Nouri al-Maliki, in the run-up to the parliamentary elections next May. In Iraqi politics, almost everybody ends up by overplaying their hand.

2 November 2017

"Fake facts!" exclaimed a senior Iraqi official in exasperation as he pointed to photographs online allegedly showing the Iranian General Qasem Soleimani in Kirkuk, orchestrating the Iraqi government retaking of the city last month. He said that in reality the picture, tweeted by a Kurdish leader as evidence of Iranian hegemony, dates from 2014.

The greatest threat to the growing stability of Iraq is the differences between the US and Iran being fought out politically—and even militarily—in Iraq. Haider al-Abadi said in an interview with me earlier this week that his greatest concern is a US-Iran crisis. He added that "it is not my

job to solve their differences, but it is my job to prevent their confrontation inside Iraq." He hoped that mutual denunciations by Washington and
Tehran would turn out to be rhetorical.

Given US hostility to Iran, the Baghdad government is alarmed by
what it sees as an attempt to portray it as an Iranian proxy manipulated
by General Soleimani and reliant on the Hashd al-Shaabi or Popular
Mobilisation Units (PMUs). "Today's offensive by Iraq, PMU Shia militia
commanded by Iranian IRGC on Kirkuk have sadly started a new war in
Iraq & Kurdistan," reads a tweet from Hoshyar Zebari. The senior Iraqi
official said that General Soleimani never meets Abadi or anybody else of
real importance in Baghdad and has also failed to get an audience with the
Shia supreme religious authority, Ali Sistani, in the holy city of Najaf. He
said: "In fact, Iranian influence over the Hashd has been going down over
the last two years because they are no longer paying most of the groups,
aside from Kata'ib Hezbollah."

The propaganda war is intense and unscrupulous with Kurdish leaders
in Erbil and much of the Arab media claiming that Iran pulls the strings
in Baghdad, though the US is the government's main military ally. The
PMUs are portrayed as sectarian death squads which are leading the offensive into Iraqi Kurdistan. One video posted online purports to show the
Kurds blowing up a bridge over the Lesser Zaab river at Altun Kupri,
where Kurdish and Iraqi forces confront each other, to block the PMUs
advancing into the Kurdish heartlands. In reality, the bridge is still standing
and the much-watched video is of an entirely different bridge in Topeka,
Kansas being destroyed in a controlled explosion to make way for new
construction.

The power of the Hashd has become more limited today than when they
were created as a mass movement three years ago by a fatwa from Grand
Ayatollah Sistani—though several paramilitary organisations like the Badr
Organisation, Asa'ib Ahl al-Haq, and Kata'ib Hezbollah, which has no
connection with the Lebanese group with a similar name but is strongly
supportive of Iran, have a much longer history. This was in June 2014
when the Iraqi army had lost Mosul to Isis and looked as if it would be
unable to defend Baghdad. The Hashd was central in defending the capital
and in early counter-offensives against Isis but has increasingly had a sec-
ondary role in military operations, which are now led by the highly trained
and experienced Counter-Terrorism Service. In the nine-month siege of
Mosul, the Hashd occupied territory outside the city, but the assault was

led by the CTS, Federal Police, and Emergency Response Division. There were no Hashd units in Kirkuk city earlier this week, though they do have joint checkpoints with the army along the road back to Baghdad.

The Hashd, who are part of the Iraqi security forces and paid for by the state, are becoming less independent and less influenced by Iran because the Iraqi government is much more powerful than it used to be. But there is no doubt that Sunni and Kurds are frightened of them and they have a nasty reputation for sectarianism and criminality. For all their claims to be obedient to the state, there is an Iraqi saying that there are four givers of the law in Iraq: the government, the religious authorities, the tribes—and the Hashd.

Qais al-Khazali, forty-three, the leader of the Asa'ib Ahl al-Haq Shia paramilitary group, denies that it is under the control of Iran or is sectarian. Dressed in a white turban and black robes, he answers questions swiftly and articulately, showing a moderation that feels out of keeping with his violent past. Once a lieutenant of the nationalist populist cleric Muqtada al-Sadr, from whom he split in 2004, he set up Asa'ib Ahl al-Haq, which rapidly gained a reputation for ferocity and close links to Iran. Arrested by the British in 2007, he was released in exchange for a British hostage in 2010. Speaking in his office in Najaf, he was keen to emphasise that his group were neither sectarian nor pawns of Iran. "It is one of their lies," he says in response to the charge of sectarian killings. "There has been no sectarian cleansing. I am adamant—we did not bring in any Shia families to a Sunni area."

He says that American forces should leave Iraq because they are no longer needed. "They don't want to leave, but we can force them to," he says. "We have experience in resistance. If there is a mandate from the Iraqi parliament and the Iraqi people, then we will stand up to them." This would be the sort of nightmare envisaged by Mr. Abadi, in which Iraqi Hashd—which the US believes are under Iranian direction—start killing American soldiers. As for the role of Iran and Soleimani in the taking of Kirkuk, Mr. Khazali says that they were supportive to Mr. Abadi and Iraqi government forces. "The reason the Prime Minister gets the credit is because he galvanised a great force to show he was serious." He says that what Soleimani did was to pass on to the Kurds that Mr. Abadi really meant business and they would not be able to resist.

As for the future of the Hashd, he says that "in future, it should be completely amalgamated with the Iraqi military and should not be involved in politics." Much here will depend on whether or not there is a prolonged confrontation with the Kurds in northern Iraq, in which case Baghdad will continue to need large military forces, including the Hashd. As of Thursday, Baghdad is threatening to end a truce and take military action after the failure of talks about the central government taking control of the borders of Kurdistan.

Speaking of more general developments in Iraq, Mr. Khazali made an interesting point. He said that after the US invasion of 2003, it was the Shia and the Kurdish communities, long opposed to and oppressed by Saddam Hussein, who held power. But this Kurdish-Shia bloc was dissolved when the Kurds voted for independence in the referendum on 25 September and cannot be rebuilt. He says it might be time for the Shia community to look to the Sunni rather than the Kurds as their new partners in running Iraq. Asked if he thought the era of wars in Iraq was over, Mr. Khazali, replied: "Iraq is similar to Alice in Wonderland—you cannot predict what is going to happen next."

PART IV. WINNERS AND LOSERS IN THE SYRIAN WAR

By the summer of 2019, war in Syria had subsided into an unsatisfactory but fairly stable stalemate, which left Bashar al-Assad in control of most of the population and all of the biggest cities. Out of about twenty-two million Syrians, ten to eleven million are in government-held areas, six million are refugees outside the country, three million are in the embattled opposition enclave of Idlib in north-west Syria, and two million live east of the Euphrates in the Kurdish zone, though the population there is half Kurdish and half Arab. Isis, which once ruled territory stretching from the outskirts of Baghdad to the Mediterranean, was defeated in the sieges of Raqqa and Mosul in 2017. It can still carry out pinprick guerrilla or terrorist attacks at home and abroad, but the caliphate declared in 2014 no longer exists. There is much sterile debate about whether or not Isis is permanently out of business or could rise again, but the decisiveness of its defeat in the great sieges of 2017 should be beyond question. It is this stalemate which was shattered in north-east Syria in October when the Turkish Army invaded, leading to a new and much more fragile stalemate.

This section describes how we arrived at this present stage of the conflict in Syria through a war dominated by sieges and blockades in the period 2016–19. In the west of the country, Assad's ground troops and air forces, backed by Russian air strikes, ground down the armed opposition, over-running or, more commonly, forcing the surrender of their strongholds. Over the same time period, the Kurdish YPG backed by the US fought a largely separate war in north-west Syria, driving Isis out of its vast but scantily inhabited territory west of the Euphrates. In both cases, the Syrian government and Kurdish-led forces relied on shelling by artillery and bombing from the air to smash armed resistance, an effective strategy which the opposition vainly tried to counter by using snipers, mines, and the suicide bomber.

I felt from an early period that Assad would stay in power and the real question was how long the agony endured by ordinary Syrians would go on. I stayed in the Christian district of Bab Touma in the Old City of Damascus to cover the Syrian side of the war, which Isis fought as if there was no common border between Syria and Iraq. Damascus was a patchwork of government and insurgent-held areas between which there was always intermittent shooting: Bab Touma was under mortar fire from the nearby opposition district of Jobar, which was an outpost of the much larger opposition enclave of eastern Ghouta. But the occasional incoming mortar rounds exploding in Bab Touma were a minor irritant compared to the systematic destruction of blockaded opposition-held districts by government artillery, the sound of whose guns would boom across the city. When I was able to enter such places like Barzeh in the north of Damascus and Daraya in the south, I found a sea of shattered ruins or streets of gutted buildings where small ornamental bushes had grown into sizeable trees during the long years of war.

A similar jigsaw puzzle of government and rebel-held districts existed all over Syria, but the former almost always had the upper hand because the opposition never linked up the thirty more enclaves where it held sway. Assad was visibly short of combat troops—I would see few convoys on the road—but he had a mobile strike force, which some authorities put at 25,000 men, that could be moved from place to place. Crucially, he was backed by ideologically driven paramilitaries from the Shia communities in Lebanon and Iraq. Assad and his government also had the great advantage of controlling a battered but still minimally functioning state machine. He held the main roads north spreading out from Damascus, which has a population of five million or almost one-third of the Syrians still in the country. Out of the three next biggest cities in Syria, he held all of Hama and most of Aleppo and Homs and could pick-off chunks of opposition territory one-by-one.

From 2012 on, I had believed that Assad was going to survive and, from September 2015, when Russia intervened militarily on his side, that he was going to win. The reason was essentially the same in both cases: all the Syrian parties to the war had become dependent on the foreign states supporting them and here Assad had a clear advantage. I wrote that he would come out on top "because the upper ranks of his regime were united, he had a powerful army, but, above all, because Russia and Iran were always more committed to his survival than Turkey, Saudi Arabia, Qatar, and the US were to regime change." This calculation was true from an early stage in the uprising and remained true in the following years.

October 2016–May 2017

7 October 2016

Across Syria, towns and districts are under siege. In the north, the Syrian army and its Shia allies from Iran, Iraq, and Lebanon, assisted by Russian airpower, have surrounded the opposition enclave of east Aleppo, where a quarter of a million civilians are under attack. If east Aleppo falls, one of the last big urban centres held by the opposition will have been eliminated. In Damascus, government forces are bringing to an end a series of long sieges, most of which began in 2012, and look close to taking full control of the capital. The administrative heart of the state, home to one-third of the population, Damascus is the key to political power in Syria, and once Assad holds all of it, he will have little reason to step down or share power with his enemies.

According to the UN, there are seventeen separate sieges underway in Syria, with nearly 600,000 people surrounded in towns or cities and often cut off from basic supplies. The degree of deprivation differs markedly from siege to siege and may change from week to week. A woman from the town of Madaya, thirty miles west of Damascus, where 43,000 people are under siege from Hezbollah, told me she had been reduced to boiling up thistle-like plants she had picked by the roadside in order to feed her family. There were no vegetables, fruit, or biscuits available in the town, but there was some meat: sheep had been slaughtered because they could no longer be fed, though most people couldn't afford the mutton. The woman, who like many others I spoke to didn't want her name published, had been lucky enough to get out of Madaya under the terms of an international agreement: one of her daughters had had her leg shattered by a bullet when she went to fetch water and needed emergency surgery in Damascus to save it from amputation.

On the outskirts of Damascus is the biggest besieged rebel enclave in Syria, eastern Ghouta, with a population of 270,000. Here, people are managing to survive without malnutrition. It is a substantial urban and agricultural area and the land is fertile; people grow their own food. Goods are smuggled in, sometimes by issuing bribes at government checkpoints, though the Syrian army is gradually advancing into the area and has reduced the extent of rebel-held territory by a third over the last year. A recent visitor described "booths selling vegetables including potatoes, cucumbers, cauliflowers, and lettuce as well as peaches and Syrian cherries, though these are expensive." The worst shortages are of seeds, spare parts for agricultural machinery, surgical kits, medicines, and educational materials for the schools. So the exact circumstances of each of these sieges differ, but the actions of government and armed opposition forces are, in most cases, similar. Government units carry out the cruel but traditional counterinsurgency strategy of separating fighters from their civilian supporters by bombing and shelling indiscriminately until the civilians flee. Those who remain are treated as committed rebels. This was the approach of the British in Malaya, the French in Algeria, and the Americans in Vietnam. (In the Middle East, it's a strategy that has been employed by the Turkish army in its fight against Kurdish guerrillas: an estimated 3,000 Kurdish villages have been destroyed since 1984 and two million people have been driven into shantytowns or forced to migrate to other parts of Turkey. Over the last eighteen months, large parts of the Kurdish cities of Diyarbakir and Cizre have been turned into ruins and flattened by the Turkish armed forces, in a series of actions that have failed to provoke an international outcry or even attract the attention of a Western media that expresses outrage when similar methods are used by the Syrian army.)

Damascus is calmer than it was two years ago: you hear the sound of mortars and artillery only occasionally. The violence feels further away than it used to. People have become accustomed to living in a permanent state of war and are coming to believe they can survive it. The mood is like that of Beirut in the 1980s, halfway through the fifteen-year civil war. Restaurants and cafés are open late into the night. Maher Jalhoun, an architecture student, told me that in one part of the Old City, "twenty new bars and eating places have opened in the last few months alone. I don't know where people get the money from." He himself was about to set off with a group of 150 people on a camping holiday in the mountains above Latakia on the Mediterranean coast. There had been fighting in the general area, but he said the place they were going to was safe.

It's clear where some people get their money from: there's the black market, and then there are remittances from family members who have found jobs in other countries—there are now up to six million Syrian refugees abroad. But overall, Syrians are poorer than they were. War makes everything more costly and official salaries have failed to keep pace with inflation as the Syrian pound has collapsed. Most families used to have a single wage-earner: nowadays, every member tries to get a job. They aren't easy to find: the unemployment rate is at least 40 percent (some have put it as high as 65 percent). Mass impoverishment isn't obvious at first, or not in the streets—but then you notice the number of booths selling second-hand clothes and shoes, a common sight in Kabul but not until now in Damascus. The influx of people from more dangerous parts of the country means that many houses and flats once occupied by a single family now have a family in every room. Ancient public baths or hammams, whose customers used to be mostly foreign tourists, are now full of Syrians who are living in a house with dozens of people and only one bathroom.

People are talking less about the progress of the war than they used to, but they complain endlessly about prices and corruption. One relatively well-off friend said he had just paid $300 to replace a broken car mirror that would have cost $70 five years ago. War itself has had an impact, but much of the damage is done by Western economic sanctions, which have disrupted trade links with foreign suppliers. Banks in Lebanon now avoid transactions with Syrians for fear that action will be taken against them by the US authorities. The situation reminds me of Iraq in the 1990s and early 2000s when UN sanctions did so much to destroy the economy but failed to weaken Saddam Hussein. Shadi Ahmed, an economic and political analyst in Damascus, says that per capita income is down by almost two thirds; 2.5 million homes have been destroyed by war. But things aren't as bad as they could be in every respect. Syria isn't isolated: Iran and Iraq have given extensive financial aid, enabling the government to maintain subsidies. Petrol is still cheaper than in Lebanon, however long the queues at the pumps. There are opportunities for some Syrians too: the souqs are doing well because they can keep prices lower than regular shops thanks to lower costs; they give employment to people whose jobs have disappeared. In a small shop in the Buzurieyah souq by the Umayyad Mosque, Abed Bitar explained that he is by profession a geologist: he had "worked for twenty-seven years in the oil and gas fields of Syria as well as in the rest of the Middle East and North Africa." Now that the Syrian oil and gas fields are largely under the control of Isis or Kurdish forces, he has turned to selling herbal medicines instead. He said there was increased demand for traditional remedies because of a widespread belief among Syrians that the only doctors who haven't left the country for better-paid employment elsewhere "have no experience or are second-rate."

I visited the 200-bed al-Mouwasat University Hospital in Damascus to see if what the geologist said was true. The hospital's director, Hashem Saker, said that "about 30 percent" of his most highly qualified staff had gone abroad, mostly to the Gulf, and pressure on the remaining staff was intense. But younger doctors were gaining experience and not everyone wanted to stay in the Gulf forever. At the Mouwasat in Damascus at least, there is no evidence of a collapse in medical services as there was in Iraq in the 1990s, when a foreign medical delegation once witnessed doctors trying to operate on a patient with scissors too blunt to cut through his skin. And plenty of young Syrians still want to train to be doctors; there are apparently twenty-one schools of dentistry in the country too. Syrian parents have traditionally favoured medicine as a profession for their children: it means financial security. But in wartime, enthusiasm for higher education has another, more immediate benefit: university students can postpone their military service.

Fear of their sons being forced to join the army is one of the main reasons Syrians become refugees—with good reason. Once in the army, it is difficult to get out and the chances of being killed or injured are high (since 2011, some 55,000 soldiers have died). Standard army pay is just fifty dollars a month, which leads to pervasive petty corruption among soldiers who try to earn enough illicitly to live on: every army checkpoint acts as a sort of privatised customs barrier with the officers in charge setting their own fees. This may be small change for a taxi driver, but it will be much higher for a vehicle carrying goods. One checkpoint in central Damascus is known to local drivers as "the million-pound checkpoint" because those manning it expect their earnings to exceed a million Syrian pounds ($4,700) a day. Another local industry flourishing thanks to the war is the manufacture of fake antiquities for sale abroad. Maamoun Abdulkarim, general director of Antiquities and Museums, says that about 80 percent of the "antiquities" leaving Syria today have been made in workshops in Damascus or Aleppo. All the really valuable treasures in provincial museums were removed before they were overrun by Isis or other armed groups, though in Palmyra, the trucks "carrying the antiquities got out only three hours before Isis captured it." The business is flourishing on both sides of the front line: in rebel-held Idlib, craftsmen specialise in making Roman and Greek mosaics, which then go through an ageing process. Sometimes, Abdulkarim said, their makers bury them and film themselves excavating them in order to convince prospective buyers of their authenticity.

Two years ago, when I last stayed in the Bab Touma neighbourhood of the Old City of Damascus, mortar bombs were landing most days. They made a sharp cracking sound as they exploded, different from the booming of government artillery targeting rebel areas from the top of Mount Qasioun, which overlooks the capital. One day a friend, also living in the Old City, phoned to say that a suicide bomber had just blown himself up a few hundred yards from my hotel, killing four people in the street between the Naranj restaurant and the Greek Orthodox Church of the Virgin Mary. Pro-rebel media were soon mentioning the fact that Assad used to eat at the Naranj, implying that this made it a legitimate target, though he certainly hadn't been there since the war began five years ago. Pro-government television, always keen to underline the anti-Christian leanings of the opposition, emphasised how close the explosion had been to the church. I walked over to where the suicide bomber had supposedly blown himself up, which turned out not really to be near either the restaurant or the church. It had happened on the pavement outside a curio shop. Across the street, there was a body on the pavement under a white sheet: people kept flicking it back to see if the dead man was a friend or relative. Just past the shop, whose owner had been wounded in the leg, there was an area covered in drying blood, though the body had been removed. I saw a dent in the pavement about three inches deep: it looked as if the explosion had been caused by a mortar round—not a suicide bomber at all. Eventually, footage from a CCTV camera nearby showed that, indeed, there had been mortar fire: the camera had caught the exact moment when the dark shape of the descending shell was outlined against the white shirt of a passer-by. He had been killed and his remains mistakenly identified as those of a suicide bomber. The men firing the mortar from the nearby rebel enclave of Jobar were probably just firing in the general direction of the Christian parts of the Old City, which they knew was either pro-Assad or at least overwhelmingly against Islamist rebels. Just as I was leaving, another mortar round hit a balcony and killed a woman standing on it.

Such incidents still happen—eight people died in a restaurant in Bab Touma when a mortar shell hit it in July—but they are rarer than they were. Many of the rebel-held districts have agreed to ceasefires or "reconciliation agreements" that amount to something close to surrender. At one point, the rebels had held much of the outskirts of the city, but they were never able to link up their enclaves or control the roads to the international airport, Beirut, or Homs. I saw one of the first of these ceasefires in Barzeh in north-east Damascus in early 2014: some local opposition fighters, who had kept their weapons, showed me around. It had once been inhabited by 50,000 people, but had been largely depopulated by bombing; many buildings were a jumble of smashed concrete floors piled on top of one another. A local commander, who called himself al-Kal, told me the government had promised to release 350 rebel prisoners following the ceasefire. "But all I have got," he said, "is three dead bodies." The shaky truce in Barzeh still holds, but I was warned that it was now too dangerous to visit.

In the last few weeks, several rebel strongholds in Damascus have surrendered on terms. The most significant is Daraya, which had a population of 80,000 before the war and was a symbol of the anti-government resistance. Only five miles from the centre of Damascus, it's now an empty shell: the remaining fighters and civilians, by now numbering only 1826, were either reconciled with the government or bused north with their weapons to rebel territory in Idlib in August. At the entrance to the district, anything that was more than a few feet off the ground had been blown up. Further in, most buildings were intact—but they had been gutted and looked uninhabitable. Once, Daraya had been known for making furniture and in a few places, broken wood-cutting machines were lying amid the debris. In every street, what had been small ornamental bushes at the start of the four-year siege were now fifteen feet high. The Syrian general who had commanded the operation said his brigade had lost 286 dead. Nobody knew how many civilians had been killed. Pointing up at the wrecked buildings, their windows now empty of glass, the general said: "They make good positions for snipers."

We drove down dark streets with heaps of rubble on either side, mostly shaded by the tall apartment blocks with an occasional strong shaft of light where a building had been demolished by a shell or bomb. One can usually tell that someone has recently been living in a neighbourhood like this by the smell or sight of rotting garbage, but here there was none. One building contained the entrance to a tunnel and nearby there was a faded message on the wall: "The martyrs of Syria are so many that they will have to build a new Syria in heaven." A few days after our visit, on the feast of Eid al-Adha, President Assad underlined the significance for him of Daraya's capture by praying at the main mosque. The military balance in Syria could turn against him again if one or more of the outside powers opposing him steps up their support for his enemies. But so long as this doesn't happen, Assad has every reason to believe that he is winning the war.

7 October 2016

The US and EU economic sanctions on Syria are causing huge suffering among ordinary Syrians and preventing the delivery of humanitarian aid, according to a leaked UN internal report. The embargo was supposed to target President Bashar al-Assad and contribute to his removal from power. Instead, it is making it more difficult for foodstuffs, fuel, and health care to reach the mass of the people.

Aid agencies cited in the report say they cannot procure basic medicines or medical equipment for hospitals because sanctions are preventing foreign commercial companies and banks from having anything to do with Syria. A European doctor working in Syria says that "the indirect effect of sanctions… makes the import of medical instruments and other medical supplies immensely difficult, nearly impossible." The revelations in the internal UN assessment of the effect of sanctions on aid delivery, entitled *Humanitarian Impact of Syria-Related Unilateral Restrictive Measures* and leaked by the investigative publication *The Intercept*, open up the US and EU to the charge of hypocrisy, after criticising Syria and Russia for impeding the delivery of UN aid supplies to besieged cities in Syria. *The Intercept* quotes an internal UN email from a senior official saying that sanctions have been a "principal factor" in degrading the Syrian health system and have contributed to a 300 percent rise in the price of wheat flour and 650 percent rise for rice, following a doubling of fuel prices in the last eighteen months.

Syria was once largely self-sufficient in pharmaceuticals, but many plants were in the Aleppo area and have been destroyed or rendered unusable by the fighting. The email says that many of the plants that survived have now been forced to close because of the impact of sanctions on obtaining raw materials from abroad and the foreign currency to pay for them. The report states that conflict in Syria is the greatest humanitarian crisis the world has seen since the Second World War, with thirteen million people, or two-thirds of the population, in need of assistance. The disaster has led to the exodus of at least five million refugees and four million internally displaced people. The report says that the chaos has produced a weakening of the state and conditions that have fostered the growth of Isis.

US and EU sanctions are contributing to this humanitarian calamity while Mr. Assad remains firmly in power. In many respects, the situation resembles that in Iraq between 1990 and 2003 when UN sanctions destroyed the Iraqi economy and helped dissolve its society while doing nothing to reduce the power of Saddam Hussein as Iraqi leader. Many critics of Iraqi sanctions argue that the mass impoverishment they produced contributed significantly to the political and sectarian breakdown after the invasion of 2003. The same process is now taking place in Syria. The report says that "in totality, the US and EU sanctions in Syria are some of the most complicated and far-reaching sanctions regimes ever imposed." It says that in parallel with the humanitarian crisis, there is this complex network of non-UN sanctions targeting the government of Syria and some entities and individuals alleged to have contributed to violence and human rights abuses. The EU has imposed wide-ranging prohibitions on commercial and banking dealings with Syria as well as control of the export of "dual use" items that might have some security application.

US sanctions are even more extensive, imposing a blanket ban on exports to Syria or financial dealings with the country. This includes foreign produced goods, of which the US content is more than 10 percent of the value of the finished item. There are supposedly means available for purely humanitarian goods to reach Syria, but, in practice, this is not the case. The report quotes numerous examples of aid agencies in Syria which have found their work made very difficult or impossible by the Kafka-esque system of licenses, export controls, risk management assessments, and other prohibitions that require expensive legal advice to navigate. For instance, the ban on "dual use" goods includes such items as drilling equipment and pipes used for water and sanitation, which require a special license—even though a shortage of fresh drinking water is a major health hazard in Syria.

The big aid agencies are universal in their condemnation of the present system and the way in which it compounds the miseries caused by the war. None of the agencies are named in the report, but one large one from the EU complains that it has to apply for a license to send goods to Syria through national government bureaucracies, but officials there do not know what the criteria is for doing so. This means endless delays and many commercial companies and banks want to have nothing to do with Syria for fear of unwittingly breaching sanctions and opening themselves up to heavy fines. These fears are not exaggerated. The report notes that "non-US banks have paid billions in US dollars in sanctions-related penalties, mostly to US regulators."

Staying within the law is also expensive. One aid agency said that the cost of legally sending laptops to their staff in Syria was greater than the laptops had cost in the first place. It is not just government-held parts of Syria that are affected. One major EU charity, partly funded by the EU itself, planned "to deliver humanitarian assistance to besieged areas inside Syria." For this, it needed to bring funds from the bank it usually used to another country near Syria, but it did not conceal the fact that the final destination was Syria. This turned out to be a mistake. The bank objected that it was at risk because of sanctions and other prohibitions. The charity concludes by saying that "the planned humanitarian assistance has still not been delivered."

In effect, the US and EU sanctions are imposing an economic siege on Syria as a whole, which may be killing more Syrians than die of illness and malnutrition in the sieges, which EU and US leaders have described as war crimes. Over half the country's public hospitals have been damaged or destroyed. Syrian doctors in Damascus told me about the difficulty in obtaining medicines and spare parts for medical equipment purchased before the war. In other parts of Syria, the health situation is far worse. The report says that "British doctors working in Aleppo have indicated that over 80 percent of those requiring urgent medical treatment die as a result of their injuries, or lack of basic care, medicine, and equipment." Nevertheless, the World Health Organisation says that brand name US medicines "cannot be procured due to the embargo situation." In general, living conditions have fallen disastrously with electricity supply about "three hours on three hours off" in the capital. Maintenance and spare parts for the electricity system have both been hit by sanctions. There are private generators, but the report says that power has "become too expensive for most Syrians, and many live without electricity."

As Syrians sit in the dark, US and EU sanctions are combining with war to destroy their country.

11 October 2016

A proposal has been put forward in the British Parliament to shoot down Russian and Syrian aircraft over eastern Aleppo in a bid to end the bombardment of this part of the city. The proposal is wholly unrealistic. The West is not going to risk a war against a nuclear power and its Syrian ally in order to help the 250,000 to 275,000 civilians trapped there. To pretend anything else is empty bombast detached from the realities on the ground. The danger of such wild schemes is that they divert attention from more realistic plans to save the besieged from further suffering and death.

The realities in Aleppo are that the city, once the industrial heart of Syria, has been split between government in the west and rebels in the east since 2012. Hospitals and health care centres are being systematically destroyed. There is an economic blockade with UN aid convoys unable to pass through government checkpoints. It is near impossible to cook such food as there is because of the lack of propane gas cylinders and kerosene. East Aleppo was first fully encircled by pro-government in forces in July when they cut the so-called Castello Road in the north of the city, which was the last link to rebel areas to the west. The main supply road from east Aleppo to Turkey had been severed in February. A rebel counter-offensive briefly broke through the siege lines in August in the Ramouseh Road in south Aleppo only for the Syrian army and its allies to re-impose the siege in September.

It looks unlikely that the encirclement can be broken by military means. The last time around, the rebels suffered heavy casualties put at around 500 dead. The lesson of all the many sieges taking place in Syria and Iraq over the last year—Daraya in Damascus, al-Waer in Homs, Ramadi and Fallujah in Iraq—is that rebel light infantry stands no chance in the long term against heavy air attack directed from the ground. The UN estimates that there are 8,000 rebel fighters in Aleppo, of which 900 belong to Fatah al-Sham, previously the al-Qaeda affiliate Jabhat al-Nusra. They can inflict heavy losses on pro-government forces in street fighting if they fight to the last man, but at the end of the day, they will lose unless there is a change in the military balance in Syria through one or more of the outside powers involved in the conflict intervening more forcefully in the air or on the ground. Assad has made clear that he is not going to relax his grip on east Aleppo, saying that he will go on fighting "with the rebels until they leave Aleppo. They have to. There's no other option." It is unlikely that anybody will stop him.

The UN Special Envoy to Syria, Staffan de Mistura, has proposed that there be mass evacuation of fighters and civilians to rebel-held Idlib province. He says that he personally is "ready physically to accompany you."

The Syrian government says that it is willing to give safe passage, but this sounds better than it is because of the extreme distrust on the rebel side of any assurances from Damascus that they will be safe from the Mukhabarat secret police now and in the future. The UN says that about half the civilians in east Aleppo are ready to leave now, but this is accompanied by understandable wariness. During the siege of the Old City of Homs two years ago, which in many ways resembles the siege of Aleppo today, I talked to a middle-aged man who had evidently been on the rebel side and two of whose sons were missing. He himself was free and living with other displaced people in a school in Homs, but he could not go to Damascus to ask about the fate of his sons because he rightly suspected that he himself—the last adult male in his family still free—would be arrested on the road and detained for an indefinite period. I said that I supposed that all men of military age were at risk. He laughed hollowly and replied that "we are all at risk, every single one of us."

This fear of the Syrian security forces is the main reason why civilians and others will not want to leave. Other reasons include the sheer danger of appearing on the streets in order to go and the attitude of the rebel fighters. In most rebel-held districts in Syria and Iraq, rebels of whatever stripe do not want civilians to depart because they act as human shields. In some cases, they are forcibly prevented from doing so and those that get out have to pay large bribes, as has happened in Mosul and Raqqa in recent months. An organised withdrawal from east Aleppo under the auspices of the UN may be the best option for the civilians remaining there, but the collapse of the Russian-US ceasefire shows how difficult it will be to arrange.

Are there alternative scenarios, if not solutions? In Syria, there usually are because there are so many players inside and outside the country, all claiming hypocritically to be acting in the interests of the Syrian people but invariably consulting their own interests first, second, and third. It is difficult to see where any outside force willing to break the siege will come from. President Recep Tayyip Erdogan, normally so belligerent on behalf of the Syrian insurgents, has been surprisingly mute about the fate of Aleppo. This is probably because he is more concerned with the threat from the Syrian Kurds and on fostering goods relations with President Putin with whom he has just signed a gas deal.

A further aspect of the Syrian crisis tends to be underestimated in the West, which is over-obsessed with Russian intervention. Iran and Shia communities in Iraq and Lebanon see the struggle for Syria as a struggle for their own existence. They provide many of the fighters attacking east Aleppo and they are not going to give up until they win.

6 November 2016
A Syrian Kurdish and Arab force backed by US air strikes has launched an offensive against Isis's de facto Syrian capital at Raqqa aimed at maximising pressure on Isis when it is already under attack in Mosul in Iraq. Anti-Isis forces advanced six miles in the first four hours of the attack, capturing many villages and farms.

The move against Raqqa, a city of 320,000 people on the Euphrates River, is by the Syrian Democratic Forces, which numbers about 30,000 fighters, of whom 20,000 are seasoned Kurdish fighters and 10,000 are drawn from the Sunni Arab population of northern Syria. The US is keen not to provoke Turkey, which has denounced the YPG as terrorists. US officers say that one reason for seeking to isolate and capture Raqqa now is that it is at the centre of planning and execution of Isis terrorist operations against Europe, the US, and the wider world and they fear such an operation is about to be launched. General Stephen Townsend, the US commander of Operation Inherent Resolve, which is aimed at eliminating Isis, said last week that "we know they're up to something. And it's an external plot; we don't know exactly where; we don't know exactly when." He added that this uncertainty was creating "a sense of urgency."

It would be in keeping with Isis's actions in the past that it seeks to counter-balance setbacks on the battlefield in Iraq and Syria by staging spectacular terrorist atrocities abroad that show that it is still to be feared and can strike when and where it wants. It carried out two suicide bombings in Iraq on Sunday, killing twenty-five people and wounding fifty in the cities of Tikrit and Samarra.

The opening of the Raqqa offensive brings with it political complications that may exceed the military difficulties because Turkey does not want Raqqa to fall to a force dominated by the YPG, which is the Syrian arm of the Kurdistan Workers' Party. The US has been trying to avoid an armed confrontation between the YPG and Turkey or Turkish backed forces, a possibility that has grown since Turkey had its local allies seize Jarabulus and a strip of territory along the Syrian-Turkish border in August. The mainly Kurdish SDF will be moving into a fertile area north of Raqqa, where the population is Sunni Arab. There are doubts among the Syrian Kurds about suffering casualties trying to take an Arab city, which they cannot keep, when they would prefer to move west and link up their present swathe of territory with the Kurdish enclave at Afrin further west, but this is being resisted by Turkey. The Syrian Kurds are doing what the US wants because their future is very dependent on US military and political support. The SDF said it had received weapons from the US, including anti-tank missiles, and some fifty US advisers are reported to be accompanying the advance to call in air strikes.

The SDF spokesman Talal Sillo was quoted as saying that "we want to liberate the surrounding countryside, then encircle the city, then we will assault and liberate it." Asked about the possibility of intervention by Turkey or its local allies, he replied: "Of course, to begin the operation, we have made sure there will be no other forces but the SDF in the operation." Underlining the complexity of the present situation, an SDF official, Rezan Hiddo, said Turkey has been an "obstacle" to the Raqqa campaign all along. He said that if Turkey moves against Kurdish areas in northern Syria, then the Kurds would stop their campaign directed at Raqqa, adding: "We cannot extinguish the fire in our neighbours' house if our home is burning."

2 December 2016

It is too dangerous for journalists to operate in rebel-held areas of Aleppo and Mosul. But there is a tremendous hunger for news from the Middle East, so the temptation is for the media to give credence to information they get second hand. The Iraqi army, backed by US-led air strikes, is trying to capture east Mosul at the same time as the Syrian army and its Shia paramilitary allies are fighting their way into east Aleppo. An estimated 300 civilians have been killed in Aleppo by government artillery and bombing in the last fortnight, and in Mosul, there are reportedly some 600 civilians dead over a month.

Despite these similarities, the reporting by the international media of these two sieges is radically different. In Mosul, civilian loss of life is blamed on Isis, with its indiscriminate use of mortars and suicide bombers, while the Iraqi army and their air support are largely given a free pass. Isis is accused of preventing civilians from leaving the city so they can be used as human shields. Contrast this with Western media descriptions of the inhuman savagery of President Assad's forces indiscriminately slaughtering civilians regardless of whether they stay or try to flee. The UN Chief of Humanitarian Affairs, Stephen O'Brien, suggested this week that the rebels in east Aleppo were stopping civilians departing—but unlike Mosul, the issue gets little coverage.

One factor making the sieges of east Aleppo and east Mosul so similar, and different, from past sieges in the Middle East, such as the Israeli siege of Beirut in 1982 or of Gaza in 2014, is that there are no independent foreign journalists present. They are not there for the very good reason that Isis imprisons and beheads foreigners while Jabhat al-Nusra is only a shade less bloodthirsty and generally holds them for ransom. These are the two groups that dominate the armed opposition in Syria as a whole. In Aleppo, though only about 20 percent of the 10,000 fighters are Nusra, it is they—along with their allies in Ahrar al-Sham—who are leading the resistance. Unsurprisingly, foreign journalists covering developments in east Aleppo and rebel-held areas of Syria overwhelmingly do so from Lebanon or Turkey. A number of intrepid correspondents who tried to do eyewitness reporting from rebel-held areas swiftly found themselves tipped into the boots of cars or otherwise incarcerated.

Experience shows that foreign reporters are quite right not to trust their lives even to the most moderate of the armed opposition inside Syria. But, strangely enough, the same media organisations continue to put their trust in the veracity of information coming out of areas under the control of these same potential kidnappers and hostage-takers. They would probably defend themselves by saying they rely on non-partisan activists, but all the evidence is that these can only operate in east Aleppo under license from the al-Qaeda-type groups. It is inevitable that an opposition movement fighting for its life in wartime will only produce, or allow to be produced by others, information that is essentially propaganda for its own side. The fault lies not with them but a media that allows itself to be spoon-fed with dubious or one-sided stories. For instance, the film coming out of east Aleppo in recent weeks focuses almost exclusively on heartrending scenes of human tragedy such as the death or maiming of civilians. One seldom sees shots of the 10,000 fighters, whether they are wounded or alive and well.

None of this is new. The present wars in the Middle East started with the US-led invasion of Iraq in 2003, which was justified by the supposed threat from Saddam Hussein's possession of weapons of mass destruction. Western journalists largely went along with this thesis, happily citing evidence from the Iraqi opposition who predictably confirmed the existence of WMD. Some of those who produced these stories later had the gall to criticise the Iraqi opposition for misleading them, as if they had any right to expect unbiased information from people who had dedicated their lives to overthrowing Saddam Hussein or, in this particular case, getting the Americans to do so for them. Much the same self-serving media credulity was evident in Libya during the 2011 NATO-backed uprising against Muammar Gaddafi. Atrocity stories emanating from the Libyan opposition, many of which were subsequently proved to be baseless by human rights organisations, were rapidly promoted to lead the news, however partial the source.

It is always a weakness of journalists that they pretend to excavate the truth when in fact they are the conduit rather than the originator of information produced by others in their own interests. Reporters learn early that people tell them things because they are promoting some cause which might be their own career or related to bureaucratic infighting or, just possibly, hatred of lies and injustice. A word here in defence of the humble reporter in the field: usually, it is not he or she, but the home office or media herd instinct, that decides the story of the day. Those closest to the action may be dubious about some juicy tale which is heading the news, but there is not much they can do about it. Thus, in 2002 and 2003, several *New York Times* journalists wrote stories casting doubt on WMD only to find them buried deep inside the newspaper, which was led by articles proving that Saddam had WMD and was a threat to the world.

Journalists and public alike should regard all information about Syria and Iraq with reasoned scepticism. They should keep in mind the words of Lakhdar Brahimi, the former UN and Arab League special envoy to Syria. Speaking after he had resigned in frustration in 2014, he said that "everybody had their agenda and the interests of the Syrian people came second, third, or not at all." The quote comes from *The Battle for Syria: International Rivalry in the New Middle East* by Christopher Phillips, which is one of the best informed and non-partisan accounts of the Syrian tragedy yet published. He judiciously weighs the evidence for rival explanations for what happened and why. He understands the degree to which the agenda and pace events in Syria were determined externally by the intervention of foreign powers pursuing their own interests.

Overall, government experts did better than journalists, who bought into simple-minded explanations of developments, convinced that Assad was always on the verge of being overthrown. Phillips records that at a high point of the popular uprising in July 2011, when the media was assuming that Assad was finished, that the long-serving British ambassador in

Damascus, Simon Collis, wrote that "Assad can still probably count on the support of 30-40 percent of the population." The French ambassador Eric Chevallier was similarly cautious, only to receive a classic rebuke from his masters in Paris who said: "Your information does not interest us. Bashar al-Assad must fall and will fall."

12 December 2016

The Syrian armed forces are close to capturing the remaining rebel-held districts in the enclave of east Aleppo, bringing them their biggest victory in five years of war. The insurgent armed forces have been retreating or giving up more readily than had been expected. It is still possible that a hard core will hold out in the ruins, but President Assad will be eager to crush any remaining resistance so he can present the fall of east Aleppo as a decisive turning point in the conflict.

Will this be true? There are so many players with such diverse agendas in the Syrian civil war that past "turning points" have turned out to be no such thing. But what is truly important about what we have just seen in Aleppo is that the outside allies of the armed opposition to Assad—Turkey, Saudi Arabia, Qatar, and, in a somewhat different category, the US—have not come to the rescue of the rebels whom they have previously supported. Over the last five years, it has been foreign powers and not domestic parties in Syria who have dictated who is winning or losing at any particular moment. When Assad was losing, he went to the Russians, Iranians, Iraqis, and Hezbollah and asked for more support. Likewise, the insurgents looked to their external allies when they were on the retreat. This time around, this has not happened. The Russian military intervention in September 2015 finally and permanently tipped the balance of power in Assad's favour.

The failed military coup of 15 July and the consequent purge makes it dubious how far President Recep Tayyip Erdogan can effectively intervene at this stage in the war. Saudi Arabia took over in 2013 from Qatar as the biggest Arab ally of the insurgency. Until quite late in the day, the Saudis and the Arab Gulf states remained convinced that Assad would be defeated and overthrown like Muammar Gaddafi in Libya in 2011. They exaggerated the likelihood of US military intervention against Assad though President Obama had made clear his wish not to be sucked into another quagmire in the Middle East after the US experience in Iraq and Afghanistan.

But there are limits to Assad's military success. This has been underlined by the recapture of the ancient city of Palmyra by Isis fighters who are once again executing captured Syrian soldiers in the streets of the modern city. The Syrian army, like all other combatants in the Iraq-Syrian civil war, is short of troops to replace casualties. This is one reason why men of military age leaving east Aleppo are being conscripted straight into the army.

The conflict was and remains a civil war, primarily sectarian between Sunni and the rest but with ethnic and social aspects. The Syrian security forces may have taken the poorest and most religious part of Aleppo, but the countryside around Aleppo is largely Sunni. Better-off urban areas tended to support the government, while the rural Sunni districts are the bedrock of the revolution. These districts are likely to fight on, particularly when government forces move against Idlib province to the west of Aleppo city. These are heavily populated Sunni areas close to the Turkish border and will probably still be able to get supplies from Turkey. The more territory the Syrian army takes, the more it will have to hold and defend. Its enemies hope it will be vulnerable to guerrilla war and will never be able to reassert its hold over all of Syria. They may be right—much depends on the attitude of foreign powers—but many Syrians have always said that the struggle for Aleppo would decide the war. They may well be right.

13 December 2016

The defeat of the insurgents in east Aleppo came faster than was expected, though there are still some districts under their control. The weakness of the resistance is probably the result of being under intense artillery fire for over a month without the ability to retaliate. Though the Syrian government and Russian air strikes have been the main focus of the foreign media, it is shelling by artillery which does most of the damage in east Aleppo and other besieged rebel strongholds in the rest of Syria.

The armed opposition were divided; different parties fought each other as recently as November. They did not have the firepower to keep the breach in the government encirclement open and the enclave began to contract rapidly under the impact of repeated attacks. The Syrian government's strategy since 2012, of surrounding rebel-held zones and depopulating them through shelling and bombing, was dictated by lack of troops. But from September on the Syrian army and paramilitary forces were numerous enough to keep up constant pressure on the rebels. It seemed possible that the rebels would make a stand in heavily populated areas in the city

centre where buildings are close together and streets are narrow. So far, this
has not happened. It may now be too late for a last stand, as happened in
the city of Homs a couple of years ago.

There is a big contrast here with east Mosul where Isis has slowed the
progress of the Iraqi army and counter-terrorism forces to a crawl, inflicting heavy casualties on them. The UN says the Iraqi army lost upwards of
2,000 dead in November alone, most of the losses being suffered in and
around Mosul city. A difference may have been that Isis is the only armed
insurgent movement in Iraq, while in Syria the armed opposition is disunited, Isis had complete control of Mosul for over two years and was able
to build up its defences, notably a network of tunnels, as well as recruiting
hundreds of suicide bombers driving vehicles packed with explosives.

Rebels will fight on in Idlib, where they are likely to get support from
Turkey, and in the south of Syria where they get aid through Jordan. But
they have been losing their enclaves in Damascus as well as Aleppo, so the
non-Isis forces will have difficulty continuing the struggle. What remains
unclear is whether or not Isis will benefit from the defeat of the rest of the
armed opposition.

14 December 2016

Ceasefires in Syria are difficult to arrange and particularly likely to collapse
because their successful implementation involves so many parties inside
and outside the country who hate and would like to kill each other. All
of these powers have their own agendas that may have little to do with
the wellbeing of those who want to leave a besieged enclave in safety. The
planned evacuation of fighters and civilians in Aleppo arranged between
Turkey and Russia and due to take place on Wednesday morning predictably failed to occur. Street fighting resumed and it will be difficult for
either side to exercise the degree of operational control necessary to get
this to stop.

Furthermore, the Syrian government wants as part of an agreement
the full or partial evacuation of two pro-government Shia towns, Fua and
Kefraya, west of Aleppo that have a population of 20,000 and have been
long besieged by the armed opposition. There are also disagreements about
the exact numbers to be brought to safety in buses to the rebel-held province of Idlib. By Wednesday night, opposition groups spoke of another
agreement being reached, but there was scepticism from some allies of
Damascus, such as Hezbollah. The situation is dangerous for everybody

inside the much-reduced rebel enclave in Aleppo and the UN says that it has evidence that eighty-two civilians have been summarily executed by pro-government forces. It believes that many more are dead. But comparisons by the US Ambassador to the UN, Samantha Power, with the Rwandan genocide of 1994 and the Srebrenica massacre in 1995 are wholly out of proportion. The most likely outcome is an evacuation of fighters and their families along with thousands of others who, for very good reasons, believe they are in danger from the Syrian security services.

The reason for believing that a ceasefire could hold if implemented and an evacuation is possible is that they have happened before and are in the interests of both the trapped rebel leadership inside east Aleppo and the government. The rebels' military position has collapsed and they do not look as if they are able to stage a last stand. They may as well save their remaining fighters, families, and supporters while they still can. At the same time, Jabhat al-Nusra, said to make up about 30 percent of 1,500 fighters to be evacuated—according to the UN—and to be in operational command in east Aleppo, has usually been the last of the armed opposition groups to agree to ceasefires that are close to surrender by their own side. The Syrian government has an interest in a ceasefire and an evacuation—as has happened previously in and around Damascus—because a massacre would mean that other besieged rebel areas would have no alternative but to fight to the end. There are probably about thirty such enclaves left. The most important of these is eastern Ghouta, a large urban and agricultural area east of Damascus, where over 250,000 people have been blockaded for four years.

The severity of the sieges varies greatly, with shortages but no starvation in eastern Ghouta in contrast to Madaya, a town west of Damascus where 43,000 people have been starving and even those with money can find no food to buy. In Deir Ezzor in eastern Syria, some 110,000 people are besieged by Isis in a Syrian government-held enclave but are receiving supplies dropped from Russian aircraft. The figures for those besieged in Syria—excluding east Aleppo—was 590,000 in September, according to the UN. The numbers are only roughly accurate because those inside an enclave have an interest in inflating them in order to get the maximum amount of aid. The UN has previously then made its own estimates of the real numbers and tried to persuade the Syrian government to allow in aid convoys with sufficient food to feed them.

The figures for fighters and civilians in east Aleppo differ widely and this may be one reason for the delayed evacuation. The UN used to estimate

250,000 to 275,000 people lived in east Aleppo and 1.5 million in government-held west Aleppo (where many also receive aid) but now appears to have reduced this to 140,000 in the east. The number of fighters had originally been estimated at between 8,000 and 10,000, which may have been too high, but many may have been killed or have already surrendered. A final reason for the government to want to bring the battle for Aleppo to a close as quickly as possible is that Isis has recaptured Palmyra and is threatening an important Syrian air base in the region. The government will want to transfer its best combat troops south to the Palmyra front as will their Russian allies, who highlighted their role in the recapture of the ancient city last March and are humiliated by its loss.

Of course, the fact that a ceasefire and an evacuation of east Aleppo is in the interests of government and armed opposition does not mean it is going to happen.

16 December 2016

It has just become more dangerous to be a foreign correspondent reporting on the civil war in Syria. This is because the jihadis holding power in east Aleppo were able to exclude Western journalists, who would be abducted and very likely killed if they went there, and replace them as news sources with highly partisan "local activists" who cannot escape being under jihadi control.

There was always a glaring contradiction at the heart of the position of the international media: on the one hand, it was impossibly dangerous for foreign journalists to enter opposition-held areas of Syria, but at the same time independent activists were apparently allowed to operate freely by some of the most violent and merciless movements on earth. The threat to Western reporters was very real: James Foley had been ritually beheaded on 8 August 2014 and Steven Sotloff a few days later, though long before then, foreign journalists who entered insurgent-controlled zones were in great danger. But the threat was just as great for local persons living under insurgent rule who criticised their actions or ideas. This is made clear by an Amnesty International report published in July this year entitled *Torture Was My Punishment*. Philip Luther, director of the Middle East and North Africa Programme of Amnesty International, says that in these areas civilians "live in constant fear of being abducted if they criticise the conduct of armed groups in power or fail to abide by the strict rules some have imposed."

Any genuinely independent journalists or activists are targeted, according to the report. Speaking of Jabhat Fatah al-Sham, a twenty-four-year-old media activist called "Issa" said, "they are in control of what we can and cannot say. You either agree with their social rules and policies, or you disappear." What follows after such an abduction was made clear to me by a political activist called "Ibrahim," who in 2015 organised a peaceful protest in support of the 2011 uprising. Such independent action was evidently unacceptable to Nusra, who kidnapped him. He says: "I was taken to the torture room. They placed me in the *shabeh* position, hanging me from the ceiling from my wrists so that my toes were off the ground. Then they started beating me with cables all over my body…after the *shabeh* they used the *dulab* (tyre) technique. They folded my body and forced me to go inside a tyre and then started beating me with wooden sticks."

Bassel, a lawyer in Idlib, said: "I was happy to be free from the Syrian government's unjust rule, but now the situation is worse." He criticised Nusra on Facebook and was immediately detained. Amnesty says the main armed opposition groups are equally severe on anybody differing from them.

There was a period in 2011 and 2012 when there were genuinely independent opposition activists operating inside Syria, but as the jihadis took over, these brave people were forced to flee abroad, fell silent, or were dead. In August 2013, I appeared on the same television programme as Razan Zaitouneh, a renowned human rights lawyer and founder of the Violations Documentation Centre, which recorded crimes and atrocities. She was speaking by Skype from the opposition stronghold of Douma in north-east Damascus where I had been the previous year, but it had become too risky for me to visit. Zaitouneh was describing the sarin poison gas attack that had killed so many people in rebel-held districts of Damascus and denouncing the Syrian government for carrying it out. She was an advocate for the non-jihadi Syrian opposition, but she also criticised the Saudi-backed Jaish al-Islam movement that controlled Douma. On 8 December, its gunmen broke into her office and seized her and her husband, Wael Hamada, and two civil rights activists: Samira al-Khalili, a lawyer, and Nazem al-Hamadi, a poet. None of the four have been seen since and are very likely dead.

It would be simple-minded to believe that this very appealing and professional PR for the Syrian armed opposition is all their own work. Foreign governments play a fairly open role in funding and training opposition media specialists. One journalist of partly Syrian extraction in Beirut told me how he had been offered $17,000 a month to work for just such an opposition media PR project backed by the British government. The dominance of propaganda over news in coverage of the war in Syria has many negative consequences. It is a genuine civil war and the exclusive focus on the atrocities committed by the Syrian armed forces on an unarmed civilian population gives a skewed picture of what is happening.

News organisations have ended up being spoon-fed by jihadis and their sympathisers who make it impossible for independent observers to visit areas they control. By regurgitating information from such tainted sources, the media gives al-Qaeda type groups every incentive to go on killing and abducting journalists in order to create and benefit from a news vacuum they can fill themselves.

30 December 2016

The new ceasefire in Syria that began on Thursday evening will not mean an end to the shooting, but it marks a crucial development in the five-and-a-half-year-long civil war. It will not stop the killing because the biggest armed opposition groups—Isis and Jabhat al-Nusra—are not covered by the agreement, and have a strong motive for making sure that it fails. But what is most important about the ceasefire is not so much what is agreed as who is doing the agreeing.

According to a draft copy of the Russian-Turkish agreement, the Turkish government "guarantees the commitment of the opposition in all the areas that the opposition controls to the ceasefire, including any type of shelling." Russia gives similar guarantees on behalf of the Syrian government and its allies. These are bland words, but what is important here is that Turkey is distancing itself from the armed opposition groups who have depended on its support or tolerance since the uprising against Bashar al-Assad started in 2011. Without such backing, anti-Assad forces may be unable to withstand Syrian government offensives in the future. In other words, there has been a decisive shift in the balance of power inside Syria against the rebels and in favour of Assad.

But the present ceasefire is not solely the result of Syrian and regional developments. The last hope of the non-Isis opposition in Syria and its foreign allies was that Hillary Clinton would win the presidential election and switch US policy to one more committed to getting rid of Assad and more hostile to Russia. Instead, they were horrified by the election of Donald Trump, a candidate even more dismissive of the non-Isis rebels, focused on destroying Isis and more favourable to a Russian alliance than President Obama. Will the US acceptance of Russia playing a dominant role in Syria be capsized by new US sanctions against Moscow and the expulsion of thirty-five Russian diplomats? Probably not, because what Trump is proposing to do openly in Syria is not much different from what Obama was doing without publicity. It is a long time since the US was seriously interested in getting rid of Assad—it has instead been concentrating on defeating Isis. This is likely to continue under Trump and might even have been done under Hillary Clinton if she had become president. At this stage, US policy in Syria and Iraq would in any case be difficult to unglue.

But in a broader sense, President Obama's measures against Russia and Secretary of State John Kerry's denunciation of Israeli policy towards the Palestinians will have an impact on every aspect of US foreign policy. This is less because of specific policy initiatives, which can be dismissed as the empty gestures of an expiring administration, but because Obama's actions are evidence that political warfare in the US post-election is not going to de-escalate. There may be a shaky ceasefire in Syria, but there is none in Washington. The Russian-US relationship in Syria will remain a mixture of rivalry and cooperation. The most important decisions here have already been taken by Obama when he did not intervene militarily against Assad in August 2013 and when he accepted Russian intervention in September 2015. But the degree of cooperation with Russia will remain in dispute between different power centres in Washington. This was already the case, which is why the Syria ceasefire negotiated by the US and Russia in September this year almost immediately collapsed in rancour. Both sides were acutely mistrustful of the other: the US claimed that Russian and Syrian planes had deliberately bombed an aid convoy bound for east Aleppo. The Russians and Syrian government suspected that US air strikes had deliberately targeted and killed sixty-two Syrian soldiers near Deir Ezzor in eastern Syria.

The present Russian-Turkish ceasefire suffers from some of the weaknesses of the two previous Russian-US ones in February and September: several of the major combatants have not signed up and are unlikely to do so because the ceasefire is directed against them. But all three of the ceasefires of 2016 have been serious, even when they failed, because they have involved major players in the conflict: Russia, US, Turkey, and, at one remove, Iran.

The interwoven crises in Syria are of nightmarish complexity and not all the arrows point towards peace. Turkey is backing away from supporting a war to overthrow Assad, but it is also weighing up the prospects for fighting the Syrian Kurds and eliminating their de facto state. Assad has signed up to the latest ceasefire, but he makes no secret of his determination to retake all of Syria. He is probably waiting for the ceasefire to collapse because of its deficiencies before resuming the offensive. Isis, which has been on the retreat in Syria and in Iraq, is by no means out of business.

The Syrian and Iraqi wars are still full of nasty surprises for all participants, as the Trump presidency may soon find out for itself. Every crisis in the region is linked to every other. One of the biggest potential crises hanging over the Middle East is not Trump's attitude to Russia, but to Iran. The role of Russia in Syria tends to be over-publicised and that of Iran, and its loose Shia coalition, tends to be under-reported. Up to the Russian military intervention in September 2015, it was the alliance with Iran that was most important to Assad. Iran certainly has not fought a long war in Syria, or in Iraq for that matter, to see the country impotent on the regional stage and divided up into zones of influence. Peace talks are to start soon in Astana, the capital of Kazakhstan, though the pro-Assad powers are not looking for power-sharing or compromise but a virtual surrender by the other side.

One does not have to spend long in Washington these days to find that, while there are many important people who detest Assad and Vladimir Putin, this feeling is far exceeded by the hatred they feel for the victors of the US presidential election. These divisions are bound to further envenom and shape policy decisions towards the crises and wars exploding in the Middle East.

23 January 2017

The Syrian peace talks arranged by Russia, Turkey, and Iran that opened today in Astana, the capital of Kazakhstan, show that Assad is winning the six-year-old war, but his final victory may be a long way off. Several participants in the conference have good reasons to fight on and Isis has recently made important advances. Representatives of some of the armed rebel groups sat on one side of a round table, while the Syrian government delegation sat on the other, but the rebels said there would be no face to face talks. The most positive likely outcome of the meeting would be a reinforcement of the shaky ceasefire that began on 29 December and has been only partially effective. The US is not taking part in the talks, in contrast to previous abortive negotiations, but has sent its ambassador to Kazakhstan, indicating that it does not oppose them.

The most important feature of the conference is that it proves that Russia's military intervention in the civil war on the side of Mr. Assad since 2015 has promoted it to being the most powerful foreign power engaged in the Syrian war. It signed a long-term agreement with Syria last Friday, which will enable it to expand its naval base at Tartous on Syria's Mediterranean coast and to increase its use of an air base at Latakia. The other big change from previous abortive peace talks is that Turkey, formerly the most important ally of the Syrian opposition, has, in many respects, changed sides.

The Turkish Deputy Prime Minister Mehmet Simsek said last week at the World Economic Forum in Davos that Turkey was retreating from its long-term policy of displacing Mr. Assad. "We have to be pragmatic, realistic," he said. "The facts on the ground have changed dramatically, and so Turkey can no longer insist on, you know, a settlement without Assad, and it's not, you know, realistic." Turkey later said that Mr. Simsek's remarks had been misinterpreted, but in practice, Turkish President Erodogan's lack of response while pro-government forces backed by Russia were recapturing rebel-held east Aleppo at the end of last year showed that Turkey had already changed its policy. Turkish soldiers are suffering heavy losses in a battle against Isis for the town of al-Bab, north-east of Aleppo. Russian planes have, for the first time, been offering air support to Turkish troops, but an Isis video showed its fighters destroying Turkish tanks and armoured vehicles.

Turkey has ensured that the Syrian Kurds are not represented at Astana, though their People's Protection Units are at the forefront of the fight against Isis in Syria. They supply the military punching power to the SDF, which are advancing towards Raqqa and is only a few miles from the Tabqa Dam on the Euphrates, the largest dam in Syria. The Syrian Kurds, who number about two million out of sixteen million Syrians still in the country, are not the only important players unrepresented at today's talks in Astana. Though fourteen rebel factions are present, including the powerful Army of Islam based just east of Damascus, the two most powerful rebel armed groups are not there: Isis and Jabhat Fateh al-Sham (JNS). JNS led the fight for east Aleppo but was unable to put up the same sort of stiff resistance to the Syrian army and its allies as Isis has been able to do against the Iraqi security forces in Mosul.

Isis has been demonstrating that it is still a powerful military force in Syria by capturing the ancient city of Palmyra for the second time in December; it has since blown up the Roman amphitheatre. On 15 January, it launched a determined assault on the Syria government enclave at Deir

Ezzor, a provincial capital on the Euphrates in eastern Syria, where 93,500 people have been long besieged by Isis, depending on supplies dropped by Russian aircraft to survive. The Isis assault partly succeeded in cutting the government-held part of Deir Ezzor in half on 17 January and captured the land on which relief supplies had previously been dropped. The UN Office for the Coordination of Humanitarian Affairs (OCHA) says that "6,000 people in east Deir Ezzor are running out of bread and food supplies." Russian aircraft have launched heavy air strikes to hold back the Isis offensive and an elite Republican Guard unit is being helicoptered in to hold the city, which remains under threat.

25 January 2017
The Turkish army is suffering unexpectedly serious losses in men and equipment as it engages in its first real battle against Isis fighters holding al-Bab. Turkish military commanders had hoped to capture al-Bab quickly when their forces attacked it in December, but they are failing to break through Isis defences. At least forty-seven Turkish soldiers have been killed and eleven tanks disabled or destroyed according to the Turkish military expert Metin Gurcan writing in *al-Monitor*. Isis have posted a video showing a Turkish tank being destroyed, apparently by an anti-tank rocket and Isis fighters looking at the wreckage of other armoured vehicles.

The Turkish military intervention in northern Syria, known as Operation Euphrates Shield, which began on 24 August last year, has also led to heavy civilian casualties. The Syrian Observatory for Human Rights, citing local witnesses, says that 352 civilians, including seventy-seven children and forty-eight women have been killed by Turkish artillery bombardments and air strikes over the last five months. Drone footage taken by Isis shows that the buildings in al-Bab, that once had a population of 100,000, have been devastated. Turkey had intended to make a limited military foray into the territory between the Turkish frontier and Aleppo city forty miles further south, which would make it a serious player in the Syrian conflict. It would drive Isis from its last big stronghold in northern Syria at al-Bab and, above all, prevent the YPG from linking up their enclaves at Kobani and Qamishli with one at Afrin, north-west of Aleppo.

The strategy has proven far more costly and slower to implement in the face of determined and skilful Isis resistance than Ankara had foreseen. It wanted primarily to rely on Arab and Turkman militiamen under Turkish operational control, though these would be nominally part of the Free

Syrian Army (FSA) umbrella group. These proxies would be backed up by Turkish artillery, air strikes, and a limited number of Turkish ground troops. The plan seemed to work in the beginning as the Turkish forces took over the Isis-held town of Jarablus, where the Euphrates River crosses the Turkish border. But swift success here came because Isis did not fight, its men retreating or shaving off their beards and melting into the local population. But when the Turkish-backed FSA advance failed to break through Isis lines in and around al-Bab, Turkey had to reinforce them with its own units, which no do the bulk of the fighting.

Turkish leaders blamed their problems partly on the US, which has failed to make more than a few air strikes in support of the al-Bab offensive. The US does not want to aid militarily a Turkish intervention aimed primarily at the YPG, who have proved the most effective US ally against Isis in Syria. Ankara is hoping that the new Trump administration will be less cooperative with the Kurds and more so with Turkey. Isis is using an effective cocktail of tactics similar to those which it employed to slow down the offensive of the Iraqi security forces in east Mosul, which took them three months to capture. These tactics include frequent use of suicide bombers driving vehicles packed with explosives (VBIEDs), often especially armoured in Isis workshops so they are difficult to stop. "Isis uses VBIEDs to disrupt its enemies' field planning, organisation, and morale," says Mr. Gurcan. "With tunnels, Isis maintains mobility, despite air attacks." As in Mosul, Isis is able to move small mobile units containing snipers, specialists using anti-tank missiles, and suicide bombers from house to house without exposing them to superior enemy firepower. The Turkish forces have been unable to encircle al-Bab and cut the main supply route to Raqqa.

Turkey benefited at this week's peace talks in Astana in Kazakhstan from being one of three foreign powers—the others being Russia and Iran—with ground troops in Syria. It had previously provided crucial aid, sanctuary, and a near open border to the Syrian armed opposition. Reinforced by diplomatic marriages of convenience with both Russia and Iran, Turkey has acquired significant influence over the outcome of the six-year-long war in Syria. But the slow military progress at al-Bab shows Turkey's growing military engagement in Syria is coming at a price—even in its initial phases.

6 March 2017

Kurdish-led Syrian fighters say they have seized part of the road south of Raqqa, cutting Isis off from its other territory further east. Isis is confronting an array of enemies approaching Raqqa, but these are divided, with competing agendas and ambitions. The SDF are now getting close to Raqqa and are likely to receive additional US support. The US currently has 500 Special Operations troops in north-east Syria and may move in American-operated heavy artillery to reinforce the attack on Raqqa.

This is bad news for Turkey's Operation Euphrates Shield as it is being squeezed from all sides. In particular, an elaborate political and military chess game is being played around the town of Manbij, captured by the SDF last year, with the aim of excluding Turkey, which had declared it to be its next target. Turkey will find it very difficult to attack Manbij, which the SDF captured from Isis after ferocious fighting last year because the SDF said on Sunday that it is now under the protection of the US-led coalition. Earlier last week, the Manbij Military Council appeared to have outmanoeuvred the Turks by handing over villages west of Manbij—beginning to come under attack from the FSA militia backed by Turkey—to the Syrian Army which is advancing from the south with Russian air support.

Isis looks as if it is coming under more military pressure than it can withstand as it faces attacks on every side though its fighters continue to resist strongly. It finally lost al-Bab, a strategically placed town north-east of Aleppo, to the Turks on 23 February, but only after it had killed some sixty Turkish soldiers along with 469 FSA dead and 1,700 wounded. The long defence of al-Bab by Isis turned what had been planned as a show of strength by Turkey in northern Syria into a demonstration of weakness. The FSA was unable to advance without direct support from the Turkish military and the fall of the town was so long delayed that Turkey could play only a limited role in the final battle for nearby east Aleppo in December.

Turkey had hoped that President Trump might abandon President Obama's close cooperation with the Syrian Kurds as America's main ally on the ground in Syria. There is little sign of this happening so far and pictures of US military vehicles entering Manbij from the east underline American determination to fend off a Turkish-Kurdish clash which would delay the offensive against Raqqa. The US has shown no objection to Syrian army and Russian "humanitarian convoys" driving into Manbij from the south. There are other signs that the traditional mix of rivalry and cooperation that has characterised relations between the US and Russia in Syria is shifting towards greater cooperation. The Syrian army, with support from Russia and Hezbollah, recaptured Palmyra from Isis last Thursday with help from American air strikes. Previously, US aircraft had generally not attacked Isis when it was fighting Syrian government forces. Seizing Palmyra for the second time three months ago was the only significant advance by Isis since 2015.

Turkey could strike at Raqqa from the north, hoping to slice through Syrian Kurdish territory, but this would be a very risky venture likely to be resisted by the YPG and opposed by the US and Russia. Otherwise, Turkey and the two other big supporters of the Syrian armed opposition, Saudi Arabia and Qatar, are seeing their influence over events in Syria swiftly diminish. American and British ambitions to see Mr. Assad removed from power have been effectively abandoned.

7 April 2017

President Donald Trump had little option but to order a missile strike against a Syrian air base after holding Syria responsible for that poison gas attack on Khan Sheikhoun that killed eighty civilians. He had criticised President Obama for being weak, slow, and indecisive when facing similar challenges, so he could scarcely do nothing when Assad appeared to breach the agreement in 2013 to hand over all his chemical weapons to be destroyed. The fact that the US has taken its first direct military action against Assad is significant, not so much because it has done much damage to the Syrian armed forces, but because it may be repeated. Senior politicians and generals in the US have been calling for air strikes to take out or at least "ground" the whole Syrian air force. This option is now more on the table than it was previously, but that does not mean that it is going to happen.

The launching of fifty-nine Tomahawk missiles that killed six people and did an unknown amount of damage at al-Shayrat air base in Homs province in central Syria is symbolic. But it is a warning that is likely to be taken seriously in both Moscow and Damascus, because full-scale American intervention against Assad is the one thing that would deny them victory in the war. Those who argue that the Syrian armed forces would not have done anything quite so foolish and against their own interests as to launch the strikes, probably underestimate the extent of the stupidity present in all armies. Despite the air strike overnight, the Assad government and the Russians remain in a strong military position because they control all the biggest cities in Syria.

The exiled anti-Assad opposition, who have little strength on the ground in Syria, has welcomed the US missile strike, saying it ended Assad's "impunity." They have called for more of the same, but if this does not happen—and it is unlikely that they will—then the political and military balance of power in Syria will not change significantly. The war is by no means over, but it has jelled and it is getting towards the endgame. It is very unlikely that Washington will want to change its present level of engagement to the point that it became involved as it did—with disastrous results for all concerned—in Afghanistan in 2001, Iraq in 2003, and Libya in 2011. The White House contrasted overnight its swift and decisive response to Assad's use of chemical weapons with the supposed feebleness of President Obama but, in reality, the policies of both administrations are much the same.

Obama was giving priority to eliminating Isis and the al-Qaeda-type movements that dominate the armed opposition and Trump is doing likewise. Obama had long ago placed getting rid of Assad on the back burner and the same is more publicly true of Trump, or so it seemed until the chemical attack on Khan Sheikhoun in Idlib province on Tuesday. Secretary of State Rex Tillerson was much criticised by interventionists in Washington for saying a few days earlier that "the fate of Assad was in the hands of the Syrian people" or, in other words, the Syrian leader was going to stay. Trump said that Tuesday's suspected chemical gas attack had changed his attitude towards Assad and developments in Syria. But this is doubtful as American policies will probably stay the same because they are working successfully and the self-declared Islamic State is getting weaker by the day. The US will probably not want to let Isis and al-Qaeda off the hook now by weakening the Syrian armed forces that remain the strongest military power in Syria. At the same time, the Americans do not intend to allow Assad to flaunt his success and, even before the chemical attack, there were reports of the US resuming aid to some opposition groups deemed to be anti-jihadi and anti-Assad.

If the Russians conclude that Assad was indeed behind the chemical attack—something they currently deny—then they will be infuriated that he has risked so much for so little. The Kremlin will be eager to continue to pursue parallel policies with Washington, something that dates back to 2015 when Obama decided not to oppose Putin's military intervention on the side of Assad. This was a critical moment in the outcome of the war. From Trump's point of view, there is a great advantage in any cross words coming from Moscow because they will counter accusations in the US that he is too close to the Russians. Democratic Party and media criticism, based on conspiracy theories claiming that Russian hackers determined the course of the election, will be deflated and Trump will have his first foreign policy success. The missile strike could do more change to the political landscape than in Syria.

3 May 2017

When Lionel Messi scored a last-minute winning goal for Barcelona against Real Madrid on 23 April, football fans in the Syrian coastal city of Tartous, who had been watching the game on television, rushed into the street to celebrate. This turned out to be a mistake from their point of view because many of the jubilant fans were men of military age, whom the Syrian security forces promptly detained in order to find out if they were liable for military service. It is unknown how many were conscripted but, once in the army, they will have difficulty getting out and there is a high chance they will be killed or injured.

Military service and ways of avoiding it are staples of conversation in Syria where government, Kurds, and insurgents are all looking for soldiers after six years of relentless war. Casualties have been heavy with pro-government forces alone losing an estimated 112,000 dead since 2011, according to the pro-opposition Syrian Observatory for Human Rights. In theory, men can escape conscription if they are the only son of a family or are studying at university, but even then, they are not entirely safe from being arbitrarily drafted.

The conscripts eat bad food and are poorly paid, earning around fifty dollars a month, which gives them little option but to live off bribes mostly earned by letting people pass through their checkpoints. Lorry drivers on the 165-mile route between Kirkuk and Baghdad were on strike in March, complaining that the main checkpoint outside Baghdad had raised its illegal fees to $1,500 per truck, which was three times the previous level. "This money does not come from individual drivers, but from the owner of the goods he carries who passes on the extra cost to the consumer in Baghdad," said a broker called Ahmed, who works as a freelance freight forwarder. He explained that the drivers were on strike not because of the bribery, but because the increased delays at checkpoints that meant the Kirkuk-Baghdad round-trip, which used to take three days, was now taking fifteen.

10 May 2017

Mr. Trump approved a plan on Monday to arm the Kurds directly, in order to enable the YPG and its Arab allies to assault and capture Raqqa. The

US will send heavy machine guns, anti-tank weapons, mortars, armoured cars, and engineering equipment to bolster the attack. Turkey has sought in vain to persuade the US to break its alliance with the Syrian Kurds. "Both the PKK and the YPG are terrorist organisations and they are no different, apart from their names," said Turkish Foreign Minister Mevlut Cavasoglu on Tuesday. "Every weapon seized by them is a threat to Turkey."

Turkey's response to the YPG and SDF successes has been to step up military engagement in northern Syria and to threaten much tougher action. On 25 April, Turkish planes launched air strikes against YPG positions killing twenty fighters, half of them women. Mr. Erodgan threatened that similar action might happen "at any time." The US said the Turkish action was "unacceptable" and was so concerned about a Turkish ground invasion that it sent patrols of US special forces in vehicles to monitor the Syrian side of the border. For their part, the Syrian Kurdish leaders said they would not take Raqqa if Turkish military action continued.

The public decision by Mr. Trump to send heavier weapons to the YPG is important primarily as a sign that the US is ignoring Turkish threats and will stick to its military alliance with the Syrian Kurds, which has served it well. This makes it difficult for the Turkish army and air force to escalate its attacks on the YPG. Mr. Erodgan is to see Mr. Trump for the first time in Washington on 16–17 May and will seek to persuade him to reverse his policy towards the Syrian Kurds, but he is unlikely to succeed. In his final days in office, President Obama had also decided to send heavier equipment to the YPG, indicating that the pro-Kurdish policy has broad support in the US. At the same time, the Americans are trying to reassure the Turks by saying that the new weapons will only be used against Isis and the quantity of ammunition delivered will be limited to what is needed for that operation. The Turks say they fear that the arms will be handed over to the PKK and used against their soldiers.

The Syrian Kurds are worried that, once Isis is defeated, the US will no longer need them and will revert to its old alliance with Turkey as a member of NATO and a major power. This would leave them vulnerable to a Turkish ground attack aimed at extinguishing their semi-independence. For now, however, the Kurds in Syria will be relieved that the US has decided to stick with them.

PART V. THE SIEGE OF RAQQA

The Syrian conflict is in practice a tangle of separate, though interrelated, conflicts in different parts of the country, each with their own separate set of players and rules of the game. Foreign powers like Russia, Turkey, Iran, and the US have their own zones of influence and their own interests, which invariably take precedence over those of the Syrian people. The nature of the conflict in north-east Syria, in which Kurds, Americans, Turks, and—before its defeat— Isis, are the main players, has until recently differed radically from that in the north-west where Russia, the Assad government, Turkey, and armed opposition in the Idlib enclave are the most important forces. But the Turkish invasion on 9 October, swiftly followed by the advance of Russian and Syrian troops and the on/off US withdrawal made a complex situation even more complicated.

Access to either government-held territory or Rojava was never easy. The government could arbitrarily deny one an entry visa: I spent tedious weeks in Beirut waiting for visas that never came because I had reported, illegally in the eyes of the government, from the Kurdish-held zone. At another moment in 2016, I drove to the crossing point into Rojava on the Tigris, where the Kurdistan Regional Government territory in Iraq abuts the Syrian Kurdish statelet, only to find that the promised permission to cross the river had not arrived.

To visit Rojava, I would fly to the Iraqi Kurdish capital Erbil and seek a permit to cross into Syrian Kurdish territory. The process was complicated by the fact that the two Kurdish administrations detested each other, making the move from one to the other tricky and unpredictable. I had influential friends among the Kurdish leaders in Erbil and could usually obtain a permit after persistent effort. Once at the river, I would, if all was well, walk down a slipway into a metal motorboat to make the short river crossing, though I could see a perfectly good pontoon bridge 300 yards downriver. I never discovered why pedestrians like myself were not allowed to use it, but it presumably had something to do with intra-Kurdish feuds.

Once on the western bank of the Tigris, I would wait to see if the Syrian Kurdish authorities had told their local officials to let me pass and, almost equally important, had sent an essential scrap of paper telling their checkpoints to let me through. Without this, I would have had to join the enormous queues of traffic at the entrance to every Kurdish-held town and village. If all was in order, I drove two hours to the Kurdish capital Qamishli or an attractive town called Amida twenty miles further west. Everything appeared so calm and well ordered that it was easy to forget that the Turkish frontier was less than a mile away and the Turks were always saying that they were about to launch an invasion. This was not an idle threat as Turkish incursions culminated in the over-running and ethnic cleansing of the Kurdish canton of Afrin in 2018. This could be a foretaste of the fate awaiting the entire Kurdish population of Rojava in the event of a full-scale Turkish invasion.

Each time I drive into Rojava, I was struck by its vastness and its instability: even when there was no actual violence I had a sense that the situation might explode at any moment: American armoured vehicles, with stars and stripes fluttering, patrolled outside the Arab city of Manbij west of the Euphrates to deter an attack by the Turks. Once fertile fields around Raqqa were empty aside from herds of sheep because the irrigation system was broken and the farmers had fled. Raqqa city was in ruins and its surviving inhabitants desperate to prove that they had always hated Isis during its years of occupation. At the same time, they did not much like their new Kurdish rulers and wondered if Assad or the Turks might be a better bet. Everywhere I had a sense of living inside a house of cards, that might collapse at any moment. Syria is often compared to a quagmire, but I wrote that a better analogy was a "great poisonous stew in which the ingredients are contending sects, ethnicities, and foreign powers that continually produce new and lethal combinations." These ingredients are not likely to change.

June 2017–March 2018

6 June 2017

"I do not think the siege of Raqqa will be as long as Mosul," says Awad, an Arab fighter in the SDF, who belongs to a military unit attacking the de facto capital of Isis in Syria. He says that "we are advancing quickly and the geographical nature of Raqqa is different from Mosul."

Awad, thirty-two, comes from Raqqa but fled to Tabqa to the west of the city last year before it was captured by the SDF and four months ago joined the SDF, which the US says has 13,000 Arab fighters in its ranks. In a phone interview, he gives a vivid description of conditions on the front line, which the SDF Raqqa Operations Room says is three kilometres away from Raqqa to the west and north and one kilometre away to the east. The US estimates that there are between 3,000 and 4,000 Isis fighters in Raqqa, who are isolated there because US coalition air strikes on 3 February destroyed the last two bridges linking it to the south bank of the Euphrates. The fighters can only cross the river by boats, but they would then be vulnerable to air attack.

"They [Isis] are mostly withdrawing [into Raqqa], though some are fighting fiercely and do not leave their positions until they are killed," says Awad. "We killed dozens when we liberated al-Mansoura [west of Raqqa] and Baath Dam [on the Euphrates, renamed Freedom Dam by the SDF]. In addition, we repelled many counter-attacks by Isis since the Tabqa battle until now." The SDF captured the Tabqa Dam, the largest in Syria at the southern end of Lake Assad, and the nearby town of Tabqa, twenty-five miles west of Raqqa, on 10 May, ending a stalemate that had lasted for several weeks. Though Isis units have been retreating in the face of SDF advances and US-led air strikes, the jihadis are still resisting strongly. Awad says that "last week, Isis fighters attacked us from behind in a village called Abu Qebab, east of Raqqa. They were hiding in a tunnel that had not been checked yet by our comrades. In that attack, we surrounded them from two sides and killed about ten of them."

It should become clear in the next few days if Isis will try to defend Raqqa strongly and risk losing many of its experienced fighters. Awad does not believe that the siege of Raqqa will be as prolonged as in Mosul and suspects that the determination of the Isis defenders may not be as high as in Iraq. He says that "the SDF made two calls last month for Isis to surrender, but those that did so were locals. No foreigners have surrendered so far." Some of the Isis units are composed of foreigners who cannot blend into the local population, or expect much mercy if they surrender. "I have been told by our officers that all the Isis snipers killed by our forces are foreigners," says Awad. "We lost some of our commanders because of these snipers and a few days ago, one of our snipers killed an Isis sniper when we fought in Mansoura, west of Raqqa."

The firepower and military expertise of the SDF is much enhanced by US support: "The US-led coalition air strikes and forces are working efficiently with us, we have many American experts who train our commanders and officers and instruct them in using new technical devices. We also have heavy weapons and armoured vehicles. Every week we receive many weapons on the three fronts around Raqqa." This supply of modern weapons, and expertise on how to use them, will determine not only the fate of Raqqa but the future ability of the Syrian Kurds to stand up to Turkish military intervention or action by Assad's forces, which are advancing into Isis-held eastern Syria.

If Turkish troops cross the border into Kurdish held territory in Syria, then the Kurds have made clear that the attack on Raqqa would cease. An alternative strategy for Turkey would be to wait before intervening in the hope that the SDF will become entangled in a long struggle for Raqqa in which it suffers serious casualties. The Turks may also calculate that once the SDF and the Syrian Kurds have defeated Isis, the US will have no more use for them and will return to its traditional alliance with Turkey.

7 June 2017

Anti-Isis forces are advancing into eastern Raqqa, and Iraqi troops have penned surviving Isis fighters into one part of the Old City in Mosul. "They are down to their last neighbourhoods in Mosul and they already lost part of Raqqa, and the Raqqa campaign from here on can only accelerate," said Brett McGurk, the US envoy to the international coalition fighting Isis. "These are critical elements in the ultimate defeat of Daesh, but this will be a long-term effort."

Predictions of impending victory, mixed with doubts about just how long this will take, are echoed by fighters in the front line as they approach Raqqa. "We broke into Raqqa from the east in just two hours," says a Syrian Kurdish fighter in the YPG, who did not want to give his name. "We advanced for 1.5 kilometres in a few hours and the centre of the city is about two kilometres away from us."

But the grim experience of the siege of Mosul is making everybody cautious about forecasting imminent victory. The YPG fighter says that Isis has withdrawn quickly and without putting up much resistance from the eastern entrance to Raqqa, but he warns that "the battle will not be as easy as many expect and maybe they [Isis] are hiding in tunnels."

7 July 2017

In the early dawn of 5 July, a 200-strong force of anti-Isis fighters launched a surprise attack on the Old City of Raqqa. Recruited mostly from survivors of a tribe that Isis massacred three years ago, the five-man assault teams, into which the attackers were divided, at first made quick progress and reached a well-known local mosque in the Old City called Othman bin Affan. Abu Imad al-Sheity, the commander of the anti-Isis group, told me in an interview by phone from the front line, that "the Daesh militants learned that the local civilians were telling us the position of their snipers. They targeted them and killed dozens. It was a horrible massacre." The UN says that there are between 50,000 and 100,000 civilians still left in Raqqa.

Sheity says his fighters "retreated to the Baghdad Gate at the entrance to Raqqa's Old City." He adds the pull-back was to protect those civilians who were still alive, but the hard-fought battles this week are a sign that Isis is still capable of defending this isolated city on the north bank of the Euphrates River. Since the SDF offensive to take the city started on 6 June, the Syrian Observatory for Human Rights says that 224 civilians have been killed by US-led air strikes.

The group that tried to fight its way into Raqqa this week is known as the Syrian Elite Forces, which belong to the FSA. But Sheity says that he and most of his men come from the al-Sheitaat tribe that lives mainly in Deir Ezzor province. In 2014, the Sheitaat resisted the rising power of Isis and were massacred with at least 900 of its members shot, crucified, beheaded, thrown down wells, and buried in mass graves that are still being unearthed. It was the worst single atrocity carried out by Isis in the war in Syria. Sheity, a young man with long dark hair, says that the losses of his tribe were even greater: "We lost about 1,700 tribesmen, including those who disappeared as well as those killed." Isis, then at the height of its power, wanted to show that it would mercilessly punish any individual or tribe which resisted the newly established caliphate. The places where the Sheitaat live is one of the diminishing number of enclaves where here Isis is still in control.

Sheity says that in some parts of the city, Isis had evacuated people before the fighting began. When Isis fighters later withdrew, they left the area behind them heavily seeded with mines. "Daesh planted mines even in the shops and bins on the corners of the streets and buildings," says commander Sheity. "They used a lot of drones dropping explosives." He thought that the clashes over the last month were the most intense since the operation against Raqqa started last year. More than anything else, Sheity says it is the Isis snipers that hold up his advance, quickly changing their positions and moving through tunnels or holes in the walls of houses. As in Mosul, where Isis blew up the al-Nori mosque last month, Isis in Raqqa has destroyed shrines to the companions of the Prophet Mohammed. Advancing from the east, commander Sheity and his men found that every trace of the tombs was gone.

At the height of their power in Raqqa, Isis had a well-organised administration staffed by well-trained experts. In a phone interview Jasim, twenty-five, a graduate of an institute of accounting in Raqqa, described to me how he had worked for two years for Isis in Mosul and Raqqa. He and his two teenage brothers (aged fourteen and sixteen) had taken advantage of an SDF amnesty and surrendered earlier this year. He joined the force attacking Raqqa two weeks ago. Jasim says that all the managers in the Isis accounting office where he worked were Iraqi, confirming that Isis was always essentially an Iraqi movement. "We Syrians were second-class employees or servants," he says. He was paid $300 a month compared to about $400 for a fighter, though both got a free monthly supply of fuel, flour, rice, and some kind of food basket. He finally fled in May this year after several abortive attempts. "I managed to flee through a smuggler, an Iraqi who was a fighter with Isis," says Jasim. "It cost me and my family members about $5,000."

6 September 2017

Al-Qaeda is creating its most powerful stronghold ever in north-west Syria at a time when world attention is almost entirely focused on the impending defeat of Isis in the east of the country. It has established full control of Idlib province and of a vital Syrian-Turkish border crossing since July. "Idlib Province is the largest al-Qaeda safe haven since 9/11," says Brett McGurk.

Hayat Tahrir al-Sham (HTS) has long been the most powerful rebel group in western Syria. After the capture of east Aleppo by the Syrian army last December, it moved to eliminate its rivals in Idlib, including its powerful former Turkish-backed ally Ahrar al-Sham. HTS is estimated to have 30,000 experienced fighters whose numbers will grow as it integrates brigades from other defeated rebel groups and recruits young men from the camps for IDPs who have sought refuge in Idlib from Assad's forces. Al-Qaeda is growing in strength in and around Idlib province, just as Isis is suffering defeat after defeat in eastern Syria and Iraq. Its latest setback was its failure on Tuesday to stop the Syrian army linking up with its enclave at Deir Ezzor, where Isis has been besieging the government-held part of the city for three years. Divided by the Euphrates, the city's complete recapture opens the way to the al-Omar oil fields that once provided half of Syria's crude production.

Deir Ezzor is only the latest Isis urban centre to be lost on the Syrian portion of the Euphrates valley, which was the heartland of its territories in Syria. Isis is everywhere on the retreat. HTS stands to benefit politically and militarily from the decline of Isis, the original creator and mentor of Jabhat al-Nusra, as the earliest of al-Qaeda's incarnations in Syria was known. Under the name of al-Nusra, the Syrian branch of the movement split off in 2013 and the two sides fought a bloody inter-jihadi civil war. If Isis is destroyed or rendered a marginal force, Sunni Arab jihadis refusing to surrender to Mr. Assad's army and intelligence service will have no alternative but to join HTS. Moreover, Sunni Arabs in eastern Syria may soon be looking for any effective vehicle for resistance, if Syrian government armed forces behave with their traditional mix of brutality and corruption. HTS will expect the many states now attacking Isis, and battering to pieces its three-year-old caliphate, to turn on them next. But they will hope to delay the confrontation for as long as possible while they strengthen their movement.

Ideologically similar but politically more astute than Isis, they will seek to avoid provoking a final territorial battle which they are bound to lose. Some Syrian specialists warn against waiting too long. "The international community must seek urgently to counter-attack HTS, which grows stronger by the day, without waiting for the complete destruction of the Islamic State," writes Fabrice Balanche in a study published by the Washington Institute for Near East Studies called *Preventing a Jihadist Factory in Idlib*. He says that HTS wants to dominate the whole Syrian rebellion and is close to succeeding.

The open dominance of an extreme Islamic jihadi movement like HTS creates a problem for foreign powers, notably the US, UK, France, Turkey, Saudi Arabia, and Qatar, previous funders and suppliers of the Syrian rebels. HTS, whose attempt to distinguish itself from al-Qaeda, has convinced few and is listed in many countries as a terrorist organisation, unlike its former ally, the Ahrar al-Sham. It will be difficult for foreign powers to do business with it, though the armed opposition to Mr. Assad has long been dominated by extreme Islamist jihadi groups. The difference is that today there are no longer any nominally independent groups through which anti-Assad states and private donors can channel arms, money, and aid while still pretending that they were not supporting terrorism.

Many of the members of this de facto alliance always disliked each other almost as much as they hated Isis. It was only fear of the latter that forced them to cooperate, or at least not fight each other. It may not be possible to recreate the same unity of purpose against al-Qaeda.

6 October 2017

Shortly before the siege of Raqqa began in June, Isis officials arrested Hammad al-Sajer for skipping afternoon prayers. Hammad, who is twenty-nine, made a living from his motorbike: he carried people and packages, charging less than the local taxis. Isis had arrested him a number of times before—mostly for smoking cigarettes, which were banned under Isis rule—but he had always been released after paying a fine or being lashed. Attendance at prayers was compulsory and he had missed the Asr, the afternoon prayer because a passenger had made him wait while he went into his house to get money for his fare after a trip to Raqqa's Old City. Hammad expected to be fined or lashed, but this time he was sentenced to a month in prison. Except it turned out not to be prison. On his first morning, "militants blindfolded us and took us in a vehicle to a place that seemed to be inside the city because it took no more than ten minutes to get there."

Hammad and the other prisoners, all of them local men, were taken to an empty house. In one of the rooms there was a hole in the floor. Rough steps led down about sixty feet before the tunnel flattened out into a corridor, which was connected to a labyrinth of other tunnels. A fellow prisoner, Adnan, told Hammad that Isis had started work on what was effectively a subterranean network a year and a half earlier. In other words, construction began in 2015, after Isis's spectacular run of victories ended and it started its long retreat in the face of Kurdish offensives backed by coalition firepower. To escape the aerial bombardment, Isis decided to disappear underground, digging immense tunnel complexes underneath its two biggest urban centres, Mosul in Iraq and Raqqa in Syria, to help it defend itself when the final assaults came.

Few people in Raqqa knew the extent of the excavations going on beneath their feet—not even Hammad, who rode his motorbike around the city every day. The entrances were always in districts from which local inhabitants had fled or been evicted. "When we got into the tunnels we were amazed," Hammad remembers. "It was as if an entire city had been built underground." Isis must have needed an army of workers to build it—but then there were large numbers of prisoners and jobless labourers to draw on. The prisoners were told as little as possible about what they were doing: anyone who asked a lot of questions was punished. Hammad saw rooms with reinforced concrete walls and ceilings, and what looked like boxes of ammunition piled up on the floor. When he asked about the boxes, he says, one of the guards "hit me on my back with a piece of cable and said: 'Don't poke your nose into things. This is not your business. Do your job and keep quiet.'" The foreign fighters on duty were silent and unapproachable, but some of the guards were locals and occasionally talked to the diggers during the ten-hour working day. "Sometimes they joked with us because they were bored and tired," he says. One day he asked one of them what all this hard work was for. "This great construction will help the lions of the caliphate to escape," he said (the "lions" were the Isis emirs and commanders). "They have a message to deliver to people and they should not die too soon."

Isis officials used prisoners to work on the tunnels when they could, but they also hired labourers. One of these was Khalaf Ali. When Isis seized the city in 2014, he was selling cigarettes in the street. "I was picked up by some militants who took me to a commander," he says. "They did not take me to prison, but they confiscated my boxes of cigarettes and said that if I sold cigarettes again, they would put me in prison and I would get thirty lashes." He started spending his days in a local square with other unemployed men; they would wait for a car or truck to stop and offer them odd jobs—moving furniture, mending broken doors or windows. In April 2016, Khalaf was sitting in the square with the others when an Isis security man said he wanted to talk to them. At first, they were nervous, but the official said they could have work if they registered their names at an Isis office. When they showed up at 7 a.m. the following day, they were told they had to agree to certain conditions: "We must not talk about what we were doing in public as it was one of the caliphate's secrets and, if we violated this condition, they would kill us as traitors." They were blindfolded and driven a short distance to an empty house, where the blindfolds were removed. It wasn't the house Hammad had first been taken to: here, there were no stairs, just a sloping tunnel about 150 feet long, which took them around sixty feet underground.

"We entered an area that looked like a residential complex," Khalaf remembers. "There were many rooms: some under construction, others finished, with concrete walls." The labourers used trolleys to move the excavated soil to a certain point in the tunnel, where other men, whom he didn't know, took charge of moving it up to the surface to be dispersed. The various teams of workers were forbidden to talk to one another. Khalaf's team was responsible for moving furniture, including sofas and beds, to completed rooms." There was electricity, though not in every room, and the corridor had lights." As the SDF advanced towards Raqqa and the American bombardment intensified, Isis doubled wages to eight dollars a day, though money was deducted if the Isis officials were dissatisfied with the quality of the work. Once Khalaf asked an Isis militant who had first had the idea of building these underground complexes. He was told that it was "our brothers in faith." "In Afghanistan," the militant said, "many attacks were repelled and failed because of the tunnels."

Hammad and Khalaf, who didn't know each other, escaped separately from Raqqa during the first weeks of the siege. Hammad fled in the early morning with a group of men, moving from house to house whenever there was a break in the fighting. They took advantage of a tactical retreat by Isis fighters to run towards the Kurdish-led forces, stopping every ten minutes to hide behind walls and the wreckage of houses until they reached safety. The SDF questioned them to make sure that they weren't Isis infiltrators, and then took them to a camp for displaced people at Ain al-Issa, north of Raqqa. Khalaf's journey out of Raqqa was even riskier: after a number of people in his neighbourhood were killed, he and thirty others decided to try to escape from the city guided by SDF radio broadcasts. Even so, Khalaf says, they were sometimes trapped inside a house by the fighting for several days. "Finally we fled, but we lost some of our friends," he says. "We saw their bodies lying there as we ran, but everybody was afraid of snipers, so we couldn't go back for them."

The siege of Raqqa has now been going on for four months. Isis fanaticism is one reason it hasn't fallen sooner, but that alone wouldn't be enough to stop the SDF, with the might of American airpower behind it. The network of tunnels connecting up bunkers, hideouts, and hidden escape routes is the key to the resistance. Isis fighters are able to move swiftly underground, shifting positions before they can be detected and eliminated by bombing or shellfire. As in Mosul, the only way for the attackers to advance without sustaining heavy losses has been to call in coalition air strikes so intense that much of the city has already been destroyed. The Kurdish general commanding the SDF, Mazlum Kobane, was quoted on 26 September as saying that his forces now hold 75 percent of Raqqa, but there are still some 700 Isis fighters and 1,500 pro-Isis militiamen in the city centre. For Isis, eventual defeat is inevitable, but they remain dangerous: last month, a group of Isis fighters in SDF uniforms killed twenty-eight SDF men in a surprise attack.

17 October 2017

Kurdish and Arab fighters have raised their flag over the last Isis stronghold in Raqqa, bringing to an end the four-month siege. A small number of Isis fighters holding out in the sports stadium were overrun by the Syrian Democratic Forces and fighting has ceased everywhere, according to an SDF spokesman.

In the last hours of fighting, the SDF cleared the National Hospital, which had operated as an Isis headquarters, where twenty-two militants were killed along with three SDF paramilitaries. Earlier, the Kurdish-led-force had captured "Paradise Square" where Isis had once carried out executions and punishments, including beheadings, after which they would leave the severed heads and bodies of their victims to rot in the sun. The SDF has raised the red and yellow flag of the Kurdish YPG forces and torn down the black flag of Isis wherever it was still flying. The UK-based Syrian Observatory for Human Rights confirmed on Monday that Isis had been completely cleared from the city.

The Save the Children charity says that some 270,000 people who fled Raqqa are in critical need of aid, have no homes to return to, and may have to stay in camps for months or years. Sonia Khush, Save the Children's director for Syria, described conditions in the camps where displaced people from Raqqa are staying as "miserable and families do not have enough food, water, or medicine." The end of the battle was marked by negotiations under which Syrian members of Isis and several hundred civilians were bussed out of the city while foreign fighters remained behind to fight to the end. The exodus of Syrian fighters may indicate a fall in the morale of Isis militants, who previously were notorious for refusing to surrender and fighting to the end. It could also mean that Isis has suffered such heavy losses that it is keen not to lose experienced fighters.

There were no air strikes on Raqqa on Monday in a further sign that the battle was over, according to the coalition spokesman Colonel Ryan Dillon. He added that "we do know that there are still IEDs and booby traps in and amongst the areas that Isis once held, so the SDF will continue to clear deliberately through areas." He later added: "We expect our Syrian Democratic Force partners to hit pockets of resistance as the final parts of the city [are] cleared."

Isis still has some sources of strength, notably the fact that its leader al-Baghdadi appears to be alive going by the latest tape-recording of his voice. The broad array of states and movements that had been focussing on wiping out Isis is breaking up, notably in Iraq, where the government recapture of Kirkuk on Monday will sharpen differences between the central government in Baghdad and the Kurdish authorities in the KRG. Overall, some of the Kurdish leaders will look for support to the Sunni Arabs. New divisions and confrontations might offer opportunities to Isis, though they will no longer be able to catch the world by surprise as they did in 2014.

8 March 2018

Cascades of broken concrete line the streets of Raqqa. Few people are about and those who are look crushed and dispirited. An eighty-year-old woman who says her name is Islim is scrabbling in the debris looking for scraps of metal and plastic to sell. She explains that she is trying to look after the wife and daughter of one of her sons, who was killed by a mine. The destruction is apocalyptic. Houses, hospitals, bridges, schools, and factories are gone, turned into heaps of broken masonry. There is no electricity and little water.

"After the war we were at zero and we are still at zero," says Dr. Saddam al-Hawidy. He complains that foreign aid organisations come and look at the ruins of the city, but then leave and are never seen again. The final siege was only the devastating culmination of years of degradation that pre-dates Isis rule. When the much-hated government rule collapsed there was nothing to put in its place. "My father died because the kidney dialysis unit in a local hospital was hit in a Syrian government air strike in 2015," Dr Hawidy said. A few districts escaped the worst of the bombing by the coalition, but none are unscathed. Inside the old walled city, we meet Ahmed Mousaqi, a middle-aged former building worker specialising in ceramics, who complains about the high price of buying a minimal amount of electricity from a private generator. He says he survived the siege, though Isis kept herding him and other civilians held as hostages from building to building. His brother Ahmed, a motorcycle mechanic, was not so lucky. "Isis fighters took over part of his house and it was hit by an air strike," he says. "He was killed along with five members of his family." He adds there is little aid available for people like him because as soon as you say you are from Raqqa, "they think you belong to Isis."

Some 150,000 people have returned to Raqqa, though they are not very visible on the streets. A few shops have reopened, but there are not many customers and business is slow. Beside an ancient ruin called "The Ladies' Castle," Basil Amar as-Sawas has a shop selling doors, some of which he makes himself, while others he buys from people whose houses have been badly damaged but they have been able to salvage some of the fittings. He says there is little money around and those who have any are reluctant to spend it while the situation remains so uncertain. Some people whose houses have survived "are selling them to businessmen because they need the money." He has two small children below school age, but for other people, the absence of schools—mostly destroyed or badly damaged—is another disincentive for thinking of a return to Raqqa.

Another danger faces those whose homes were not hit in the battles: Isis was notorious for its copious use of mines and booby traps. Its fighters specialised in placing well-concealed bombs in the homes of people known to oppose their organisation, and who had fled the city, but were likely to return when the siege was over. One member of the local council was killed when he impatiently went home before the limited demining operation had cleared his house. A reason why so little aid is distributed is the difficulty of finding distribution points for food and medicine that have been declared safe. Sarbast Hassan, an electrical technician working to restore the electricity supply, says that "we can't even work in the city because of the mines."

There is an extra charge of fear percolating everywhere in Raqqa that makes it different from the many other Syrian cities ravaged by war since 2011. It stems primarily from the three-and-a-half years of sadistic and pitiless Isis rule, which has left everybody in the city traumatised. "Daesh is in our hearts and minds," says Abdel Salaam, who is in charge of social affairs for the council. "Five-year-old children have seen women stoned to death and heads chopped off and put on spikes in the city centre." Others speak of sons who killed their fathers, and fathers who did the same to their sons. Some of these atrocity stories may be exaggerated but, given the Isis cult of cruelty, many of them are likely to be all too true.

The memory of Isis terror will never go away and is accompanied by a more concrete fear that some of the movement have survived and are reorganising. Commander Masloum, one of four SDF field commanders in charge of security in Raqqa, dismisses this as an exaggerated rumour and says that there have been no recent Isis attacks in the city. He had investigated reports of "sleeper cells," but so far these had turned out to be untrue. Even so, security is tight and a curfew begins at 5 p.m., after which everybody must be off the streets. The roads leading to the city have checkpoints every few miles manned by locally recruited security forces.

In other Syrian cities bombed or shelled to the point of oblivion there is at least one district that has survived intact. This is the case even in Mosul in Iraq, though much of it was pounded into rubble. But in Raqqa, the damage and the demoralisation are all-pervasive. When something does work, such as a single traffic light, the only one to do so in the city, people express surprise.

Reminders of the grim rule of Isis are everywhere. The tops of the pointed metal railing surrounding the al-Naeem Roundabout are bent outwards because that is where severed heads were put on display. A couple of hundred yards away is what looks like a square manhole, which is the entrance into an elaborate system of tunnels which Isis dug under Raqqa. The horrendous past of the city has been succeeded by the prospect of a dangerous and uncertain future. "People here are frightened of everybody:

Isis, Kurds, and the Assad regime," says a local observer. They may prefer the Kurdish-led SDF to Isis, but the choice between the Kurds and the Syrian government is more difficult to make. "They know that the Assad regime will be more merciless towards anybody who had dealings with Isis, though they may just have been selling them food or other goods," says one frequent visitor to the city. "On the other hand, they have never liked the Kurds and at least the Assad regime is Arab like them." Like most Syrians, the people of Raqqa are faced with a choice of evils—and nobody knows more about what evil rulers are capable of doing than they are.

PART VI. TWO LAST STANDS: AFRIN AND EASTERN GHOUTA—EQUAL MISERY, UNEQUAL COVERAGE

On a green hillside in Afrin in northern Syria, Arab militiamen allied to the Turkish army, which invaded this Kurdish enclave have captured a group of terrified looking Kurdish civilians. The unformed and heavily armed militiamen are shouting "pigs," "pimp," and "PKK pigs," all the while chanting "Allah Akbar (God Is Great)." The Kurds, their hands raised in the air, are led away by the militiamen and their fate is unknown.

There were many such videos and still photographs from Afrin in early 2018 taken by Kurds and members of the Turkish forces showing the shelling and bombing of houses, the mangled bodies of children killed by the explosions, and others of Kurdish civilians being herded away. One horrific selfie taken by a militiaman showed him staring at the camera while over his left shoulder was a burned-out civilian car in which sat the corpse of the driver, his white teeth thrown into relief because the rest of his body is burned black. If any of these images were coming out of eastern Ghouta, they would have been leading every television newscast and dominating the front pages. Nikki Haley, then the US ambassador to the UN, would have been holding up pictures of dead and dying children. But because these events were happening in Afrin and not in eastern Ghouta, in the same country but 200 miles apart, they were almost entirely ignored by both media and foreign politicians.

Afrin was seeing the beginnings of a tragedy that could be every bit as bad or worse than anything witnessed in eastern Ghouta in 2018 or east Aleppo in 2016. Coming upon pictures of children buried under broken concrete, one had to search for additional information to know if the deaths were of Kurds killed by the Turkish bombardment in northern Syria, or people in eastern Ghouta slaughtered by Syrian government shells and bombs at the same time and in much the same way. The greatest difference between the two situations was that the atrocities in Damascus were publicised by the media across the world, while in the Kurdish case, they were regarded as scarcely worth a mention.

Over a single week in March in Afrin, the siege of heavily populated areas tightened and the death toll rose—220 dead and 600 injured civilians according to the local Kurdish health authority—and the suffering was going get a lot worse. The Turkish advance was speeding up, something the Kurds believe was happening because Turkey knew that international attention was focused exclusively on eastern Ghouta. The Turkish forces announced that they had captured the large and strategically placed town of Jinderes, south-west of Afrin City. The latter is the largest urban centre in the enclave where most of the population driven from the villages in the countryside had taken refuge. Such was the chaos in Syria that nobody knows how many people are trapped in Afrin with the UN giving a figure of 323,000 and Kurdish leaders saying that it was closer to one million.

Afrin is about three times larger in area than eastern Ghouta before the latest Syrian government assault, but, as we have seen in other sieges in Syria and Iraq, civilian casualties go up as the besiegers press people into smaller and smaller zones. The water pumping station in Afrin City was hit, reducing the availability of drinking water. As with eastern Ghouta, there was a grisly argument about whether or not the local inhabitants were free to leave Afrin or were being detained as "human shields." Elham Ahmad, the co-president of the Syrian Democratic Council, which administered Kurdish-controlled areas and has just returned from Afrin, denied this and told me that people were free to leave.

Another reason why the Kurds in Afrin fled was the nature of the Turkish forces that invaded Afrin on 20 January. There were regular Turkish troops and special forces, but also as many as 25,000 Free Syrian Army fighters. Evidence from the front line and from former FSA and Isis members suggested that many of these were battle-hardened Islamists who had previously fought with or along-side Isis and al-Qaeda. They detested the US-backed Kurds, who held 25 percent of Syria, as one of the reasons for the Islamist defeat in the struggle for Syria. The departure of the Kurds had the advantage from Turkey's point of view of establishing a powerful Sunni Arab bloc north of Aleppo, which would be under its influence. The Kurds of Afrin could end up like the Greeks in Cyprus who fled or were driven from the northern part of the island by the Turkish invasion of 1974 and are still trying to return to their homes and lands forty-four years later.

I used to attribute such partisan coverage of the war to the greater skill and resources of the Syrian opposition in recording and publicising very real atrocities committed by the Syrian government and its allies. But in Afrin, there is no shortage of film of the suffering of civilians, but it simply is not widely broadcast or printed.

February–April 2018

20 February 2018

Syrian artillery and aircraft are bombarding eastern Ghouta, the last big rebel enclave, which is just to the east of Damascus. Some 127 people were reported to have been killed on Monday alone. By Tuesday evening, that figure was said to have doubled. The strength of the attack by shellfire, bombs, and missiles is more intense than anything seen in the area for several years, suggesting that an all-out ground assault is in prospect or, as in east Aleppo just over a year ago, there will be a last-minute attempt to negotiate a mass evacuation.

The siege of eastern Ghouta could be the last of the big sieges that have characterised the war in Syria for the last five or six years and has made it such a destructive conflict. Early on in the war, government forces adapted the strategy of abandoning opposition strongholds, surrounding them and concentrating pro-government forces in defence of loyalist areas, essential roads, and important urban areas. The rebel enclaves were sealed off with checkpoints and the people inside were subjected to regular bombardment. Once there were many such areas, almost encircling Damascus, which has a population of around five million. Some districts, like Daraya in the south of the capital, were emptied out early and their buildings still stand but are gutted and uninhabitable. Other opposition enclaves, notably those in north Damascus, have been levelled by gunfire or demolition teams so hardly a single building stands more than a few feet high.

Eastern Ghouta is just a few miles to the east of the capital and is an extensive urban and agricultural area with an estimated population of 400,000, which was loosely besieged after 2013. There were shortages of medical supplies, machinery spare parts, and other high value items though not of basic food supplies. But last year, the government tightened the siege, closing the informal tunnel system through which fuel and food had been coming in. By January this year, the cost of a basket of essential food items in eastern Ghouta was 780 percent higher than in government-held areas a few miles away.

Besieged rebel areas have been falling one by one, the fighters and the civilian population sympathising with them often going to Idlib in north-west Syria. In Daraya, they left in the summer of 2016 and east Aleppo fell at the end of the same year. Eastern Ghouta has held out longest because it was large, strongly held, and could grow part of its own food. But the rebel factions in control were divided, occasionally fought each other, and had no strategy to counter the Syrian army's steady advances other than firing mortars into pro-government districts like Christian Bab Touma in the Damascus Old City.

Living conditions have been deteriorating because of lack of goods or, even when they are available at high prices, people have no money to pay for them. Where food is permitted to enter the eastern Ghouta enclave, it is subjected to a high fee for every kilo imported. Aid workers say that nobody died of starvation in January, but many people are suffering from malnutrition. As shelling and air strikes intensified last month, all schools closed.

With Syrian government forces either victorious or not engaged in full-scale combat in much of the country, it has more soldiers and airpower to concentrate on remaining rebel strongholds in eastern Ghouta and Idlib. But there is a growing confrontation between Assad and Turkey in the northern Kurdish enclave of Afrin. Turkish artillery has been shelling on Tuesday the government-held entry point to Afrin down which pro-government fighters armed with heavy machine guns have been driving as part of their new alliance with the Kurds.

26 February 2018

Ghafour, forty-three, tells me he just wants to get out of what the UN has dubbed "hell on Earth." But at a checkpoint, a rebel commander made clear he wouldn't be allowed to go. Syrian rebels and government forces are both preventing civilians fleeing the bombardment of eastern Ghouta, he told me. A teacher of Arabic, Ghafour spoke of their abortive attempt to escape.

"I live in Douma [in the north of eastern Ghouta] and have three children who are all under fifteen," he says. "I tried to send my family out, but the opposition militants prevent all families leaving." He adds that even the extensive networks of independent smugglers, who used to bring goods secretly into eastern Ghouta and sometimes smuggle people out, would not help him because they work with the rebel movements in control of eastern Ghouta. "I tried but in vain," he recalls, describing how one of the local rebel commanders, probably from the Army of Islam that controls this part of the besieged enclave, caught Ghafour and his family last Thursday when they were trying to move from Douma to another opposition-held district further west called Harasta. "He shouted at me and said, 'You should stay here and support our fight against the regime, and you should not even send your wife and children away. If we send our families out, our morale will go down and we will lose.'"

Ghafour returned home with his family and says that they expect to be killed at any moment. Even so, he is sympathetic to the rebels who are stopping him and his family escaping. "I am not fighting myself, but I go and see the fighters nearby and offer help in case it is needed," he says. He is fearful of government reprisals, saying that it is dangerous even to use the Syriatel mobile network because "calls are recorded by the regime." "A friend of mine was arrested last month because of some calls he made in Douma before moving from there to regime-held areas," he adds. He says that it has now become impossible to cross from Harasta or Douma to government-held territory, as had previously been possible, because "the regime will not let them go to its areas." As a result, he and his family remain in their house, terrified and confused about what will happen next after a week of continual shelling and bombing. "I lost two friends of mine in Shafouniya yesterday in an air strike," he says.

Ghafour was speaking just as the UN Security Council passed its resolution demanding a thirty-day ceasefire in Syria, which has led to some easing of the bombing and shelling that has already killed 500 people in eastern Ghouta over the last week. This was also before allegations that Syrian government forces had been using chlorine gas.

This is confirmed by a UN-backed report called *Reach*, which says: "Women of all ages, and children, reportedly continued to be forbidden by local armed groups from leaving the area for security reasons." This has been the pattern in all the many sieges in Syria conducted by all sides who do not want their own enclaves depopulated and wish to retain as much of the civilian population as possible as human shields.

But Ghafour is right in thinking that he and his family would have a great deal to be frightened of even if they did manage to make their way to government lines. Men of military age, in particular, are likely to be detained because they are suspected of being rebel fighters or because they are liable to be conscripted into the Syrian army. Detention might be immediate or happen later at any one of the thousands of government checkpoints. These often act like border crossings and ill-paid soldiers and police will look for a bribe, especially from those who come originally from rebel-held areas. But there is another reason why people fleeing eastern Ghouta might be in danger in government-held Damascus. Seven years of civil war has ensured that Syrians on different sides, many of whom will have lost relatives in the violence, regard each other with undiluted hatred. In Damascus, the shellfire and bombing are largely by the government into rebel areas, but there is also outgoing fire from eastern Ghouta, mostly from mortars, into government-controlled districts.

Rania, twenty-two, a fourth-year student of English literature at Damascus University, explained to me what had happened in her area and what was the local reaction to it. She lives in the Dwel'a neighbourhood, which is a government-held area but located between two opposition-controlled zones, Ayn Tarma to the north and Mukhayyam Al Yarmouk to the south. "Our neighbourhood has been shelled once or twice a week by opposition militants since last year, but since last week the shelling has intensified and is happening every day," she says. She and her friends have been stranded in their houses for a week and cannot even go out to buy food. The army, and local young men willing to take the risk, have been supplying them. "People are being killed every day in our neighbourhood," Rania says. "Yesterday, a shell hit the balcony of our neighbour's house and killed his daughter, who was a university student."

There are similar incidents every day. One house near to Rania's was hit by a rocket and a mother and her three-year-old child were killed. As a result of this, Rania says that people in her district speak about "what is happening in Ghouta in a very negative way." This means they are all in favour of the use of maximum force against it. She says that "a shopkeeper in our locality lost his son in Ghouta. He was serving in the Syrian army and, while he and his unit were trying to break into eastern Ghouta, he was killed along with several other soldiers. The shopkeeper and many who lost their sons say that even the children of Ghouta should be killed because 'if they grow up, they will be terrorists as well.'"

1 March 2018

The Turkish attack on Afrin is likely to have the same devastating outcome as the Syrian army siege of eastern Ghouta, destroying everything but failing to capture the area, says a senior Syrian Kurdish leader. The official says it was inevitable that Afrin would come under siege, comparing it to eastern Ghouta, adding that Afrin has a single supply line controlled by the Syrian government and the Russians, "but they could block the way at any moment."

Aldar Khalil, co-chair of the Movement for a Democratic Society, the Syrian-Kurdish dominated organisation that controls 30 percent of Syria, also predicted that the war in Syria may last "another four years until a new balance of forces becomes clear." Based in the city of Qamishli, Mr. Khalil says there are signs of a resurgence by Isis, whose fighters have taken advantage of the diversion of Kurdish forces to face the Turkish invasion of Afrin on 20 January, to make attacks in Deir Ezzor province. "It used to be we who were attacking Isis, but now we are losing fighters every day and we have had 170 killed since the start of the Turkish operation," says Mr. Khalil. Reports from the ground in eastern Syria and from former Isis strongholds in northern Iraq confirm that the movement, which appeared wholly defeated a few months ago, is showing renewed activity.

Mr. Khalil has a bleak but highly informed view of the future of Syria, believing that there is a lot more fighting to come. He is adamant that the YPG will fight to the end for Afrin city and will never surrender. Given the dedication and battle experience of its combatants, who have been fighting Isis since 2015, a prolonged and bloody siege of Afrin is in prospect. The Syrian government sent a force of militia into Afrin to oppose the Turkish-backed forces earlier this month, but Mr. Khalil says their number was small and the action was symbolic. He does not see it as opening the door to a wider agreement between the Damascus government and its Kurdish minority, which would be an essential development if peace is to be restored. He says that the Kurds often sent conciliatory messages to the Syrian government, but have yet to receive a positive response.

The problem for the two million Syrian Kurds, a persecuted and marginalised minority before 2011, is that the war between Assad and the armed opposition has enabled them to make great political and military gains, which will be difficult to retain. Syrian government forces withdrew from most of the Kurdish region in 2012 to concentrate on defending strategically more important areas. The YPG began to advance but came under ferocious attack by Isis in 2014 which tried to capture the Kurdish city of Kobani. The Kurds defended it heroically, but the siege was broken by the intervention of the US air force at the cost of the destruction of 70 percent of Kobani.

A crucial question since the fall of Raqqa has been whether or not the US would withdraw its 2,000 advisers and air support and abandon the Kurds. Mixed signals have been coming out of Washington on this. But Mr. Khalil sounds confident that the US is not going to go. "I don't think the US will leave Syria to the Russians," he says. At one time, Russia had a few troops in Afrin to deter a Turkish invasion and these were backed up by the Russian air force and anti-aircraft missile defence systems in northern Syria. Mr. Khalil says the reason that the Russians gave a green light to a Turkish invasion was in retaliation for the drive of the Kurdish Arab forces into Deir Ezzor, depriving Mr. Assad of Syria's biggest oil fields. Mr. Khalil is convinced that the Russians will do nothing to stop the Turks, even if they attack Syrian government forces in Afrin. Russia's close relationship with Turkey is too valuable to Moscow for it to put it at risk. "Even if all of Assad's army goes to Afrin, Putin will not defend it," says Mr. Khalil.

Afrin has an estimated population of about 400,000, which is much the same as eastern Ghouta. So far, the Turkish advance has been slow. In the last few days, despite the UN Security Council resolution calling for a thirty-day truce in all of Syria, Turkish forces have been taking the borders of Afrin. There are air strikes every day, but on Afrin city only once or twice a week, though it is being hit by artillery. This is likely to change as the Turkish army and associated Arab militias try to fight their ways into urban areas and suffer heavy casualties. The outlook for Afrin, which has so far survived the seven-year war in Syria untouched, looks grim.

Mr. Khalil is sure that the next great battle of the Syrian war will be fought in Afrin. He does not think that the Turks will attack the town of Manbij further east, as they have often threatened to do, because of the US military presence. He describes a Syrian political landscape in which all the players still believe they can be successful, making his belief that the Syrian war still has at least four more years to run sound horribly convincing.

2 March 2018

Manbij is a good place to understand the jigsaw puzzle of competing fiefdoms into which Syria is now divided and the reasons why the multiple wars that have torn the country apart will go on for several more years. A largely Arab city with a population of 300,000, it is situated east of Aleppo and west of the Euphrates River but has been effectively controlled by the Kurds since they captured it from Isis after a long siege in 2016.

Turkey has been repeatedly threatening to attack Manbij to end the Kurdish presence, though the Kurds, for their part, say they are no longer in control but have handed over power to a local body called the Manbij Military Council. The Turks claim that this just means that the Kurds have changed their uniforms, but the council, which has about 5,000 fighters, acts in concert with US troops, so, if Turkish troops and the local militias they work with do advance, it will be at the risk of a shooting war with the US. The Americans in Manbij are certainly very visible and this is presumably intentional. We saw a convoy of five armoured vehicles, the lead one carrying the Stars and Stripes, racing towards Manbij from the bridge across the Euphrates. Mohammed Abu Adel, the leader of the Military Council, says the US soldiers never go into the city "but are very active in the front lines."

After seven years of war, Syrians are used to living in a state of permanent crisis, so the prospect of a Turkish assault has had only a limited impact. Ibrahim Kaftan, the co-chairman of the executive council running the city, says that when Turkey invaded the nearby Kurdish enclave of Afrin on 20 January, "about 80 percent of the people here thought the Turks were going to attack us, but now they are more optimistic." In the crosshairs of the Turkish army and its militia allies, Manbij may be, but for all that, it is a surprisingly bustling place. The streets are crowded and the shops are piled high with everything from oranges to wheelchairs. A few buildings have been reduced to heaps of rubble, blown up by US air strikes targeting Isis during the siege of the city, but there is not the devastation that you see in the Kurdish city of Kobani on the other side of the Euphrates. The most striking sign of the Isis presence is a large cemetery in the centre of Manbij, where its militants systematically smashed all the tombstones, which they saw as idolatrous.

Despite the Turkish threat, Manbij has become a boomtown thanks to the chronic political fragmentation and instability, which as ruined most Syrians. A prosperous trading city on the main highway to the east of the country, it had no great advantage before 2011 when Syria was united. But

today it has the unique benefit of standing at the entrance to the vast territories to the east of the Euphrates. "We are the only gateway for the Kurds,"
says Kaftan, who explains that businessmen from Aleppo had poured into
the city to profit from the trade with the Kurds.

The Syrian jigsaw puzzle is even more complicated than is portrayed by
those neat maps shown on television in which different factions are shaded
in contrasting colours. Groups that are fighting each other in one part of
the country are fighting side by side in another. The country has the feel of
medieval Italy in which every city and town had its own distinct politics,
along with some powerful foreign sponsor. One quickly gets used to living
in a world of competing authorities. For instance, we left Qamishli early
in the morning, but to get to the main highway, we went down a winding
country road. This is because we wanted to avoid the old link road which
goes past Qamishli airport, still held by the forces of President Assad under
a mutually beneficial agreement. Assad wants to retain a foothold in north-
east Syria and the Kurds want to have the option of flying to Damascus,
since otherwise they are isolated.

The problem for the Kurds in Syria is that they have been almost too successful militarily. To hold onto at least part of their gains, the Kurds need
continuing US support. Probably, the US will stick with the Kurds because
it would be ashamed, at least in the short term, to abandon them. Doing
so too swiftly would also deter other potential US allies in the Middle East
who might fear a similar fate. What is interesting and perhaps ominous
about Manbij is that control of this small city has become an issue that
could see US and Turkish troops shooting at each other. The same pattern
is visible in the rest of Syria where fierce local disputes, such as the attempt
by the Syrian government to batter eastern Ghouta into submission, turns
into an international confrontation.

Yet the wars in Syria have now gone on for so long that they are almost
impossible to end. A few issues have been decided: Assad is going to
stay in power in Damascus, but his power is not going to extend to the
whole country. Isis has been defeated, overwhelmed by the sheer number
of its enemies. But Russia, the US, Turkey, and Iran have become so
embroiled in Syria that they cannot afford to see their local allies and
proxies destroyed.

Driving across the rain-soaked plains that the Kurds conquered over the
last three years, one is struck by their great extent but also by their vulnerability. One day, Damascus and Ankara may unite to destroy them,

and US willingness to guarantee their security is bound to ebb in time. A city like Manbij may benefit briefly from the political breakup of Syria, but it is too close to too many front lines and will find it difficult to survive. The same could be said of Syria as a whole.

4 March 2018

Suleiman Khalaf, also known as Abu Fadi, was killed ten days ago in a fight with Isis in eastern Syria when the vehicle he was in was hit by a heat-seeking missile. "He was driving a bulldozer which was building an earth rampart when Isis hit it with a missile we call a 'fuzia,'" said Baran Omari, the commander of his unit in the YPG. "Isis attacked us in the village of Bagin in Deir Ezzor province," he explained, adding that his men had been able to kill those who fired the missile. He described Khalaf, who was about fifty when he died, as a very brave man because he had the peculiarly dangerous job of constructing tactical earth fortifications in the middle of battles.

Omari, whose name is a nom de guerre, was standing beside Khalaf's newly dug grave in the military cemetery in the city of Qamishli. There is a poster with a picture of the dead man at one end of the grave, which is decorated with artificial red and yellow flowers. He pointed to half a dozen fresh graves nearby and said that they belonged to YPG fighters who had been killed recently fighting Isis. This should not be happening because Isis was supposed to have been decisively defeated last year when it lost Raqqa and Mosul, its de facto capitals in Syria and Iraq, respectively. The self-declared Isis caliphate, the size of Great Britain only three years ago, had shrunk to a few enclaves in the deserts of eastern Syria and western Iraq.

But it is turning out that the enemies of Isis had written it off too early. There are an increasing number of fights, like the one in which Khalaf died. A senior Kurdish official in Syria says that 170 of their forces have died in combat with Isis in the past six weeks. On 19 February in Iraq, Isis ambushed an intelligence unit of the Hashd al-Shaabi in the Hawijah district west of Kirkuk and killed twenty-seven of them. Western diplomats say that they are worried by the increasing number of pinprick attacks, which means that Isis is beginning to get back in business. In Qamishli, the first Isis car bomb in six months killed five people and wounded seven last month.

There are other signs of an Isis resurgence in its old strongholds. A recent visitor to Deir Ezzor province warned that "local people talk of an Isis comeback and you should not be on the roads after 3 p.m., because that is when the SDF abandon their checkpoints for the night." Similarly, in

Hawijah, government officials are reported to be spending the night in Kirkuk, where they are safe from Isis assassination squads.

The main cause of the rebirth of Isis, though still limited in scale, is not difficult to detect. Those who claimed to have destroyed the movement last year were dividing the lion's skin when it was badly wounded but not quite as dead as they believed. After declaring victory prematurely, they became diverted by other crises. In Iraq, it was the Kurdish referendum on independence that provoked the Baghdad government to send its forces that had been fighting Isis to retake Kirkuk and other territories disputed with the Kurds on 16 October. Najmaldin Karim, the Kurdish former governor of Kirkuk, says that the Iraqi security services never really secured Hawijah, traditionally a hardcore Isis area, because they were too busy confronting the Kurds. In Syria, it was the Turkish invasion of the Kurdish enclave of Afrin north of Aleppo on 20 January, which suddenly made the military situation more favourable to Isis. Asked if Isis is getting stronger, Aldar Khalil says: "Go look at our cemeteries. Every day we lose five, seven, or eighteen martyrs. Isis are now the ones doing the attacking, while we used to be the ones who were on the offensive."

The Arab-Kurdish SDF is said by the Americans to have a strength of 57,000 fighters, but this is not large, given the sheer size of the Kurdish-held territories. Many YPG Kurds are being transferred from confronting Isis in Deir Ezzor to fighting the Turkish invasion of Afrin in the northwest. Elham Ahmad, co-chairman of the Syrian Democratic Council, which helps administer the Kurdish-held area, comes from Afrin, where her family still lives. She says that "the front against Isis is fractured. My relatives who were fighting Isis in Deir Ezzor know they must go back to Afrin to fight the Turks there."

The re-emergence of Isis is still only in its early stages. In Raqqa, where Isis held out for four months until 20 October last year, there are rumours of Isis "sleeper cells," but there have been no attacks, says Masloum, an SDF field commander in the city. Even so, he is taking no chances and there is a curfew that starts at 5 p.m. This does not necessarily imply that there is any great threat from Isis, but is a testament to the terror people in the city feel in recalling the sadistic and merciless rule of the movement. "Their security men used to mask their faces so we don't know who they were and they may still be living here," said one local observer nervously.

It is unlikely that Isis will ever come back in full force because of its heavy losses, reputation for mindless savagery, and lack of external support.

But it can still do a lot to stir up ethnic and sectarian hatred since many Syrians suspect people from Raqqa as secret Isis supporters and likewise in Iraq in respect to Mosul. Communal punishment of Sunni Arabs in Hawijah after the killing of the twenty-seven Hashd, mostly Shia from Basra, might provoke a backlash favouring Isis recruitment.

5 March 2018

Sieges are a merciless business, never more so than in Syria. As a UN aid convoy entered eastern Ghouta, the World Health Organisation said that Syrian government security had forced the removal from its trucks of "all trauma kits, surgical, dialysis sessions, and insulin." Some 70 percent of the medical supplies being sent were rejected according to a WHO official.

There is something disgustingly mean and vicious in targeting those who will die without dialysis or insulin. Depriving the sick of their last hope of life illuminates in the grimmest of ways how the siege of eastern Ghouta, as in the other sieges that have been such a feature of the wars in Syria and Iraq, puts unbearable pressure on the weak and the vulnerable. The aid convoy had already been cut back in size from food for a month for 70,000 to 27,500 people, though there is meant to be a second convoy in a few days. Even if this is not again depleted by government security forces, it is far too little for the 393,000 people estimated to be in this besieged eastern part of Damascus, though the chaos is such that nobody knows the true figure.

The siege is following much the same course as that of east Aleppo in 2016. The Syrian government is determined to retake the rebel-held zone by indiscriminate shelling and bombing combined with cutting off all supplies of food, fuel, and medicine. It is making a ground assault that is crumbling the edges of the beleaguered enclave which is being systematically squeezed to death. The aim of the multiple assaults is to chop the area into smaller pieces that can be dealt with separately. Sporadic aid convoys in such circumstances are really only a public relations ploy by the Syrian government and the Russians to ease the pressure of outraged international opinion. They do not affect the overall military course of the siege.

The US-led air war is supposedly more humane and directed solely at military targets. But I was in Raqqa last Sunday and the overwhelming impression is of universal destruction similar to that of the carpet-bombed German cities in the Second World War. Proof of this is emerging. A detailed study of 150 air strikes by *The New York Times* last year revealed that, while the US air force claimed that one in 157 of its air strikes led to civilian deaths, the real figure was probably one in five. In the Qayara district south of Mosul, the US said its aircraft had killed one civilian, but the real figure was forty-three dead, twenty-four of them women and children.

What should now be done to limit civilian casualties in eastern Ghouta? As in east Aleppo, the enclave's fall is inevitable and anything that prolongs the battle there will only lead to more dead and disabled. Humanitarian corridors are needed, but these are not much good without UN monitors ensuring the ceasefire is real. Most of the discussion is about what should happen to the civilians, but the outcome of these sieges is invariably determined negotiations between the besiegers and the armed opposition defenders. In past sieges, these have been given the choice of an amnesty of some description or evacuation with light weapons to a rebel stronghold, almost invariably Idlib in the north-west of Syria. None of these past prescriptions quite fit eastern Ghouta because of its size and because rebel fighters like the Army of Islam, which controls Douma, the largest population centre under attack, do not have another base to which they can go. But even the most successful evacuations are stories of misery and terror, which will continue so long as the war in Syria goes on.

Where foreign powers could do the most good is by preventing such sieges starting in the first place. Once besieger and besieged are locked in unequal combat, there is little the outside world can do about it, aside from a general wringing of hands.

7 March 2018

In a field beside an abandoned railway station close to the Turkish border in northern Syria, Kurdish fighters are retraining to withstand Turkish air strikes. "We acted like a regular army when we were fighting Daesh with US air support," says Rojvan, a veteran Kurdish commander of the People's Protection Units. "But now it is us who may be under Turkish air attack and we will have to behave more like guerrillas." Rojvan and his brigade have just returned from forty-five days fighting Isis in Deir Ezzor province and are waiting for orders which may redeploy them to face the Turkish army in Afrin. Rojvan says that "we are mainly armed with light weapons like the Kalashnikov, RPG [rocket-propelled grenade launcher] and light machine guns, but we will be resisting tanks and aircraft." He makes clear that, whatever happened, they would fight to the end.

Kurdish and allied Arab units are streaming north from the front to the east of the Euphrates, where Isis is beginning to counter-attack, in order to stop the Turkish advance. Some 1,700 Arab militia left the area for Afrin on Tuesday and Turkey is demanding that the US stop them. The invasion is now in its seventh week and Rojvan and his fighters take some comfort in the fact that it is moving so slowly. But the Turkish strategy has been to take rural areas before moving methodically to surround and besiege Afrin City and residential areas.

The Syrian Kurds believe they are facing an existential threat. They believe Turkey wants to eliminate not just the enclave of Afrin, but all of their Syrian territories. Some think that defeat will mean the ethnic cleansing of Kurds from Afrin, which has traditionally been one of their core majority areas. They cite a speech by President Recep Tayyip Erdogan made the day after the start of the invasion started, claiming that "55 percent of Afrin is Arab, 35 percent are the Kurds ... and about 7 percent are Turkmen. [We aim] to give Afrin back to its rightful owners." There is a suspicion among Kurdish leaders that Erdogan plans to create a Sunni bloc of territory north and west of Aleppo, which will be under direct or indirect Turkish control. The Kurdish leaders are convinced that Erdogan is determined to destroy their de facto state in the long run but differ about the timing and objectives of the present attack. Elham Ahmad believes that the Turkish assault on Afrin, if successful, will set "a precedent for a further Turkish military advance."

"Our convoy of 150 civilian cars was hit by a Turkish air strike," Ahmad said. "We ran away from the cars, but thirty of them were destroyed and one person killed." She is angry that the outside world is exclusively preoccupied with the bombardment of eastern Ghouta by President Bashar al-Assad's forces, but ignores similar bombing and shelling in Afrin where, she says, 204 civilians had been killed, including sixty-one children, as of last weekend.

There is a sense of phoney war on the front line between the forces of the Manbij Military Council and the Turkish army and its allied anti-Assad militias, who are dug in three or four miles north of the city. Most of the front lines in the Syrian civil war are a depressing scene of abandoned and half-wrecked buildings, even when there is no fighting going on. The Manbij front is idyllic by comparison, though just how long it will stay that way is another question. This is a fertile, heavily populated country with a Mediterranean feel to it, its hills and small fields full of olive trees, pines, poplars, and almond trees, which are covered in little white flowers. There are tractors on the roads and, just behind the front, we drove through the

Arab village of Dadat, whose streets are full of cheerful-looking children excited by the sight of military vehicles.

A trench and rampart gouged out the hillside by bulldozers zigzags upwards through a green field to a fortified position on a hilltop. Peering through gun slits in a sandbagged post on top of an earth bank, one could see Turkish positions not far away on the far side of the Sajur River. "They have tanks and artillery on every hilltop and they fire randomly with heavy machine guns every night," says Farhat Kobani, a local commander whose orders come from the Manbij Military Council. The Turkish army is backed up by Ahrar al-Sham, whose men act as auxiliaries. These exchanges of fire do not seem very serious because everybody, at least in daytime, is standing upright in easy range of the other side and Farhat says his men have not suffered any dead or wounded. Phoney war is often derided, but there is a lot to be said for it when compared to the real thing—and, unfortunately, that may not be too far away.

12 March 2018
Syrian Arab militiamen leading the Turkish attack on Afrin are threatening to massacre its Kurdish population unless they convert to the variant of Islam espoused by Isis and al-Qaeda. In the past, such demands have preceded the mass killings of sectarian and ethnic minorities in both Syria and Iraq. In one video, a militia fighter flanked by others describes the Kurds as "infidels" and issues a stark warning, saying "by Allah, if you repent and come back to Allah, then know that you are our brothers. But if you refuse, then we see that your heads are ripe and that it's time for us to pluck them." Though the Kurds in Afrin are Sunni Muslims, Isis and al-Qaeda traditionally punish those who fail to subscribe to their beliefs as heretics deserving death.

"The video is 100 percent authentic," said Rami Abdulrahman, who heads the Syrian Observatory for Human Rights which released it, in an interview with me. He adds that he is very concerned about the fate of some Yazidi villages in Afrin captured by the advancing Turkish forces, saying he has seen videos taken by the militiamen themselves in one of which "an elderly Yazidi man is questioned by them, asking him how many times he prays a day." Such interrogations of Yazidis by Isis to prove that they were not Muslims often preceded the killings, rapes, and the taking of Yazidi women as sex slaves when Isis seized Yazidi areas in northern Iraq in 2014. Mr. Abdulrahman, who is the leading human rights monitor in Syria with a network of informants throughout the country, says he is worried that international attention is entirely focused on the Syrian army assault on eastern Ghouta and "nobody is talking about" the potential slaughter of the Kurds and other minorities in Afrin.

He says that the two situations are similar since "President Bashar al-Assad's forces have taken 60 percent of Ghouta and Erdogan's forces have taken 60 percent of Afrin." He says that as many as one million Kurds may be threatened and adds that it is becoming extremely difficult for them to escape from Afrin because Syrian government checkpoints on the only road leading south to Aleppo "are demanding bribes of up to $4,000 per family to let people through." Mr. Abdulrahman points to growing evidence drawn from videos taken by themselves of militiamen claiming to be members of the FSA that the units advancing ahead of regular Turkish troops are extreme jihadis. This has previously been asserted by a former Isis member in an interview with me last month who said that many of his former comrades had been recruited and retrained by the Turkish military. He said that Isis recruits had been instructed by Turkish trainers not to use their traditional tactics, such as the extensive use of car bombs because this would identify them as terrorists. He suspected that Isis fighters would be used as cannon fodder in Turkey's war against the YPG and then discarded.

As the Turkish army closes in on Afrin and the Syrian army penetrates deeply into the opposition stronghold of eastern Ghouta, people in both areas fear that they will be the victims of enforced demographic change. One Kurdish observer in Iraq said that he thought Mr. Erdogan, who has claimed that the majority in Afrin is not Kurdish, will "bring in Turkmen and others to replace the Kurdish population." Motives for refusing to leave are also much the same. "I will never leave Ghouta," said Haytham Bakkar, an anti-government journalist living there, speaking just as the present Syrian army assault was getting underway. "We have lived here for hundreds and thousands of years. Here our grandparents lived. Here are our houses and tombs. We were born here and we will die here. Our souls and roots are here."

Bakkar says that most people in eastern Ghouta are convinced that their departure is part of a broader government plan to make drastic demographic changes whereby their property would be given to others. He says that even if people survived the dangerous journey out of the area, they did not want "to watch TV news and see strangers living in our homes." Kurds make a similar calculation, but it is also becoming extremely dangerous for them to try to flee. Precedents have already been set for ethnic and sectarian cleansing all over Syria since 2011 as those in control oust members of other communities.

The YPG spokesman Nouri Mahmoud said that the Kurds feared a genocide was in the making and complained that "the international media focus on eastern Ghouta has given the Turks the opportunity to step up their attack on Afrin without the rest of the world paying much attention." The Kurdish authorities are trying to publicise the sufferings of civilians in Afrin, but are so far not having much success. None of the foreign players in the Syrian crisis show any sign of intervening against Turkey. Kurdish leaders say they believe that Russia, Iran, and Turkey have agreed that Turkey will get Afrin, possibly in exchange for the Turks agreeing to drop their support for the one big remaining anti-Assad enclave in Idlib.

18 March 2018
The first act of the fighters of the FSA was to bulldoze the statue of a Kurdish mythological hero in the centre of Afrin. Some 200,000 Kurds have fled from their enclave over the past few days, many suspecting that they will never be permitted to return. If they are right, they will join the six million Syrians displaced since 2011 and a similar number who have become refugees outside the country. Given that the Syrian population in that year was about twenty-three million people, more than half have lost their homes in seven years of violence.

Afrin was easy pickings for Turkey. The FSA says it was able to enter the city without resistance from three directions on Sunday morning, though another report claims that some fighting is still going on. The commanders of the YPG were evidently convinced that Afrin was indefensible and pulled out because they had no alternative. If this was the case, then they were wise not to fight to the finish in a battle they were bound to lose with heavy loss of life. The outcome of the struggle for Afrin was evident from the moment the Turkish invasion began on 20 January. For the Turks, this may have been an easy victory, but it is still a victory. It will make them a more important player in the Syrian crisis, but they could overplay their hand.

President Erdogan is triumphant, maybe too triumphant. He said on Sunday that "in the centre of Afrin, symbols of trust and stability are waving instead of rags of terrorists." Destruction of Kurdish symbols in the city is not a good sign for the future.

19 March 2018

Erdogan is threatening to follow up the capture of the Kurdish enclave of Afrin by launching an across-the-board military offensive against the remaining Kurdish-held areas in northern Syria and the main Yazidi population centre in the Sinjar region of Iraqi Kurdistan. He claimed that the next target of Turkish troops would be the cities of Manbij and Kobani. Unlike Afrin, both places are protected by the US air force, backed by 2,000 US specialised ground troops.

Mr. Erdogan undoubtedly intends in the long term to eliminate the de facto Kurdish state, but it is unlikely that he will seek a confrontation with the US. Speaking soon after the Turkish invasion of Afrin on 20 January, General Joseph Votel, commander of the US Central Command, said that withdrawing US forces from Manbij was "not something we are looking into." The Turkish leader threatened that his country's troops could cross into Iraq to drive out Kurdish militants from Sinjar if the Iraqi government did not oust them from there itself. The area is under the strong influence of the YPG, which intervened militarily in 2014 to protect the Yazidi community who were being massacred, raped, and enslaved by Isis.

The threat of a widening offensive against Syrian Kurdish forces is probably a manoeuvre by Mr. Erdogan to divert attention from the situation in the Kurdish enclave of Afrin. "The people with cars are sleeping in the cars, the people without are sleeping under the trees with their children," Hevi Mustafa, a top member of the Kurdish civil authority in the Afrin area, told a news agency. The UN says that 98,000 recently displaced people from Afrin have registered with it at three centres outside the enclave. Another report said that 120,000 Kurds are not being allowed to enter Syrian government-held territory and are unable to return to Afrin. The US State Department said it was "deeply concerned" by the humanitarian situation.

There may be less than meets the eye in a Turkish promise to leave Afrin once military operations are over. "We are not permanent there [in Afrin] and we are certainly not invaders," said Bekir Bozdag, a deputy prime minister. "Our goal is to hand the region back to its real owners after clearing it of terrorists." The reference to "real owners" may refer to a Turkish claim that many Arabs have been driven out of Afrin in the past and will now recover their homes, a form of enforced "re-Arabisation" that would take advantage of the flight of much of the Kurdish population. A Turkish military withdrawal, even if it took place, would not mean much because Turkey and Turkish-controlled territory surrounds Afrin on three sides and the FSA units, which would presumably stay in Afrin, take their orders from Turkey.

Turkish-led forces are carrying out widespread looting of government offices, shops, and homes in Afrin as well as stealing vehicles, such as farm machinery, tractors, and trailers according to the Syrian Observatory for Human Rights. It says that the looting and arrests are fuelling growing resentment among displaced people. Pictures from the area show tractors being driven away by uniformed militiamen.

The Kurdish YPG, which did not make a final stand in Manbij, says that it will revert to guerrilla warfare, something in which its commanders have great experience. But this may not be easy to do in a place like Afrin, which is isolated from the main Kurdish-held territory east of the Euphrates River. Guerrilla attacks are likely to provoke retaliation against the remaining Kurdish civilian population who might then leave Afrin and further open the door to ethnic cleansing.

11 April 2018

Every atrocity in the Syrian civil war provokes a furious row about whether it happened and, if so, who was responsible for carrying it out. The merciless brutality of all sides combines with partisan reporting and lack of access for independent investigators to make it possible for doubts to be generated about even the most blatant war crime. One good rule is that participants in the war are often accurate about the crimes of their opponents while they invariably lie or are silent about their own.

This rule appears to hold good in the case of the poison gas attack on the city of Douma on 7 April, which killed at least thirty-four people and possibly twice as many. The Russian military claim that the attack was faked by pro-opposition activists and that samples taken from the site of where the civilians died were not toxic. The Syrian government issues blanket denials when accused of using poison gas. But there is mounting evidence from neutral observers to confirm that chlorine was used last Saturday. The World Health Organisation says that local health authorities in Douma, with whom it is cooperating, confirm that on the day of the alleged bombing they treated 500 patients with the symptoms of exposure to toxic chemicals. It reports that "there were signs of severe irritation of mucous membranes, respiratory failure, and disruption to the central nervous systems of those exposed." Other evidence for the gassing of civilians is cumulatively convincing: large gas cylinders, like those used in past chlorine gas attacks, were filmed on the roof of the building where most bodies were found. Local people report that Syrian government helicopters were seen in the area at the time of the attack. Such helicopters have been used in chlorine gas bombings in the past.

The Russian and Syrian government accounts of what happened, varying between saying there were no attacks or that evidence for them has been fabricated, are contradictory. A Russian spokeswoman said on Wednesday that the use of "smart missiles" on Syrian government forces could be an attempt to destroy the evidence. The allegations of fabrication are generalised and non-specific and amount to a conspiracy theory for which no evidence is ever produced, other than to throw doubt on the partiality of those who say that chlorine was used. It is true that many of the sources cited by the Western media as if they were bipartisan eyewitness accounts are committed supporters of the opposition. But the Russian and Syrian governments have never produced any counter-evidence to give credence to the elaborate plot that would be necessary to fake the use of poison gas or to really use it but put the blame on Syrian government air power.

The most convincing reason advanced by those who argue that Assad's forces did not carry out the attack is that it was entirely against their interests to do so. They have already won militarily in Douma and the second of two convoys carrying thousands of Army of Islam fighters and their families left for Turkish-controlled northern Syria today. And this latest success brings Assad within sight—though it is still a distant one—of a complete victory over his enemies. For all the furore about the proposed missile strike on Syrian forces—likely to happen in the very near future—it is difficult to see what it will achieve other than as a general sign of international disapproval of the use of chemical weapons. Hawks in the US and Europe may want to use the occasion to reopen the door to armed intervention in the Syrian civil war with the aim of weakening or displacing Assad, but the time for this is long past if it was ever there.

There is a widely held myth that US air strikes against government forces in 2013, which President Barack Obama is blamed for not having carried out, would have brought the war to a different and happier conclusion. But such air strikes would only have been effective if they had been conducted on a mass scale and on a daily basis in support of ground troops. These would either have been Sunni Arab armed opposition forces, which were already dominated by al-Qaeda-type movements, or the US army in a rerun of the Iraq War of 2003.

13 April 2018

The most important point about the impending missile strikes in Syria by the US, Britain, and France is being missed, despite wall-to-wall media coverage. The purported aim of the attack is to deter Assad from using chemical weapons as a weapon in the Syrian civil war. But the history of this savage conflict, in which half a million people have died, shows that all sides employ every possible method to kill or maim their enemies. Preventing the use of one type of armament, and that not the most important, will make little difference.

The only way to stop the deployment of poisoned gas in Syria is to stop the use of all weapons by bringing the war to an end. But in the run-up to military action against Assad's forces, there is depressingly little discussion about how this might be done. Insofar as there is discussion, it is to the effect that either the air strikes will not change the balance of power on the ground, or they will somewhat weaken Assad and prevent him winning a decisive victory in the war. This is the same old discredited policy that the US and its Western allies have pursued for the last five years, since they realised that the armed opposition to Assad was dominated by various al-Qaeda clones, which would replace him if he ever fell from power.

In cooperation with Turkey, Qatar, and Saudi Arabia, they helped the rebels sufficiently to keep the war going against Assad, but not enough for them to win. As early as August 2012, a report by the Defence Intelligence Agency (DIA), the Pentagon's intelligence arm, stated that "the Salafists, the Muslim Brotherhood, and AQI [al-Qaeda in Iraq] are the major forces driving the insurgency in Syria." It is worth reading in full the DIA report which forecasts "the possibility of establishing a declared or undeclared Salafist principality in eastern Syria." This was two years before Isis declared the Islamic State.

Some conspiracy theorists conclude that the US covertly supported the rise of Isis and al-Qaeda, but a more credible accusation is that Washington and its allies created the conditions in which they flourished. This was a calamitous error in judgement: when the Syrian army withdrew from northern and eastern Syria in 2012, it created a vacuum that was swiftly filled by al-Qaeda fanatics. Revolt in Syria restarted the sectarian civil war in Iraq. Isis captured Raqqa and Mosul, spread to the rest of the Islamic world, and began its terrorist attacks in Western Europe.

The same catastrophic mistake is now being made again as Western military forces ready themselves to attack Syria. Contrary to the pretence by the governments of the US, UK, and France that their great concern is the sufferings of the Syrian people, their actions will simply deepen these because their only likely impact will be to lengthen the war. Even supposing they succeed in doing something to curtail the use of poison gas by Assad, this has so far killed an estimated 1,900 Syrians out of a total of half a million who have died violently since 2011.

Ending the war is the only way to reduce civilian casualties, and everything else is hypocrisy and pretence. What is really killing people in Syria is the war which Western powers stoked year after year with the intention that neither side would win. Their real concern in firing missiles at Assad's forces is as a demonstration of power in the face of defiance by Syria, Russia, and Iran. Aside from making this gesture, they do not really want to change the present toxic situation in Syria. This may explain their hesitation in beginning the missile strikes.

It is easy enough to condemn the US, UK, and France for their past failings, but what could they really do to help Syria? They need to accept in public, as they have long done in private, that Assad is going to hold onto power. In control of Damascus, Aleppo, and the biggest Syrian cities, he is not going to be removed by anything less than a US-led land invasion along the lines of Iraq in 2003. His victory is becoming irreversible, but international recognition of it should be conditional on the return to their homes of the refugees, a quarter of the pre-war population, along with an internationally monitored amnesty and freeing of prisoners. The Syrian Kurds would like a deal with Damascus giving them regional autonomy since however much they dislike the Assad government, they are even more frightened of a Turkish invasion.

Syria is being destroyed because it has become the arena in which international and regional rivalries are fought out. Foreign intervention fuels the civil war and the civil war entraps outside sponsors of local Syrian proxies in their fiercely fought sectarian and ethnic battles. In many ways, the role of foreign intervention in Syria today resembles that of outside powers in the Balkans before 1914. It is a highly dangerous situation. Syrian, Russian, Israeli, US, Turkish, British, and French aircraft and missiles will have to manoeuvre to avoid shooting each other down. As in the Balkans a century ago, some of the most violent and embittered people in the world—in this case, the different sides in the Syrian civil war—are in a position to generate friction that could see the coalitions headed by the US and Russia tumble into an unwanted conflict.

Negotiations to end the Syrian war in general, not just the side issue of chemical weapons, should be the priority, but these are difficult and not just because of the complexity of the issues. The media is to blame for presenting the civil war as a simple fight between evil (Assad) and good (anybody opposed to Assad). This demonisation makes the compromises necessary to bring peace near impossible because nobody dares be seen shaking hands with the devil.

14 April 2018
"Big noise on the stairs, but nobody comes into the room," runs an old Chinese saying. This is an apt description of the very limited air strikes on Syria launched by the US, Britain, and France overnight, which came after apocalyptic tweets from President Trump and threats of military retaliation by Russian diplomats. In the event, the fears of a "Russian-American clash" and runaway confrontation leading to a "third world war" have turned out to be overblown. They did not look quite so exaggerated earlier in the week when Trump tweeted about US missiles: "Get ready Russia, because they will be coming, nice and new and 'smart.'" The Russians hinted that their retaliation might include American targets.

Of all the options available, the US-led coalition chose the one involving minimal action and geared not to provoke Russia or Iran. This was a one-off attack on three suspected Syrian chemical weapons facilities, one in Damascus and two west of Homs. It was more of a gesture of disapproval than an attempt to damage Assad's military machine. Hours after the missiles had struck, his supporters were understandably demonstrating their defiance in the centre of Damascus. Trump, reportedly under pressure from his military chiefs, may have chosen the most cautious option, but in fact, there were no good options.

Yet the military balance of power really has changed in Syria over the last week, although the reason for this has largely passed unnoticed internationally because of the focus on the gas attack in Douma and its consequences. The big development is that Douma, the last armed opposition stronghold in eastern Ghouta, surrendered to the Syrian armed forces on 8 April. The remaining Jaysh al-Islam fighters have been taken by bus to Turkish-held territory in northern Syria during the course of the week. This is Assad's greatest victory of the war, surpassing in importance even the recapture of East Aleppo.

Possibly it was the Syrian government's frustration at the continued resistance of part of Jaysh al-Islam, the Saudi-backed jihadi movement in Douma, that led it to use chlorine gas. It had done so before without provoking an international reaction, but this time authentic-looking video was broadcast around the world, showing dying children gasping for breath. The pictures provoked a wave of international fury, which culminated in the US-led air strikes. If the Syrian government's purpose in launching a chemical weapons attack was to force the final surrender of the Douma rebels, then it succeeded. Within hours of it happening, Russian military police moved into Douma to supervise the departure of rebel fighters and to suppress looting by government forces. On 12 April, the Syrian national flag was finally raised over a building in central Douma and the long siege was over.

18 April 2018

The Yazidis are now facing forcible conversion to Islam under the threat of death from Turkish-backed forces. Islamist rebel fighters, who are allied to Turkey and have occupied Yazidi villages in the Afrin area, have destroyed the temples and places of worship of the Kurdish-speaking non-Islamic sect, according to local people. Shekh Qamber, a sixty-three-year-old Syrian Kurdish Yazidi farmer who fled his town of Qastel Jindo in Afrin, described to me what happened to Yazidis, who refused to leave their homes. He said that some were forcibly brought to a mosque by Islamists to be converted, while others, including a seventy-year-old man he knew, were being lured there by offers of food and medical attention.

Even the place names of Yazidi villages are being changed. Mr. Qamber recounted a conversation he had with an Islamist militant who had arrested and questioned him near the town of Azaz when he was trying to escape. He was asked by his interrogator where he was from and he replied that he was from Qastel Jindo. The Islamist said: "it's no more Qastel Jindo. It's al-Quds now. We will give it the name of Palestine's capital. These areas were occupied by the infidels and now it is [going] back to their original owners and original names ... We came here to regain our lands and behead you." Mr. Qamber recalls that he replied to this threat to kill him by saying that what would happen would be by god's will. His interrogator responded: "Shut up! You are infidel. Do you really know or believe in god?" Mr. Qamber said that he believed in one god, and soon after, he was released because, he believes, he was old and sick. He eventually found his way to the main Kurdish enclave in north-east Syria.

Mr. Qamber says that the majority of the people in villages around Qastel Jindo, which fell early during the Turkish invasion, are Yazidis. He says that some villagers fled, but others risked staying because they did not want to lose their houses and lands. Those who remained were later "taken to the mosque and given lessons in Islamic prayer." In addition, "there were temples and Yazidi worship houses, but all have been blown up and destroyed by the militants after they entered the village." The Yazidi religion is a mixture of beliefs drawn from Zoroastrianism, Judaism, Christianity, and Islam. Mr. Qamber said he had spoken to people from the Yazidi villages of Burj Abdalo, Basufane, Faqira, and Tirende and they all said, "the militants are teaching the Yazidis the Islamic prayer."

Mr. Qamber puts part of the blame for what is happening on his own people who returned to their homes after the initial advance of the Turkish army and its Arab auxiliaries. He says that they ought to have known better, going by the terrible fate of the Yazidis in Sinjar [Shingal in Kurdish] in northern Iraq in August 2014 when it was overrun by Isis. He asks: "Why don't they learn from the experiences of Shingal where the Yazidi women were taken as sex slaves and our dignity and honour taken?" Asked about the present concerns of the Yazidis, many of whom are in refugee camps in northern Syria and Iraq, Mr. Qamber said that after the defeat of Isis as a territorial entity they "expected that the Turks will attack us, either directly as they did before in Turkey in the 1970s, or indirectly using their allied Islamist Jihadi groups, like Daesh or other groups like the so-called Free Syrian Army."

Only a limited amount of information has been coming out about conditions in Afrin since it was finally captured by the Turkish army and its Arab allies. The UN Office for the Coordination of Humanitarian Affairs (OCHA) in its latest report on the Afrin crisis on 16 April says that 137,000 individuals have been displaced from Afrin, while 150,000 remain there, of whom 50,000 are in Afrin City and 100,000 in the countryside. It says that the movement of people is heavily restricted and many who want to return to their homes are not being allowed to pass through checkpoints, which, though it does not identify who is in charge of them, must mean the Turkish military or their Arab auxiliaries inside Afrin, since they are the only authority there.

Reports by the Syrian Observatory for Human Rights (SOHR), widely seen as neutral or pro-opposition, citing multiple sources in Afrin confirm Mr. Qamber's account of sectarian and ethnic cleansing by the Turkish army and its Arab allies. It says that it has reliable information that "the resettlement of the displaced people of eastern Ghouta in the Afrin area is still continuing." It says that Abdul Nasser Shamir, the military commander of Faylaq al-Rahman, one of the most important armed groups previously fighting the Syrian government in eastern Ghouta, has been settled along with his top commanders in a town in Afrin. Other displaced people from eastern Ghouta are being moved into houses from which their Kurdish inhabitants have fled and are not being allowed to return according to SOHR. It says that refugees from eastern Ghouta object to what is happening, saying they do not want to settle in Afrin, "where the Turkish forces provide them with houses owned by people displaced from Afrin."

The eastern Ghouta refugees say they resent being the instrument of "an organised demographic change" at the behest of Turkey which would, in effect, replace Kurds with Arabs in Afrin. They say they reject this plan, just as they reject any demographic change orchestrated by the Syrian government and Russia in their own home region of eastern Ghouta, where shelling killed about 1,800 civilians and injured some 6,000. The SOHR notes that the ethnic cleansing by Turkey of Afrin is being carried out "amid a media blackout" and is being ignored internationally.

Mr. Qamber is living safely with his wife Adula Mahmoud Safar to the east of Qamishli. But he is pessimistic about the future, expecting Turkey to invade the rest of Rojava. He says that many Turkish officials say that "if the Kurds live in a tent in Africa, that tent should be destroyed." He adds that because the Turks and their Arab allies see the Yazidis as both infidels and Kurds, they are doubly jeopardised and will be the biggest losers in any future war waged by Turkey against the Kurds.

PART VII. BEHIND ENEMY LIES: WAR REPORTING IN THE AGE OF FAKE FACTS

Governments have openly or covertly expanded their efforts to control the news during the very period when the ability of journalists and news organisation to check what they are saying has dropped precipitously. The decline has been so steep because it is the outcome of more than one development. In the first place, reporting conflicts has become more dangerous compared to when I first started writing about "the Troubles" in Northern Ireland in the early 1970s. I used to joke then that there was no group of gunmen without a press officer ready to promote their views and explain how their violence was purely retaliatory and a response to repeated provocations by the other side. "Get your retaliation in first," was a cynical Belfast saying of the day.

Moving to Beirut during the civil war a few years later, I found militia leaders equally happy to give interviews and provide letters of accreditation, allowing one to pass safely through their checkpoints. The main risk at this point in one's travels—the actual battlefields of Lebanon were a different and more dangerous matter—was that reporters had to carry many of these letters so there was the risk that one would mix them up and inadvertently hand one addressed to right-wing Christian militiamen by their commander to left-wing Muslim fighters or vice versa.

Compare the comparative ease of access then to Syria today, where it is almost impossible for foreign journalists to enter territory held by the armed opposition, other than that of the Kurds, because of the risk of being killed or kidnapped. Reporting can be outsourced to local "citizen journalists," but they can only operate under license from al-Qaeda type groups that do not tolerate dissent of any kind and those attempting to give an even-handed version of the news can pay a heavy—possibly fatal—price.

There is an important point to be made here about what distinguishes objective news reporting from propaganda. People unfamiliar with the way news is gathered often imagine that propaganda is all about invented tales and "fake news" such as the Kuwaiti babies story or Muammar Gaddafi's non-existent *mass rape campaign and, of course, propaganda often consists of credible lies designed to have maximum political impact. But these are atypical events: it is much more common for propaganda to consist of true but carefully selected facts repeatedly publicised that show one's own side in a positive light and one's opponents as the face of evil. Since every side commits atrocities in war—and the wars in Iraq and Syria have been of peculiar brutality—it is possible to give publicity to these horrors with complete accuracy, but still give a distorted and propagandistic view of what is happening.*

In east Aleppo and eastern Ghouta, for instance, the world was rightly moved by pictures and videos of injured and dying children in hospitals following bombing and shelling by the Syrian government and its Russian allies. There is no need to imagine that any of this was concocted, but in both cases, one seldom, if ever, saw pictures of armed Syrian and foreign jihadis. The BBC and CNN would try to verify the authenticity of atrocity videos from areas their reporters could not enter except at the risk of their lives, but this rather missed the point; all these videos might be true, but that truth would be highly selective.

Another aspect of partisan selection of the facts in the wars in Iraq and Syria underlines the need for independent, well-resourced, and professional journalism. There was copious media coverage of civilian casualties caused by Syrian and Russian air strikes on rebel-held places like east Aleppo, eastern Ghouta, and Homs, which were internationally condemned. But there was near silence about heavy civilian casualties, amounting at times to a media blackout, in the cities of Mosul in Iraq and Raqqa in Syria when they were being besieged by the US-led coalition and defended by Isis. I had visited both places after they had fallen and had witnessed the utter devastation of large parts of them caused by shelling and bombing by the coalition forces.

I knew that civilian loss of life must be horrendous because of the level of destruction, the evidence of survivors, and the fact that people trapped inside Mosul during the siege whom I had spoken to by phone had all been killed by the end of it. I was sure of this but I could not prove it, and the US air force, which carried out the vast majority of the air strikes, vigorously denied that it had killed many people who were not Isis fighters. Then, in a classic piece of professional journalistic investigation, Azmat Khan and Anand Gopal writing a long piece for The New York Times *magazine, visited the sites of nearly 150 air strikes near to Mosul, which were carried out between April 2016 and June 2017. They found that the death rate from air strikes was thirty-one times greater than that acknowledged by the US air force, which carried out the great majority of the strikes. In one residential district called Qayara, they found that it claimed that it had killed just one civilian, but the true figure, only discovered after painstaking interviews with eyewitnesses and review of videos, was forty-three: nineteen men, eight women, and sixteen children aged fourteen or younger.*

April 2018–August 2019

20 April 2018

During the bombing of Baghdad in January 1991, I went with other journalists on a government-organised trip to what they claimed was the remains of a baby milk plant at Abu Ghraib, which the US had just destroyed, saying that it was really a biological warfare facility. Walking around the wreckage, I found a smashed-up desk with letters showing that the plant had indeed been producing "infant formula" milk powder. It had not been very successful in doing so, since much of the correspondence was about its financial and production problems and how they might best be resolved. It did not seem likely that the Iraqi government could have fabricated this evidence, though it was conceivable that in some part of the plant, which I did see, they might have been manufacturing biological weapons (BW).

I was visiting a lot of bombed-out buildings at the beginning of the US-led air campaign and I did not at first realise that "the Abu Ghraib baby milk factory" would become such an issue. I was more impressed at the time by the sight of a cruise missile passing quite slowly overhead, looking like a large black torpedo. But, within hours of leaving Abu Ghraib, the true purpose of the plant there had become a topic of furious controversy. The CNN correspondent Peter Arnett, who was on the trip, had reported that "whatever else it did, it [the plant] produced infant formula." He saw a lot of powdered milk and, contrary to the Pentagon claim that the place was guarded like a fortress, we could only see one guard at the gate. Arnett did not deny the US government version that the place was a BW plant, but he did not confirm it either. He simply reported that "it looked inno-cent enough from what we could see."

Even such mild dissent from the official US version of the bombing turned out to be unacceptable, producing an explosion of rage in Washington. Colin Powell, the US chief of staff, expressed certainty that the Abu Ghraib plant had manufactured BW. The US air force claimed that it had multiple sources of information proving the same thing. Arnett was vilified as an Iraqi government stooge by the US government. "This is not a case of taking on the media," said the White House spokesman Marlin Fitzwater. "It's a case of correcting a public disclosure that is erroneous, that is false, that hurts our government, and that plays into the hands of Saddam Hussein." US news outlets, none of which had correspondents in Baghdad, vigorously toed the official line. *Newsweek* derided Iraq's "ham-handed attempt to depict a bombed-out biological weapons plant near Baghdad as a baby-formula factory."

It took years for the official version of the bombing to fall apart. Even though I had been in the plant soon after it was destroyed, I could not prove that it did not produce biological weapons, though it seemed to me highly unlikely. Media interest waned rapidly: the best study I could find about how the destruction of the milk factory was spun by official PR is a piece by Mark Crispin Miller, from which the quotes above are taken, published in 2003.

Proof came slowly, long after public interest had waned. A Congressional report in 1993 on US intelligence successes and failures in the Gulf War revealed the shaky reasoning behind the US air force decision to bomb the site. It turned out that "mottled camouflage" had been used on the roofs of two known BW facilities. The report said: "at the same time, the same camouflage scheme was applied to the roof of the milk plant." This was enough for the US air force to list it as a target. Confident official claims about multiple sources of intelligence turned out to be untrue. One has to burrow deep into an unclassified CIA paper on Iraq's BW programme to find a sentence admitting that another plant, which was the real centre of Saddam Hussein's BW effort, was unknown to the US-led coalition and "therefore was not attacked during the war, unlike the Abu Ghurayb (sic) Infant Formula Plant (the *Baby Milk Factory*) that the Coalition destroyed by bombing in the mistaken belief that it was a key BW facility."

The story of the Abu Ghraib baby milk factory is worth retelling because it underlines—in the wake of the US, British, and French air strikes on alleged Syrian BW sites on 14 April—the need for permanent scepticism towards claims by governments that they know what is happening on the ground in Syria or anywhere else. But government duplicity is scarcely new and denunciations of it may obscure an even greater danger. Look again at the attack on Peter Arnett's story by the White House spokesman Marlin Fitzwater who was wrong—and Arnett was right—in saying that it contained "a disclosure that is erroneous, that is false." But he adds correctly that it was a disclosure "that hurts our government and plays into the hands of Saddam Hussein."

So it was in a minor way, and this brings us to a toxic attitude towards those who question the official version of events increasingly common in Britain and the US. It is overwhelming freedom of speech in Hungary and Poland and has already triumphed in Turkey and Egypt. In all cases, opinions diverging from those of the powers-that-be are branded as disloyal and unpatriotic and "false facts" are being spread by "useful idiots," to use two ghastly clichés much in use. Marginalisation of dissenting is followed by its criminalisation: Turkey once had a flourishing free press, but now any criticism of Erdogan or words or actions of which he disapproves can be labelled as "terrorism" and punished accordingly.

There is much tut-tutting in Britain by the commentariat about the spread of authoritarianism in the Middle East and Eastern Europe, but less so about the growing limitation on what can be freely expressed at home. Increasingly, anything less than full endorsement of the government line about the poisoning of the Skripals in Salisbury or the suspected gas attack on civilians in Douma in Syria is characterised as support for Putin or Assad.

A telling instance of this new authoritarianism is the denunciations of a party of Christian clergy and peers who have been visiting Syria to meet church dignitaries and government officials. This is an understandable mission for concerned British Christians because Christians in Syria can do with all the solidarity they can get as they are forced to flee or are kidnapped or murdered by Isis, al-Qaeda, or the Muslim Brotherhood. Like many Syrians, they see their choice as not being between good and bad but between bad and worse. They generally prefer survival under Assad to likely extinction under his enemies. Visiting embattled members of the depleted Christian community in Syria is a good thing to do. And, yes, it could be said that the presence of British Christians in Damascus is very marginally helpful to Assad, in much the same way that Peter Arnett's truthful report on the baby milk in Abu Ghraib must have pleased Saddam Hussein. The

Foreign Office said the Christians' visit was "not helpful," but then helping the British state should not be their prime concern.

None of the arguments currently being used in Britain and the US to smear those sceptical of the governmental and media consensus are new. The Bolsheviks used to denounce people who said or did things they did not like as "objectively" being fascists or counter-revolutionaries. When those being denounced, often only a preliminary to being shot, replied that they were no such thing, the Bolsheviks would reply: "tell us who supports you and we will tell you who you are." In other words, the only thing that matters is what side you are on.

5 June 2018

Air and artillery strikes by the US and its allies inflicted devastating loss of life on civilians in the Isis-held city of Raqqa, according to an Amnesty International report. It contradicts claims by the US, along with Britain and France, that they precisely targeted Isis fighters and positions during the siege. "On the ground in Raqqa, we witnessed a level of destruction comparable to anything we have seen in decades of covering the impact of wars," says Donatella Rovera, a senior crisis response adviser at Amnesty. She says that the coalition's claim that it had conducted a precision bombing campaign that caused few civilian casualties does not stand up to scrutiny. She quotes a senior US military officer as saying that "more artillery shells were launched into Raqqa than anywhere since the end of the Vietnam War."

The air and artillery strikes by the US and its allies killed many civilians—the number is unknown because so many bodies are buried under the ruins according to the report. Citing the testimony of survivors, it contradicts assertions by the US-led coalition that it took care to avoid targeting buildings where civilians might be present. Witnesses say that again and again their houses were destroyed although there were no Isis fighters in them or nearby. "Those who stayed died and those who tried to run away died. We couldn't afford to pay the smugglers: we were trapped," says Munira Hashish. Her family lost eighteen members, of whom nine were killed in a coalition air strike, seven as they tried to escape down a road mined by Isis, and two were hit by a mortar round, probably fired by a SDF unit. She says that she and her children only escaped "by walking over the blood of those who were blown up as they tried to flee ahead of us."

Many families were hit more than once by air strikes and artillery as they fled from place to place in Raqqa, vainly trying to avoid being close to the front lines, but these were often changing. The Badran family lost thirty-nine members, mostly women and children, as well as ten neighbours, killed in four different coalition air strikes. "We thought the forces who came to evict Daesh would know their business and would target Daesh and the leave the civilians alone," said Rasha Badran, one of the survivors. "We were naive."

Many cities have been destroyed in the wars in Iraq and Syria since 2011, but the destruction is worse in Raqqa than anywhere else. Streets are simply lane-ways cut through heaps of rubble and broken masonry. The few people on the streets are dazed and broken, and this has not changed much in the months since the city was captured from Isis. The claim by the coalition that its air strikes and artillery fire were precisely targeted against Isis fighters and their positions is shown up as a myth as soon as one drives into the city. I visited it earlier in the year and have never seen such destruction. Given the level of violence in Iraq and Syria, it is difficult to prove that one place is worse than another, but this has now been established with a wealth of evidence in this Amnesty report entitled *War of Annihilation: Devastating Toll on Civilians, Raqqa—Syria.*

The report, based on 112 interviews and visits to forty-two strike locations, was sharply criticised by a coalition spokesman even before it was published. US Army Colonel Sean Ryan was quoted by news agencies as inviting Kate Allen, the director of Amnesty International UK, to "personally witness the rigorous efforts and intelligence gathering the coalition uses before any strike to effectively destroy Isis while minimising harm to civilian populations." Although the report cites the detailed evidence of many surviving witnesses whose family members were killed in air strikes, Colonel Ryan says that allegations of indiscriminate and disproportionate bombardment were "more or less hypothetical." The reality in Raqqa, despite claims of the precise accuracy of modern weapons and great concern for civilian life, is that the ruins look exactly like pictures of the aftermath of the carpet bombing of cities like Hamburg and Dresden in the Second World War.

US forces fired 100 percent of the artillery rounds used against Raqqa and over 90 percent of the air strikes, but British and French aircraft were also involved. The Ministry of Defence says the UK carried out 275 air strikes and killed no civilians at all. Despite pledges that civilian loss of life would be thoroughly investigated, Amnesty says there is no sign of this happening. A consequence of the assertion by the coalition that they seldom harmed civilians, there has been little humanitarian support for people returning to Raqqa. Aid agencies say that one problem is finding a safe place where there are no unexploded munitions or mines to distribute provisions. The report says that many residents ask: "Why those, who spent so much on a costly military campaign which destroyed the city, are not providing the relief so desperately needed."

An MoD spokesman said: "Keeping Britain safe from the threat of terrorism is the objective of this campaign and throughout we have been open and transparent, detailing each of our nearly 1,700 strikes, facilitating operational briefings and confirming when a civilian casualty had taken place. We do everything we can to minimise the risk to civilian life through our rigorous targeting processes and the professionalism of the RAF crews but, given the ruthless and inhuman behaviour of Daesh, and the congested, complex urban environment in which we operate, we must accept that the risk of inadvertent civilian casualties is ever-present."

21 September 2018
A ceasefire seldom gets a good press. If it succeeds in ending violence or defusing a crisis, the media swiftly becomes bored and loses interest. But if the fighting goes on, then those who have called the ceasefire are condemned as heartless hypocrites who either never intended to bring the killing to an end or are culpably failing to do so.

Pundits are predictably sceptical about the agreement reached by Vladimir Putin and Recep Tayyip Erdogan in Sochi on Monday to head off an imminent offensive by Assad's forces directed against rebels in Idlib province. This is the last enclave of the armed opposition in western Syria, which has lost its strongholds in Aleppo, Damascus, and Daraa over the past two years. Doubts about the accord are understandable because, if it is implemented, the anti-Assad groups in Idlib will be defanged militarily. They will see a demilitarised zone policed by Russia and Turkey eat into their territory, "radical terrorist groups" removed, and heavy weapons ranging from tanks to mortars withdrawn. The rebels will lose their control of the two main highways crossing Idlib and linking the government-held cities of Aleppo, Latakia, and Hama.

There is a striking note of imperial self-confidence about the document in which all sides in the Syrian civil war are instructed to come to heel. This may not happen quite as intended because it is difficult to see why fighters of al-Qaeda-type groups like Hayat Tahrir al-Sham should voluntarily give up such military leverage as they still possess. The Syrian government has said that it will comply with the agreement but may calculate that, in the not so long term, it will be able to slice up Idlib bit by bit as it did with other rebel enclaves. What is most interesting about the agreement is less its details than what it tells us about the balance of forces in Syria, the region, and even the world as a whole. Fragile it may be, but then that is true of all treaties which General Charles de Gaulle famously compared to "young girls and roses—they last as long as they last." Implementation of the Putin-Erdogan agreement may be ragged and its benefits temporary, but it will serve a purpose if a few less Syrians in Idlib are blown apart.

It is difficult to remember now, when Russia is being portrayed in the west as an aggressive predatory power threatening everybody, the extent which it was marginalised seven years ago when NATO was carrying out regime change in Libya. Russia was in reality, always stronger than it looked because it remained a nuclear superpower capable of destroying the world after the fall of the Soviet Union in 1991 just as it was before. It should be difficult to forget this gigantically important fact, but politicians and commentators continue to blithely recommend isolating Russia and pretend that it can be safely ignored. The return of Russia as a great power was always inevitable but was accelerated by successful opportunism and crass errors by rival states. Assad in Syria was always stronger than he looked. Such wishful thinking and flight from reality continues to this day. Miscalculations by Washington, Paris, and London have provided Putin with ideal political terrain on which to reassert the power of the Russian state. The agreement signed by Russia and Turkey last Monday deciding the future of Idlib province is a token of how far Russia has come out on top in Syria. Putin is able to sign a bilateral agreement with Turkey, the second largest military power in NATO, without any reference to the US or other NATO members. The accord means that Turkey will increase its military stake in northern Syria, but it can only do so safely under license from Moscow.

As has happened with North Korea, President Trump's instincts may be surer than the vaunted expertise of the Washington foreign policy establishment and its foreign clones. They have not learned the most important lesson of the US-led intervention wars in Iraq and Syria, which is that it is not in western interests to stir the pot in either country. Despite this, they argue for continued US military presence in north-east Syria on the grounds that this will weaken Assad and ensure that any victory he wins will be pyrrhic. Everything that has happened since 2011 suggests the opposite: by trying to weaken Assad, western powers will force him to become more—not less—reliant on Moscow and Tehran. It ensures that more Syrians will die, be injured or, become refugees and gives space for al-Qaeda clones to re-emerge.

Russian dominance in the northern tier of the Middle East may be opportunistic but is being reinforced by another process. President Trump may not yet have started any wars, but the uncertainty of US policy means that many countries in the world now look for a reinsurance policy with Russia because they are no longer sure how far they can rely on the US. Putin may not always be able to juggle these different opportunities unexpectedly presented to him, but so far, he has had surprising success.

11 October 2018
"People in Idlib hate all those with power over them," says Ahmad Abu Omar, thirty-three, a history teacher living in the province. He says that the three million people of Idlib fear a return of government forces, but are almost equally hostile to the armed opposition groups now ruling Idlib because they have spread violence and chaos. He sees Turkey and Russia as acting solely in their own interests.

Abu Omar, living in Idlib city, told me via WhatsApp that the mood in the city is one of war-weariness and disillusionment. "At the beginning, you could see the youth rushing to fight [against government forces]," he says. "But now nobody cares about fighting and religious belief can no longer motivate people to fight for those in control here [the armed opposition]." Abu Omar, who does not want his real name published because of fear of retribution, was speaking as Russia and Turkey were implementing the terms of their agreement. They have established a demilitarised zone fifteen to twenty kilometres wide to separate opposition and Syrian government forces, which is being monitored by Turkish and Russian patrols. Opposition heavy weapons such as tanks, rocket systems, and mortars have been withdrawn, along with 1,000 fighters. Other provisions of the agreement include the withdrawal of the most militarily effective opposition group, the al-Qaeda linked Hayat Tahrir al-Sham, by 15 October as well as the opening of the M4 and M5 highways linking the government-held cities of Aleppo, Hama, and Latakia.

The city's residents are sceptical about the motives of local and foreign players in Idlib, but they are grateful that a new round of the fighting has been averted for the moment. They see themselves as facing a choice of evils. Abu Ahmad Bakour, forty-seven, who tries to eke out a living as a day labourer in Idlib, says: "We don't understand what is happening in our region, but we are all happy that there is no fighting and no bombardment." He dislikes the continuing rule by opposition militias, said to number some 90,000 fighters, as much as the prospect of a return of Syrian government authority. "If we people are asked whom we would prefer to rule us, then we would say the Turkish rather than the Syrian government," he says. Mr. Bakour is fearful of the Iranian militias on the government side whom, he is convinced, would kill Sunni Arabs like himself and "put us in mass graves" if they ever recaptured Idlib.

He is trenchant in his criticism of the many opposition groups that have held Idlib city since 2015 and the rest of the province for even longer. "We are tired of war and of the militant groups that use the name of Islam to control us," he says. "They are just stealing money and strangling the people by what they do." Abu Omar agrees with Mr. Bakour's rage against both the Syrian government and the armed opposition, though he does not go along with his preference for Turkish rule. He says that less than 10 percent of people in Idlib are pro-Turkish and that the rest "realise that Turkey is playing for the region for its own benefit."

People in Idlib are not starving, but they are very poor, particularly in the cities and towns where there is little work. In Idlib city, there are many, like Mr. Bakour, who sit in the squares and roundabouts hoping to be hired as day labourers, which will earn them the equivalent of about two dollars for a day's work. Others wait beside the road selling fuel, much of which comes from the Kurdish-held oil fields in eastern Syria. Nobody is building anything, so there are no construction jobs, but some skilled workers and professionals, such as doctors, nurses, electricians, and car repairmen, earn good money providing essential services. The best jobs are with aid organisations that pay between $200 and $700 a month in dollars.

Idlib shares a border with Turkey, but it is not isolated from the rest of Syria despite many government checkpoints in and out of the province. Sieges in the wars in Syria and Iraq seldom amount to a complete blockade of people and goods entering or leaving. This is because checkpoints act more like privatised customs posts. Government and opposition pay their forces too little to live on, so their men depend on bribes. It will be a blow to the armed opposition if they lose the revenues from their control of the M4 and M5 highways under the Turkish-Russian agreement. "Many agricultural goods, especially olives, tomatoes, and potatoes, are exported to regime areas and industrial goods, including canned goods, pharmaceuticals, clothes, and shoes come back," Abu Omar says. He says that Syrian goods and produce are mostly cheaper than those coming from Turkey. This flourishing two-way trade means that when fighting has closed the roads in and out of Idlib, prices in its markets have gone down rather than up because output can no longer be exported to the rest of Syria. When trade is free flowing, tomatoes sell in Idlib for the equivalent of seventy US cents a kilogram, but, when the checkpoints are closed, the price drops to thirty cents. Olive oil likewise costs six dollars a litre normally, but when there is fighting, the price is half that in Idlib.

The Turkish-Russian ceasefire agreement in Idlib is holding, though the Syrian government speaks of it as a temporary arrangement. But it is Mr. Putin and Mr. Erdogan who decide what will happen in Idlib and neither of them wants the deal to collapse. Almost unnoticed, the remnants of the armed opposition, once promoted by the West and regional powers as the future rulers of Syria, is losing any autonomy it still retained and, if it has a future, it will be as auxiliaries to the Turkish army. Mr. Assad has not yet entirely won the war, but the opposition have certainly lost it.

Meanwhile, people in Idlib distrust all sides and with good reason, but, as Abu Omar says, they "are happy with any solution that stops them again becoming the victims of displacement, destruction, and war."

23 August 2019

War reporting is easy to do, but difficult to do well. It faces many of the difficulties of peacetime reporting, but in a more acute—though more revealing—form. No one taking part in an armed conflict has an incentive to tell the whole truth and every reason to say only what benefits their own side. This is true of all types of journalism, but in times of military conflict, the propaganda effort is at its most intense and is aided by the chaos of war, which hobbles anybody searching for the truth about what is really happening.

Military commanders are often more aware than reporters of the complexity and uncertainty of news from the battlefield: the Duke of Wellington cited such reasons to explain why he doubted if a truly accurate account of the Battle of Waterloo could ever be written. During the American Civil War, the Confederate General "Stonewall" Jackson made a somewhat different and more acerbic point: surveying the scene of recent fighting, he turned to an aide and asked: "Did you ever think, Sir, what an opportunity a battlefield affords liars?"

He meant that war opens wide the door to deliberate mendacity because it is so easy to make false claims and so difficult to refute them. But there is more at work here than "the fog of war" that is so often conveniently blamed as the cause of misinformation. This over-used phrase exaggerates the accidental nature of the confusion and understates the extent to which propaganda, the deliberate manipulation of information, has always been a central component of warfare but never more so than at present. Propaganda tends to get a bad press and is the subject of much finger-wagging, but it stands to reason that people trying to kill each other will not hesitate to lie about each other.

The fashion popularised by President Trump for denouncing news contrary to one's own interests as "fake news" has heightened perception that information, true or false, is always a weapon in somebody's hands. This is correct, but this does not mean that objective truth does not exist and that it cannot be revealed by good journalism. The glib saying that "truth is the first casualty of war" is a dangerous escape hatch for poor reporting or for unthinking acceptance of a self-serving version of reality spoon-fed by the powers-that-be to a credulous media. On the contrary, there is nothing inevitable about the suppression of the truth about wars, or anything else for that matter, though it is much in the interests of governments to seek to demoralise its critics by pretending that, even when they do reveal important truths, their efforts are so puny as to be marginal and ineffective. Journalists, individually and collectively, will always be engaged in a struggle with the propagandists that will sway backwards and forwards but in which the victory of either side is never inevitable.

As a general proposition, this is true, but I have had the depressing sense since the First Gulf War in 1991 that it is increasingly the propagandists who are winning this contest and that it is accurate journalism, in the shape of eyewitness reporting, that is on the retreat. The causes of this are diverse: politics, finance, and technology have combined to squeeze and even eliminate those whose job it is to find out what is truly going on and to pass on news of it to the public.

These ill-winds blow from many directions but their collective impact is to blight all types of on-the-ground newsgathering: casualties include the press in the US and Europe as well as my own field of foreign reporting, a speciality which, in the last two decades, has been increasingly dominated by war reporting. Since 1999, I have been writing about Chechnya, Afghanistan, Iraq, Libya, and Syria, conflicts which are sometimes referred to as the post-9/11 wars, but in certain important respects predate the destruction of the Twin Towers. Before that, I worked in Northern Ireland, Lebanon, and Israel.

Reporting wars is by its nature always going to be difficult and dangerous work, but it has got more so. Coverage of the Afghan and Iraqi was often inadequate, but not as bad as the reporting in Libya and Syria or its near absence in Yemen. This absence of essential information fosters misconceptions not just about matters of detail but about more fundamental questions, such as who is really fighting whom, for what reasons, and who are the winners and losers.

This ignorance is often portrayed as something afflicting the general public, while the powers-that-be, the "political class," the controllers of "the deep state," who have their burrows in the Pentagon, Whitehall, and the Kremlin, really do know what is going on. Unfortunately, sad experience shows that this is not true and politicians like Tony Blair and George W. Bush in Iraq in 2003 take momentous decisions in large part on the basis of an ill-informed and misleading media consensus that they themselves have done much to create. Intelligence chiefs do not like to contradict their political masters and shape information to fit their needs. This was true of David Cameron, Nicolas Sarkozy, and Hillary Clinton when they came together in 2011 to sanction the overthrow of Muammar Gaddafi by NATO in Libya. It should have been obvious from the beginning that the rag-tag militias on the ground were in no position to replace him and anarchy would be the inevitable outcome of the war. In Syria, political leaders and media organisations convinced themselves that the fall of Assad was inevitable, while anybody with real experience on the ground in Syria could predict from 2012 on, with a fair degree of certainty, that this was not going to happen.

One should not be too dewy-eyed about standards of reporting fifty years ago when most news organisations in Vietnam dutifully toed the official line about the impending victory of the US and its allies. The media invariably exaggerates its own ability to find out the truth and speak that truth to power. Its willingness to criticise is also limited because newspaper proprietors are usually part of that power or would like to be. But in Vietnam, journalists were thick enough on the ground and free enough to operate to include a fair number of perceptive dissenters who contradicted official optimism and predicted that the US was heading for disaster. In contrast with the present, there were then more newspaper owners, particularly in the US and UK, willing to see their journalists challenge the official line.

Sadly, the balance of forces has changed since Vietnam away from independent-minded journalism and towards those who act as the messenger boys and girls for government views. The change for the worse is detectable, though I do not want to be too much of a journalistic Casandra and there is nothing new about controlling the news or spreading "fake facts." Ancient Egyptian pharaohs inscribed self-glorifying and mendacious accounts of their battles on monuments in which their defeats are lauded as heroic victories.

What is new about war reporting in recent decades is the much greater sophistication and resources that governments deploy in shaping the news. Where governments do not have their own heavily manned press offices, they hire private PR companies. After Vietnam, the US military convinced itself—wrongly to my mind—that it had lost the war because of hostile media coverage. They were determined not to let this happen again and one could sense this approach at work in the Gulf War of 1991, a conflict that set a pattern for war reporting in the coming years.

Life was not difficult for propagandists in that early period: Saddam Hussein was easy to demonise because he was genuinely demonic. On the other hand, the most influential news story of the Iraqi invasion of Kuwait and the US-led counter-invasion was a fake. This was a report that, in August 1990, invading Iraqi soldiers had tipped babies out of incubators in a Kuwait hospital and left them to die on the floor. A Kuwaiti girl working as a volunteer in the hospital told the US Congress that she had witnessed this horrific atrocity. Her story was hugely influential in mobilising international support for the war effort of the US and its allies. In reality, the Kuwait babies' story was a fiction. The girl who claimed to be a witness turned out to be the daughter of the Kuwait ambassador in Washington. Several journalists and human rights specialists expressed scepticism at the time because purported eyewitness accounts were full of holes, but their voices were drowned out by the outrage provoked by the tale. It was the classic example of a successful propaganda coup: it was geared to be lapped up by the media, could not easily be disproved, and, when it was shown to be false—long after the event—it had had its intended and immense political impact in creating support for the US-led Coalition going to war with Iraq.

Twenty years later, in Libya, fabricated atrocity stories played an even more central role in persuading people that Gaddafi was a monster who had to be overthrown. The media uncritically ran with the story of a woman in Benghazi who claimed to have carried out a survey of Libyan women in opposition areas recaptured by Gaddafi's forces and to have found that a high proportion of them said they had been raped by Libyan troops on official instructions. It was weeks before Amnesty International, Human Rights Watch, and a UN committee published well-researched reports saying that they had found no evidence that a survey had taken place and that the women who said she had conducted it had been unable to put them in touch with a single rape victim. But by then, the news agenda had moved on and I believe I was one of the few correspondents to highlight the reports discrediting the original atrocity story.

It is not entirely fair to blame reporters for being spoon-fed propaganda. If a story—like that of mass rapes in Libya—is leading the TV news and is the top story in newspapers around the world, it is difficult for them to ignore it or discredit it. It may smell bad to them, but they cannot disprove it and their news editor will be harrying them to follow it up.

———

In the case cited above, the Libyan opposition and their NATO backers had succeeded in establishing themselves a credible source of information, while any denial by the pro-Gaddafi forces was treated with suspicion. I had seen the same process at work in Iran earlier in 2011. There were reports from opposition sources in exile saying that protests were sweeping the country and there was some substance in this. There had been a demonstration of 30,000 protesters in north Tehran on 14 February—recalling the mass protests against the allegedly fixed presidential election of 2009—that had caught the authorities by surprise. It had also led to hopeful commentary by Western pundits suggesting that the Arab Spring uprisings might be spreading to Iran and regime change was in the offing.

By the time I got to Tehran a few days later, nothing much appeared to be going on, though there were plenty of bored-looking riot police standing around in the rain doing nothing. It looked as if the protests had dwindled away, but when I checked the internet, I found this was not so. Opposition spokesmen were claiming that protests were taking place every week, not just in north Tehran but in other Iranian cities. These accounts appeared to be confirmed by videos running online, showing protesters resisting baton-wielding riot police and militiamen. I met some friendly Iranian correspondents working for the foreign media and asked why I was failing to find any demonstrations. The reporters were well-informed, but could not work because their press credentials had been suspended by the Iranian authorities. They laughed when I described my vain pursuit of the anti-government protests, explaining that I was failing to find them because they had ceased earlier in the month.

One journalist usually sympathetic to the opposition said that "the problem is that the picture of what is happening in Iran these days comes largely from exiled Iranians and is often a product of wishful thinking or propaganda." I asked about the videos online and he said that these were frequently concocted by the opposition using film of real demonstrations that had taken place in the past. He pointed to one video, supposedly filmed in the middle of winter, in which trees covered in leaves were visible in the far background. I asked the journalists if this was not the fault of the Iranian government which, by suspending the credentials of local report-ers who were credible eyewitnesses, had created a vacuum of information which was swiftly filled by opposition propagandists outside the country. The stringers agreed that to some extent this was so, but added gloomily that, even if they were free to report, their Western editors "would not believe us because the exiles and their news outlets have convinced them that there are big protests here. If we deny this, our bosses will simply believe that we have been intimidated or bought up by the government."

I was to recall my experience in Iran many times in the coming years in Syria as I tried to write objectively—but somewhat contrary to the media consensus—about developments there during the long war.

A further weakness in the reporting of these post-9/11 wars is not really the fault of the participants. In all of them, political developments have been just as important as military action, but this is obscured by what I call the 'twixt-shot-and-shell' style of reporting. News organisations and the public are both attracted by the melodrama of war, but it can be very misleading.

I reported the war in Afghanistan in 2001–2002 at a time when the international media was giving the impression that the Taliban had been decisively defeated. Television showed pictures of bombs and missiles exploding on the Taliban front lines and the Northern Alliance opposi-tion forces advancing unopposed into Kabul. But I followed the Taliban retreating south to Kandahar and it became clear to me that they were not a beaten force, but their units were under orders to disperse and go home. They knew that they were over-matched and it would be better for them to wait until conditions changed in their favour. By 2006 the Taliban were back in business, and by 2009, it was already becoming too dangerous to drive beyond the southernmost police station in Kabul because of the risk of roving Taliban patrols suddenly establishing pop-up checkpoints on the road to Kandahar.

These obstacles to the accurate reporting of wars are great but they are also surmountable. Many of them are not new: consider how the First World War was misreported. But for the media to push-back effectively requires experienced well-resourced journalists on the ground capable of investigating all aspects of a conflict.

But this is exactly what is not happening and the trend today is in the opposite direction. There are far fewer professional journalists in the field: publications have disappeared, foreign bureaux are closed or are manned by a skeleton staff. The number of employees in US newspaper newsrooms fell by 45 percent in the decade up to 2017 according to a survey. As war reporting becomes more dangerous, it gets more expensive and the money to pay for it is no longer there. "In more than 40 years of reporting," writes Sammy Ketz, the recently retired Agence France-Presse bureau chief in Baghdad and one of the most experienced journalists in the Middle East, "I have seen the number of journalists on the ground steadily diminish while the dangers relentlessly increase. We have become targets and our reporting costs more." Bulletproof jackets and drivers who rightly demand danger money need to be paid for. But, as advertising migrates from news organisations to internet platforms like Google and Facebook, the flow of essential but expensive information from the battlefronts of the Middle East has gone down. Many of those who used to report from the region are out of a job and whole areas of the world have fallen off the media map. When news organisations do pay for eyewitness reporting, they do not necessarily profit from their investment because the benefits are hijacked by the internet giants, which themselves employ no journalists.

The decline of foreign reporting will continue until the internet platforms share a part of their vast revenues with those organisations which gather the news. Ketz describes the present situation graphically as being as if "a stranger came along and shamelessly snatched the fruit of your labour. It is morally and democratically unjustified." Freedom of expression is not of much use unless there are the news outlets with the means and the reach to transmit essential information to the world at large.

After decrying the difficulties that may frustrate anybody trying to accurately report wars, one must ask a more basic question: How far do the efforts of the media in general, and of the war correspondent in particular, really matter? Does the quality of journalism, now under threat, significantly affect conflicts for good or ill, or do they simply add melodramatic detail? Would they take much the same course because their direction is determined by long-standing political, religious, social, and economic pressures? At the end of the day, the US and Britain would have been in terrible trouble in Afghanistan and Iraq, regardless of how these wars were reported. This query has some truth in it, but the nature and depth of these troubles were the fruit of unforced errors and miscalculations that were by no means predetermined. Looking back over armed conflicts that I have reported over half a century, starting with Northern Ireland, I can see that their ferocity and length were radically affected by the extent to which the media succeeded or failed in presenting a true picture of what was going on.

The conflict in Northern Ireland is a good example of this: the Troubles, as they came to be called, lasted for thirty years between the first civil rights marches by Catholics in Derry in 1968 to the Good Friday Agreement in 1998. I went to Northern Ireland in the first year of the conflict when I was eighteen years old and moved to Belfast for three years in 1972 to work on my PhD about the development of Irish nationalism in Ulster at the Institute of Irish Studies, which is part of Queen's University. Even by the grisly standards of Northern Ireland, it was a particularly violent period. It should have been evident that, so long as the Catholic community in the province felt oppressed by a Protestant-dominated local government supported by the British state and army, that there would be no peace.

But it was much less inevitable that the instrument for Catholic opposition to the status quo should have been the Provisional IRA and Sinn Fein. That they should have become the centre of resistance had everything to do with the decision of the British government to send in its army in support of a sectarian Protestant and unionist government in 1970. The incursions of the British Army and Royal Ulster Constabulary into Catholic areas in pursuit of "terrorists" were wholly counter-productive and were a recruiting sergeant for the Provisional IRA. Successes by the security services against "the men of violence" were regularly trumpeted by the main outlets of a largely right-wing British media, but simply served to stoke the violence and ensured that it continued for thirty years.

The way the British media ignored or misreported acts of injustice by the British state and its local unionist allies was a central reason why the UK endured the longest and most violent guerrilla conflict in Western Europe since the Second World War. Events like internment without trial, Bloody Sunday, the imprisonment of innocent people for bombs attacks which they had not carried out in England—the Birmingham Six and the Guildford Four—delegitimised the British government and legitimised the IRA in the eyes of a significant portion of the Irish population.

Ed Moloney, one of the most experienced and best-informed journalists reporting from Northern Ireland for much of the Troubles, believes that this misreporting of events lengthened and deepened the conflict. Journalists and news outlets knew with a fair degree of certainty that those jailed for the Birmingham and Guildford bombings were innocent, but dared not say so because they feared being pilloried as IRA sympathisers. He himself says he might have been sacked from his job as a Northern Ireland correspondent for his newspaper, *The Irish Times*, if his prediction of a surge of electoral support for the Provisionals thanks to the hunger strikes in 1981 had not been confirmed by results at the polls.

I saw the same pattern repeated in wars in the Middle East and beyond: what were civil wars provoked, complicated, or exploited by foreign intervention, were portrayed as black-and-white conflicts between a demonic dictator or movement (Saddam Hussein, Taliban, Muammar Gaddafi, Bashar al-Assad) fighting a pure-as-snow popular or democratic opposition. Sometimes, it was the other way around and it was the powers-that-be who were the white hats (the Iraqi and Afghan governments after 2003) under attack by "terrorist" gangs, supposedly representing only a tiny portion of the population but mysteriously never lacking new recruits. The Iraq and Syrian wars were prolonged multi-layered conflicts—much more complicated than Northern Ireland—which even seasoned Iraqi and Syrian politicians had difficulty understanding. The international media had a bad beginning in Iraq in 2002–2003, when it, for the most part, credulously accepted that Saddam Hussein possessed weapons of mass destruction which was the justification for the war against him. In the following years, press coverage never appeared to recover from these early missteps and get a grip on what was happening on the ground.

The absence of on-the-ground eyewitnesses fosters ignorance and this, in turn, opens the door to more conflicts. Wars are started by those who think they can win them and they believe this because they have swallowed too much of their own propaganda. In almost all the wars I have written about since 9/11, those who decided to fight in Afghanistan, Iraq, Libya, Syria, and Yemen had no idea of what they were getting into.

What can be done about this? Will people be better or worse informed about wars in the future? The sucking away of advertising revenues by the internet giants from those who try to find out the truth is proving a killer blow to many publications. Is this a passing phase, or will a way be found to make sure that those publications that gather the news are rewarded for their efforts? The prospects are not encouraging: in 2019, for the first time in the US, digital advertising companies like Google and Facebook are predicted to receive more advertising revenue—$129 billion compared to $109 billion—than newspapers, TV, and radio combined. This leads to newsrooms ever-shrinking in terms of size and quality.

Not all the arrows point in the same direction: the internet has vastly democratised the distribution and consumption of news and loosened the control of monopoly news organisations. When I needed a just-issued Pentagon report in a hurry recently, I could access it online and read it in the space of a few minutes as can anybody else. Forty years ago, when I was on the *Financial Times*, I would have had to wait days to get the report and I would have had to go to the *FT* office to obtain clipping files from its library. Such information true or false is today instantly available to everybody and is consequently much more influential than in the pre-internet past. Is there more "fake news" around? Of course there is because there is much more news of all sorts available. But what I find the most truly menacing is not the increase in fake news but the diminishing means of refuting it, the "de-professionalisation" of journalism about which I wrote earlier.

Newspapers and other media depend on advertising and have done so for 200 years, but if that revenue is siphoned off by those who produce no news themselves, then the ability to counterpunch effectively against fake news will disappear and we enter an age of increasing ignorance and credulity.

I still relish watching a TV recording dating from pre-internet times in 1991 which illustrates this point, though the situation has since got worse.

In it, my late friend Christopher Hitchens demolishes Charlton Heston, who was a strong supporter of the bombing of Iraq, in a famed television encounter. Hitchens asked Heston to name the countries which shared a common border with Iraq. "Kuwait, Bahrain, Turkey, Russia, Iran," was Heston's response, which would have been a big surprise to the Russians and Bahrainis who don't have such a border and the Syrians and Jordanians who do.

"If you are going to bomb a country, you might at least pay it the compliment of finding out where it is," replied Hitchens, delivering the knockout blow. The exchange elicited much mockery of Heston at the time, but the decline of foreign reporting means that there are going to be more and more people who will share his enthusiasm for bombing places that they cannot find on the map.

PART VIII. IRAQ AT THE END OF WAR

The two key dates marking Iraq's return to violence and instability are 1 October 2019, when pro-Iranian elements in the Iraqi security forces and paramilitary units shot and killed peaceful protesters, and 3 January 2020, when the US killed Iranian General Qasem Soleimani at Baghdad International Airport. The first date marks the end of civil peace that had been increasing over the previous three years as Isis was defeated. In the three months up to the end of 2019, 669 protesters were killed and 24,488 were injured according to the Iraqi War Crimes Documentation Centre. The death of Soleimani three months later confirmed the fear of Iraqis that their country was becoming the arena in which the US-Iran confrontation would be fought out.

Prior to these developments, physical security in Iraq had been getting better, but, given Iraq's spectacularly violent past, the improvement was comparative. When sectarian killings were at their height twelve years earlier, a hundred people were being slaughtered every day. Young men were particularly vulnerable and would sometimes have a small symbol, such as an olive tree, tattooed on their skin so that their bodies could be identified, even if their faces were mutilated beyond recognition by their killers.

Gruesome memories were still fresh in the minds of Iraqis: as recently as 2014, columns of Isis fighters, who had just captured Mosul, were advancing speedily towards Baghdad, posting online revolting videos of their massacres to terrorise and demoralise anybody resisting them. It was scarcely surprising that people in Baghdad were only slowly readjusting to the ebbing of violence after the recapture of Mosul in 2017. Iraq was now suffering less violence than at any time since the US invasion of 2003, but, talking to them, I was struck by how fear was receding more slowly than the reality. I had great respect for Iraqis' well-honed survival instincts and knew that permanent pessimism about the future has been a safe bet in Iraq ever since Saddam Hussein assumed total power in 1979 and began the Iran-Iraq War a year later. A friend in Baghdad once told me, "No Iraqi can be proved to be paranoid because in our country *there is always something to be frightened of." Habits of wariness and suspicion were slow to disappear: I was in the countryside near Taji, formerly a Sunni insurgent stronghold north of Baghdad in 2018. I met a farmer who said, "I know people from here who have not been to Baghdad for ten years because they are frightened of being picked up at government checkpoints." Driving back from Taji, somebody in the car asked me to "take off your seatbelt—no Iraqi ever wears one and it identifies you as a foreigner."*

I know that itch of constant anxiety about one's safety: as security deteriorated after 2003, I would drive around Baghdad in one car, deliberately grubby and beat-up looking to avoid attracting attention, with a second car to see if we were being followed and to warn us by hand radio. I would hang a couple of shirts from a hook by the window, as people do when they are returning from the dry cleaner, but the real reason was to make it difficult to see me in the back seat of the car, without suggesting that we were trying to hide anything.

Such precautions go on longer than are strictly necessary, because nobody wants to find out the hard way that they have made premature and over-optimistic assumptions about the absence of danger. Yet confidence was slowly returning in Baghdad in the 2016 to 2019 period as new restaurants, clothes shops, and shopping malls opened. Isis bombers were no longer getting through to Baghdad after losing their old Iraqi bases. "Suicide bombers have been trying for months to cross the Syrian border and make their way to Baghdad, but they are being stopped there or in the desert before they get here," said a government security official. Isis was weaker and more easily penetrated by informants and, even if a single bomber did succeed, there was no return to the multiple attacks of a few years earlier.

Improved security meant that people could focus more on the innumerable other things that were wrong with Iraq. I first came to Baghdad in 1977, just before everything went sour. The physical appearance of the city had not changed much since then because there were few new big buildings. Resources were instead poured into wars or were stolen by those in charge of reconstruction. As a result, an infrastructure built for two million people in Baghdad was now used by four times as many and the city has some of the worst traffic jams in the world. Oil revenues had risen because of increased production and higher world prices but this was not enough to do much about forty years of neglect.

Mudher Salih, financial adviser to the former Prime Minister Haider al-Abadi, said, "Iraq has between 400,000 and 420,000 young people entering the labour force each year and there are few jobs for them." He explained that some 4.5 million people work for the government, which cannot afford to hire

more, and 6.5 million for the private sector, which is often archaic and oper-
ates in the grey market. Great numbers of unemployed or underemployed young
men—fewer women are to be seen—mill about in the streets. In Sadr City,
the great Shia working-class enclave in Baghdad, locals say that even among
those who can afford to get married, the divorce rate is going up because jobless
husbands cannot support their family. The best jobs are in the army and police
where an officer earns three times as much as a teacher, but these have all been
snapped up. The impulse to flee Iraq and its troubles is overwhelming for many,
though frustrated by lack of work visas. Buying a local phone in the Karrada
district, I met Rami, who was wearing a blue T-shirt with the slogan "I Choose
Leave" printed on the front in large white letters. The T-shirt must have been
intended for the British referendum campaign of 2016 but, perhaps because of
over-supply in the UK, had ended up being sold in Baghdad, where its slogan
has a different implication. I asked Rami if he knew the meaning of the words
on his T-shirt and, though he did not speak much English, he said that he
did understand them and they precisely expressed his ambition to leave Iraq. I
mentioned that the declaration on the T-shirt had originally referred to Britain
leaving the European Union which Rami found amusing, though he said he
had never heard of the Brexit referendum.

Iraqis, freed from the terror of Isis, were enraged by their corrupt and incompetent government, but these grievances might have gone on festering for years
had General Soleimani not ordered his forces to shoot the protesters.

November 2017–September 2019

5 November 2017

It is one of the most shocking of many sadistic videos shot and publicised by Isis in which its gunmen are seen executing their victims. It shows scenes from the Camp Speicher massacre on 12 June 2014 when Isis murdered 1,700 army recruits in a former palace compound of Saddam Hussein on the banks of the Tigris River near Tikrit.

Columns of terrified young men are filmed being driven at gunpoint by masked Isis gunmen dressed in black towards mass graves, which the victims can see are already filled with bodies. Others are beaten as they stumble down stone steps onto a small dock under a bridge on the Tigris. As each one is dragged forward by a guard, he is shot in the head by a man with a pistol so he falls into the water. The ground where the killings are taking place is covered in blood. It is worth forcing oneself to look at this disgusting video again as Isis is driven by Iraqi security forces out of its last strongholds in the deserts of western Iraq. The movement, now defeated and almost eliminated, revelled in its cruelty and boasted of its mass killings in order to terrorise its opponents. The Camp Speicher massacre was its worst single atrocity in Iraq or Syria.

The slaughter of the young recruits happened a few days after Isis had unexpectedly captured Mosul; its military units were racing south towards Baghdad against little opposition as the Iraqi army disintegrated. Its gunmen were greeted by many Sunni as liberators in places like Tikrit, the city near which Saddam Hussein was born and grew up. It was here that as many as 10,000 army recruits were being trained at an air force academy. They were told to go home by their commanders who themselves fled in circumstances that still cause controversy and anger. The young men, who were from all over Iraq, changed into civilian clothes and those carrying weapons were told to leave them behind at the camp.

Isis gunmen captured many of the recruits as they walked along the roads heading home and divided them into Shia and Sunni before loading the Shia into trucks. It is not known when they realised they were going to die because many were told at first that they would be let go where they could get transport to Baghdad. Instead, they were taken to an area where Saddam Hussein had built several palaces where he and his family could enjoy a fine view across the Tigris. Some of the palaces were in ruins, shattered by US bombing, and the rest were abandoned.

The site of the killings may have been chosen because of its associations with Saddam Hussein. Hayder al-Baldawi, a member of a committee commemorating the massacre, says: "It was an act of revenge for the execution of Saddam and the fall of his regime. Many of the killers were identified later as coming from Tikrit, Baath party members, and people from Saddam's Albu Nasr tribe and other pro-Saddam tribes, who joined up with Isis."

There are many massacre sites: on the flat ground by the river, large pits have been excavated where the recruits were killed and their bodies covered with earth and stones. At one place, they were shot on top of a low cliff so the bodies fell in a heap on the ground below. Another site is some way away, high up on a bluff overlooking the river, near Saddam Hussein's giant ruined Salahudin palace, where today there is a stretch of rough ground and a deep hole with a tree in the middle distance on the edge of a cliff. We compared this to a still from the Isis propaganda video that shows the same tree, but the foreground is carpeted in dead bodies so numerous that one cannot see the ground. Many of the dead have their hands tied behind their backs and there is a black Isis flag in one corner of the picture.

A watchman pointed to where he had just found a bit of blood-matted hair stuck to the side of a rock, which he believed must date from the massacre.

It is not clear how many died: Isis claimed that it had killed 1,700, though the number of bodies so far identified is lower. Mr. Baldawi says that "the Ministry of Health does not have enough money to pay for DNA kits, so bodies can be identified for certain." He puts the number of dead at 1,935, of which 994 bodies have been found and, of these, 527 have been identified and 467 are under medical examination. In addition, some 941 are still missing, though these figures are difficult to verify because the search for the bodies only began in March 2015, eight months after the killings, when government forces recaptured Tikrit.

The search for the perpetrators of the massacre has gone on ever since with thirty-six alleged killers executed in August 2016 amid allegations that they had not received a fair trial. Defence lawyers were not able to speak to the accused and walked out. The United Nations Assistance Mission for Iraq (UNAMI) issued a negative report on the conduct of the trial, saying that there had been a "failure to investigate allegations of torture." Nevertheless, there have been no counter-massacres and the government and NGOs have made concerted efforts to get the Tikrit Sunni tribes to reconcile with the families of the victims.

Tribal leaders said that individuals from tribes had taken part in the massacre, but denied it was a communal Sunni attack on the Shia. They said that Sunni officials from Tikrit had also been targeted and killed by Isis. Some Sunni had helped Shia escape. Reconciliation is helped because Tikrit is wholly Sunni and members of the two sects are not intermingled as they are in other parts of Iraq, where neighbourhood revenge killings have been frequent. Tikrit, with a population of 160,000, looks relaxed and suffered only limited damage during its recapture compared to other Sunni cities like Ramadi and Mosul.

Identifying who on the government side was responsible for allowing so many unarmed Shia recruits to be captured remains a divisive political issue. Victims' families want to know who were the senior officers who ran away, leaving their sons to be murdered by Isis. This is not just an issue between Shia and Sunni, but between Shia and Kurd, relations between the latter being particularly fraught in the wake of the government reoccupation in September of Kirkuk and the disputed territories.

Nouri al-Maliki, the prime minister at the time of the killings, said to me that he has a simple explanation for what happened: "In fact, the Speicher massacre occurred because the commander there was a Kurd and he received orders from [then-Kurdish President] Masoud Barzani to withdraw with his [Kurdish] men and they left everything in chaos and disorder and the massacre happened." This account has the advantage of excusing Mr. Maliki and his government for any responsibility for the collapse of the Iraqi armed forces in the area, which enabled Isis to slaughter so many young men.

14 December 2017

Isis has been defeated: it lost its last town, Rawa, close to the Syrian border, on 17 November, and surviving Isis fighters have retreated to hideouts in the western desert. In the past, Isis would respond to military setbacks by putting on a show of strength and stepping up the bombing of easy-to-attack civilian targets. This time that hasn't really happened. The great Shia pilgrimage of Arbaeen—when six or seven million people from all over Iraq walk to the holy city of Karbala over a twenty-day period—has just ended: it usually provides an opportunity for suicide bombers to mingle with the crowds and kill large numbers. But this year there were only two such attacks, and in both cases, the bombers were shot dead, with no pilgrims killed. People in Baghdad worry that Isis may be preparing some spectacular atrocity, like the bomb in a refrigerator truck that blew up in the Karada district of the capital on 3 July 2016, killing 324 people. But the IS-held towns and villages around Baghdad, where suicide bombers used to be trained and where vehicles were packed with explosives, have now all been captured by government forces. Isis probably no longer has the capacity to launch multiple attacks in markets, mosques, or crowded streets.

The mood in Baghdad is less edgy than it was. But forty years of war and emergency have made Iraqis dubious about a swift return to peaceful life. There are still checkpoints everywhere; buildings likely to be targeted are protected by walls of concrete blocks. Senior officials and diplomats continue to live inside the heavily defended Green or International Zone, a forbidden city which can only be entered with a difficult-to-obtain permit. Security restrictions have cut down the number of usable roads in the city centre, which leads to some of the world's worst traffic jams, which are exacerbated by an uncontrolled increase in the number of yellow-painted taxis—a way for jobless Iraqis to make a bit of money. A few new buildings are under construction, but most of Baghdad—the biggest city in the Arab world after Cairo, with a population of eight million—looks much as it did when I first visited in 1977. The last spurt of construction was during Saddam's early years when he borrowed money from the Gulf states to prove to Iraqis that he could modernise their country with new hotels and government offices while at the same time fighting the disastrous war with Iran that he started in 1980.

Baghdadis are less afraid of suicide bombers and sectarian death squads than they were, but this makes them all the more aware that they live in a shabby, run-down city choking on traffic and uncollected garbage. Past Iraqi governments used the war as an excuse for this, but the truth is that ever since 2003, funds allocated for development have been systematically siphoned off by the political elite. "Corruption is swallowing us up," Shirouk al-Abayachi, an MP who speaks up about the failures of public services, told me. "It is no worse now than it was four or five years ago," she said, but the difference then was that the oil price hadn't yet fallen, and "we still had a huge budget to pay for things." People are now more resentful of the corruption because the reduction in political violence means they no longer "have to give all their attention to trying to keep their families and children safe."

But political violence isn't the only kind. Little attention is paid in the foreign media to the effect on Iraqis of non-political crime, or the government's failure to provide adequate protection through the police and the courts. Nobody trusts the dysfunctional legal system. The uncertainties of everyday life make people feel vulnerable, and rumours of new threats abound. At the moment, people are talking about a supposed rise in the number of children being kidnapped for ransom—though the Interior Minister, Qasim al-Araji, told me he knows of only three such kidnappings recently; two of the hostages were released. The fears are driven by memories of the not so distant time when kidnapping was a major criminal industry in Baghdad. Nobody wants to take a chance with the safety of their children: I used to stay in a hotel near the entrance to Baghdad University in the Jadriyah district but this time I had to go elsewhere, since twice a day the road is impassable for hours at a time as parents drop off and pick up their student offspring, frightened that they will be abducted if they walk the streets alone. The Iraqi state is becoming stronger, and its authority less fragmented, but Iraqis' mentality has been shaped by four decades of chronic instability and it will take time for people to accept that they really are safer than they used to be.

Iraqis have good reason to be pessimists. Throughout many people's lifetimes, a new crisis has arrived as soon as the previous one came to an end. The eight-year-long Iran-Iraq War ended to general joy in 1988 after 250,000 Iraqis had been killed. But two years later, Saddam invaded Kuwait. After he was defeated there in 1991, he crushed Shia and Kurdish uprisings, as UN sanctions that amounted to a thirteen-year blockade ruined the Iraqi economy. The US-led invasion of 2003 got rid of Saddam but started a new round of wars. These ebbed in 2008 only to reignite in

2011 and reach a peak of horrific violence with the Isis victories of 2014. Isis has now been defeated, but Iraqis aren't sure whether, yet again, this is only a temporary respite. Their caution is understandable, but this time there really is a strong chance that the cycle of wars, both international and civil, is coming to an end. That's because winners and losers are now emerging in Iraq and in the region around it.

Inside Iraq, the Shia have defeated rival communities, and in both Iraq and Syria, the Sunni coalition of Saudi Arabia, Qatar, Turkey, and their local allies has failed in its aims and broken up. The Shia axis—a generalisation, but a useful one—has come out on top. Last month, as Iraqi government forces were taking Rawa in western Iraq, the Syrian army captured Abu Kamal, the last IS-held town in eastern Syria. Bashar al-Assad is here to stay. The significance of the fact that Iranian leaders now control a "corridor" through friendly territory all the way from the Afghan border to the Mediterranean, passing through Iran, Iraq, Syria, and Lebanon is often exaggerated (if the corridor was so important, how were they able to win wars without it?), but the verdict on the question of who will hold power—the question that was posed in Iraq in 2003, and in Syria in 2011—is now in.

An unintended outcome of the US and Britain overthrowing Saddam in 2003 was the creation of the first Shia government in the Arab world since Saladin defeated the Fatimids in 1171. But the Sunni never fully accepted it, nor did the Kurds, though early on a Shia-Kurdish power-sharing bloc was held together by opposition to Saddam and his regime. Until the second half of this year, Iraq had a peculiar political geography, as, in effect, three states in one country: a Shia-dominated government in the centre and south, with quasi-states in the north and west, each with a larger army than most member states of the UN. The Kurdish quasi-state had been gradually expanding its authority ever since Saddam lost his hold on Iraqi Kurdistan in the wake of the Gulf War in 1991. The Isis caliphate was a much later creation, established after the capture of Mosul in 2014, and at its height accounted for about a quarter of Iraq, including all Sunni-majority areas, as well as a similarly sized zone in Syria.

In the last few months, this situation has been transformed.

Not so long ago, when asked about the future, Baghdadis would commonly reply that "Iraq is finished." American politicians argued that the country should either be broken up or continue as the loosest of federations. This notion that Iraq is a failed state is now being replaced by growing self-confidence on the part of the Shia majority: the Iraqi state has been reborn, they insist, and belongs to them. There is an outpouring of nationalist celebration in the Iraqi media, even if it is not necessarily an accurate guide to what Iraqis actually think. It was significant that many of the millions of Shia pilgrims taking part in the Arbaeen walk were carrying the Iraqi national red, white, and black tricolour as well as their traditional green, black, red, and white religious flags. Shia religious identity is becoming more closely connected with Iraqi national identity. Once, nationalism was the province of the Sunni, who would denigrate the Shia as "Safavids," a derogatory term referring to the dynasty that ruled Iran between the sixteenth and eighteenth centuries, not true Iraqis.

The fact that the Sunni and Kurdish defeats have been so complete gives the Shia little reason to share power with them. "The problem with Iraqis is that they have all been victims of oppression at one time or other," said a senior official in Baghdad, a veteran of the struggle again Saddam. "So, when they do get power, they feel they have the right to treat everybody else as badly as they were once treated themselves." But it is a rule of Iraqi politics that no community is strong enough to monopolise power for very long. Saddam slaughtered the Kurds and drove them from their lands, but they survived and he was executed. Some Iraqi leaders are aware of the danger: Speaking of the Iraqi government's response to the referendum for Kurdish independence, Haider al-Abadi told me he was doing everything he could to avoid permanently alienating the Kurds: "I gave orders to our security forces that there should be no bloodshed. We did not want to fight the Peshmerga." On the other hand, Abadi is demanding that the Kurdish leaders give up control of their borders, oil exports, and international flights; the Peshmerga will largely come under the command of the central government, and state employees in Kurdistan will be paid directly from Baghdad. Given the triumphalist atmosphere, Abadi, who faces a parliamentary election in May, could do nothing else and probably doesn't want to. Yet dismissing the Kurds' national demands, which they fought for and then voted for by a huge majority, is beginning to create a counter-reaction.

Western governments and media tend to treat the wars in Iraq and Syria as if they were driven by different dynamics, similar though they have been in many respects. This skewed analysis stems partly from the fact that the West opposed Syria's government and supported Iraq's. In Iraq, the rebels were condemned; in Syria, until a late stage in the war, the armed opposition was treated sympathetically. But both insurgencies became dominated by Isis or al-Qaeda-type organisations. The Syrian and Russian bombardment of civilians in east Aleppo was widely covered in the West, while the destruction of parts of Mosul by Iraqi artillery and US aircraft was played down. A distorted picture of the war became conventional wisdom: in reality, the strategy in both countries was similar and was adopted for similar reasons: the Syrian and Iraqi government forces and the Syrian and Iraqi Kurds were all deploying limited numbers of combat troops, and they were able to advance only with the support of the massive firepower provided by American and Russian air strikes. This way of making war has been successful, and Isis has been defeated, but it has involved a high level of destruction and heavy civilian loss of life.

The wars in Syria and Iraq were linked from the beginning. Nouri al-Maliki, Iraq's prime minister between 2006 and 2014, was frequently criticised for overseeing the repression that drove the Sunni in Iraq into supporting Isis, but he sees the renewed Sunni uprising as having been driven by the Syrian war. "It began in Syria," he says, "when Saudi Arabia and some other countries"—he means Turkey and Qatar—"in co-ordination with the Americans and others decided to remove the Syrian regime by armed force." The war in Syria fuelled sectarianism everywhere, particularly in Iraq, where local Sunni leaders were convinced that Assad's regime in Damascus would soon fall. Regime change in Baghdad would then follow. "I spoke to Obama, Petraeus, Biden, and Clinton," Maliki says, "but they all thought Bashar would only last two or three months." He says he tried to negotiate with Sunni leaders in western Iraq, but they believed that their moment had come. "Negotiations failed," he says. "Their slogans were: 'We are coming to Baghdad! You are not Muslims! You are not Arabs! You are Persians! Leave Baghdad!'" Maliki has an interest in playing down his own responsibility for the rise of Isis and the fall of Mosul, but it is true that from 2011 onwards, Iraqi leaders were saying that if the civil war in Syria continued it would destabilise Iraq.

The rebellion has now been defeated in both countries as Isis is squeezed out of its last strongholds. The Sunni in Iraq and Syria may not have been responsible for the rise of IS, but they will suffer the consequences of its defeat. Saudi Arabia, Qatar, and Turkey gave essential support to the anti-government forces in Syria without caring much if they were al-Qaeda clones. All three have now retreated from the war, with Turkey focusing on blocking the Syrian Kurds from getting their own state and Saudi Arabia correctly but hypocritically—since the Saudis did the same—accusing Qatar of funding terrorism in Syria and elsewhere. Suddenly the wars in Iraq and Syria are coming to an end. Iraq is on good terms with all its neighbours. The cycles of conflict that have torn Iraq apart for so long may soon be over.

Even if war has come to an end, Iraqis have been changed by it. In the Soviet Union, it used to be said that anybody over a certain age couldn't avoid having had an interesting life: they had experienced revolutions, invasions, civil wars, purges, and famines. Much the same is true of Iraqis over the age of forty, who since 1979 have lived through three foreign wars and at least half a dozen civil wars. Many, including the best educated, have fled abroad, joining an Iraqi diaspora that has spread all over the world. There are signs of regression, such as the introduction in parliament of a bill that would legalise the marriage of girls over the age of eight. Qasim Sabti, the owner of the Hewar, the last private art gallery in Baghdad, told me that material reconstruction may come, but it won't be enough. "It will take a century for us to recover," he says, "however many shopping malls they build."

29 June 2018
Iraq has put to death thirteen people convicted of terrorism offences hours after Prime Minister Haider al-Abadi ordered the execution of hundreds of prisoners on death row in retaliation for the killing by Isis of eight members of the security forces. The hangings are aimed at quelling public anger over signs that Isis is re-emerging as a threat after the group showed eight captives, who were badly bruised and looked as if they had been severely beaten, on a video last weekend and said that they would be killed unless Sunni women prisoners were released by the government within three days. The government says that autopsies on the bodies of dead men, six of whom belonged to the logistics department of the Hashd al-Shaabi, showed that they were shot and killed before this deadline expired. Iraqi security forces now have good intelligence about Isis plans and person-nel after luring back to Iraq five senior Isis leaders it had captured and interrogated.

Isis advances are mainly in Diyala, Salahuddin, and Kirkuk provinces north of Baghdad, where Isis fighters can often recruit local guides from Sunni displaced from their villages who are looking to return. Ahmed

Abdul Jabbar al-Kraiym, head of the Salahuddin provincial council, said at a press conference this week that dozens of people have been killed and kidnapped in Salahudin. He warned of "a catastrophic situation in the province if the government does not deal with the increasing presence of Daesh militants, as some families have started to leave their homes because of the extremist militants." Blaming the government and security forces for the deterioration of the security situation in his province, Mr. Kraiym said that the security forces "are busy with smuggling fuel and taking bribes from the citizens at checkpoints, while neglecting the security file."

The kidnapping on the main road north of Baghdad and the discovery of the eight mutilated bodies, which were booby-trapped with explosives, is reawakening fears that political leaders have been diverted from finishing off Isis by the jockeying for power by different parties before and after the general election in May. To prove that it is reacting forcefully, the Iraqi authorities for the first time on Friday released pictures of the condemned men, dressed in yellow or black, blindfolded and facing a wall with their wrists handcuffed behind their backs, as well as a picture of the actual hanging.

Earlier, Mr. Abadi had called for "just retribution" against all prisoners sentenced to death for terrorism who had exhausted the appeals process. The government has not said how many prisoners might be executed, but the number on death row is reported to number 300, of whom 100 are foreign women convicted of belonging to Isis. The number for those already executed is also unknown, according to Belkis Wille, the Baghdad-based senior Iraq and Qatar researcher for Human Rights Watch. She said that a serious concern is that "the vast majority of cases rely solely on confessions and that torture is extensively practised to extract these confessions."

She said that despite this, lawyers for the accused have told her that appeals against death sentences on the grounds that the accused were tortured into confessing are almost always rejected by the courts.

2 July 2018

"I once rescued a friend from drowning when he was swept away by the force of the current as we were swimming in the Diyala River," says Qasim Sabti, a painter and gallery owner in Baghdad. "That was fifty years ago," he recalls. "I went back there recently and the water in the Diyala is so shallow today that a man could walk across it with his dog."

The rivers of Iraq, above all the Tigris and Euphrates, are drying up. The country is becoming more arid, and desertification is eating into the limited amount of agricultural land. Dams built upriver in Turkey, Syria, and Iran since the 1970s have reduced the flow of water that reaches Iraq by as much as half and the situation is about to get worse. On 1 July, Turkey will start filling the Ilisu Dam on the Tigris and this will cause another decline in the inflows to our country of about 50 percent," says Hassan Janabi, minister of water resources. He says that Iraq used to get thirty billion cubic metres from the Euphrates, but now "we are happy if we get sixteen billion cubic metres."

As Iraq begins to recover from forty years of wars and emergencies, its existence is being threatened by the rapidly falling water levels in the two great rivers on which its people depend. It was on their banks that the first cities were established 8,000 years ago and where the flood stories of Gilgamesh and the Bible were first told. Such floods are now a thing of the past—the last was in 1988—and each year the amount of water taken by Iraq's neighbours has been rising. This pattern started in the 1970s when Turkey and Syria built dams on the Euphrates for hydroelectric power and vast irrigation works. It is the latter which choke off the water supply to Iraq. The same thing happened a little later to the Tigris, whose major tributaries are being dammed by Iran. Iraqi protests have been ineffectual because Saddam Hussein and the successor government in Baghdad were preoccupied by wars and crises that appeared more important at the time. By now it is getting too late to reverse the disastrous impact on Iraq of this massive loss of water.

"This summer is going to be tough," says Mr. Janabi, a water resources engineer by training who was in charge of restoring the marshes in southern Iraq after 2003. Some smaller rivers like the Karun and Kark that used to flow out of Iran into Iraq have simply disappeared after the Iranians diverted them. He says: "We used to get five billion cubic metres annually from the Karkhah, and now we get zero." Iraq was once self-sufficient in food, but now imports 70 percent of its needs. Locally grown watermelons and tomatoes are for sale beside the road or in the markets, but most of what Iraqis eat comes from Iran or Turkey or is purchased by the government on the world market. This amount is set to increase this year because the filling of the Ilisu Dam in Turkey is forcing the Iraqi government to restrict the growing of rice and wheat by farmers in order to conserve water used for irrigation. This man-made drought is only the latest blow to hit Iraqi farmers.

Imad Naja, a returned colonel in the Iraqi air force, inherited his small family farm near Awad al-Hussein village outside Taji fifteen years ago, where he at first grew wheat and other crops as well as taking up beekeeping and fish farming. He produced half a ton of honey a year and dug a fish pond close to his house. "I feel sad that I put so much work into my farm and look at it now," he says, explaining that three-quarters of his land is no longer cultivated because it cannot be irrigated. Mr. Naja grows alfalfa for sale as animal feed in the remainder, but his beehives lie discarded in one corner of his garden and there are no fish in the pond. He makes more money from hiring out a football pitch he has built behind a high-wire fence than he does from agriculture. "I get some water from a well that we drilled ourselves, but it is salty." Iraq has a complex network of irrigation channels built over the last century to carry water from the Tigris and Euphrates. One such channel, named 43, runs close to Mr. Naja's house and, on the day we visited, was full of muddy water that comes from the Tigris. Mr. Naja says this may look good, but he is only getting the water for two days each fortnight, which is not enough to cultivate all his land. "I could manage if I got water for seven days out of fourteen but not less," he says.

As with everything else in Iraq, security or the lack of it plays a central role in the villages around Taji. This is a Sunni area which used to be a stronghold of al-Qaeda in Iraq and later of Isis. Mr. Naja had been the local leader of al-Sahwah, the paramilitary Sunni movements allied to the US against al-Qaeda a dozen years ago. As Isis advanced south after capturing Mosul in 2014, Taji was heavily fought over, with checkpoints blocking the roads and making travel dangerous. Mr. Naja looks relaxed about his own security, but he has moved his wife and five sons and daughters to Erbil, not only for their safety but because he wants his children to go to good schools not available locally. The problem is that Erbil used to be two hours' drive from Taji, but clashes between Kurdish and government forces last year cut the main road and he has to make a long diversion, so the trip now takes six hours. Nevertheless, Mr. Naja is planning to restock his fish pond.

Can anything be done by Iraq to cope with Iraq's chronic shortage of water? The government does not have enough political leverage in Turkey and Iran to get a greater share of the water which previously flowed into Iraq. Mr. Janabi shows a report on how to successfully manage water in Iraq over the next twenty years. It is a hefty volume, but he said that it is merely the introduction to a complete study of the water crisis that weighs thirty-five kilos. This apparently explains how Iraq's water problems could be alleviated, though at a cost of $184 billion (£140 billion) that the government does not have.

Iraqis are all too aware that the failing supply of water is changing the very appearance of their country. Mr. Sabti has just opened an art exhibition in Baghdad in which ninety landscape paintings by Iraqi artists show pastoral views of rivers, lakes, marshes, palm groves, crops, and vegetation. "We need to preserve the memory of these places before the Tigris and Euphrates dry up," he explains. "Some of them will disappear next year because there will be no water."

4 July 2018

"We are very much scared," says Hamid Aftan al-Hammad, an Albu Nimr tribesman from the city of Hit in western Iraq. "At night we lie on the roofs of our houses with our weapons waiting to be attacked again." He fears the return of Isis, which massacred at least 864 members of his tribe when they controlled the area where they live—a city a hundred miles west of Baghdad in the middle of the vast Sunni Arab province of Anbar, which sprawls across western Iraq.

Mr. Hammad points to a patch of open ground between the palm trees on the far bank of the Euphrates River, which divides Hit. "It was there that they killed forty-five of our people," he says, going on to list those members of his immediate family who were murdered, including two teenage cousins executed in the main square of the city and two uncles who tried to escape into the desert but have disappeared and are assumed to have been captured and killed by Isis. Compared even to the many other Isis atrocities, the hunting down of the Albu Nimr, a pro-government Sunni tribe, was relentless and genocidal. Sala Segur Omar al-Nimr, a teacher who lived through the final months of his tribe's resistance, described how they dug trenches and built sand barriers in a hopeless attempt to defend themselves, but it was not enough. They faced thousands of better armed Isis fighters. When resistance finally collapsed in October 2014, those who could not flee fast enough "were slaughtered, many of them elderly, disabled, or very young children. They even killed our farm animals."

There is little violence today in Hit, a city with a population of 90,000. But the hatred and fear generated by the savage rule of Isis still divides its people. Borhan Khalil, a local journalist, says that "there is still this division between pro- and anti-Isis families." Foreign fighters may have belonged to Isis, but the great majority were locals and longtime neighbours of those they killed. Mr. Khalil says that families whose houses were blown up by Isis—often because they had worked for the Iraqi government—have frequently taken over, with official approval, the houses of Isis supporters who have since fled. This is a further cause of anger and division.

The change of ownership is announced by messages scrawled on the outside wall of a house. One such message by a gate in central Hit reads: "This is the house of the fleeing terrorists now occupied by Fuad and his brother." Inside the house, which looks spacious and well kept, Haitham al-Ad al-Nimr, a member of the government security services, and his brother Fuad have been living there since they took it over a year ago. "Our own house was completely demolished by Isis," says Mr. Nimr, who denies that he knows the identity of the people he has replaced. He explains that "they had fled long before we got here." He is not worried by the prospect of the dispossessed trying to take their property back one day, or of Isis launching a successful counteroffensive in Anbar. Others are not so sanguine: Hamid Aftan al-Hammad, whom we met when he was about to cross the Euphrates in a boat because the bridge had been destroyed, says Isis families whose sons had been fighters were coming back to the area and, even if the fighters were not with them, they "will still back their sons."

The Iraqi government is trying to defuse the issue of what happens to families with a record of supporting Isis in the past, but without much success. This is particularly true in Hit, where the Albu Nimr reckon they lost about 1,000 people, with the same number of disappeared, shot in the desert as they tried to escape, or had their bodies thrown down wells. Mr. Hammad is enraged that two of his brothers had been thrown out of a house they had taken over and were now living in tents because a family they alleged were Isis supporters had now reoccupied it. He says they deserved better from a government they had fought for: "One of my brothers has a crippled arm and lost three fingers when he was shot by an Isis sniper."

Why was Isis so determined to wipe out this particular tribe? Isis certainly wanted to show that any resistance to them would provoke pitiless revenge. The Albu Nimr were an obvious target because their tribesmen had joined the army and police after the US-led invasion of 2003. They did so at a time when the other Sunni tribes of Anbar were at the heart of resistance to the US occupation and the Shia-dominated government in Baghdad. As Isis made its spectacular advance in 2014, the Albu Nimr were isolated, outgunned, and outnumbered.

Asked why Isis had been able to win so quickly, one of the Albu Nimr tribal leaders, Sheikh Na'eem al-Gu-ood, told me in March 2015 that "the main reason is that 90 percent of the tribes in Anbar collaborated with Isis or joined them except for ourselves." By that time, he said that 864 Albu Nimr members had been killed. Once Isis seized Mosul and the Iraqi army in northern Iraq disintegrated, the jihadis were able to capture plenty of heavy weapons. The Albu Nimr say they begged the government and the Americans for arms and air strikes but received nothing. Well-off people in Hit were able to flee but those without money were forced to stay and endure Isis rule. They say this was so cruel and murderous that Isis lost its popular support. Mr. Khalil believes that everybody in Anbar—and not just the Albu Nimr—would today fight Isis because "Isis denounces everybody in government-held Iraq, which these days is almost the whole country, as infidels who deserve to be killed, so nobody wants them back."

This is comforting, but Isis is a fanatical militarised cult that has never sought popularity and spreads its faith through force. The terror it inspired in the past still lives on: a small surge in Isis killings and kidnappings in recent weeks reverberated throughout Iraq. People in Hit say they have confidence in the Iraqi army as non-sectarian, but they know that Sunni Arabs are regarded with suspicion. "As soon as I travel outside Anbar and show my Anbar ID at a checkpoint, I am held for hours," says one source.

7 July 2018

Iraqis disagree about many things but on one topic they are united: they believe they live in the most corrupt country in the world, barring a few where there is nothing much to steal. They see themselves as victims of a kleptomaniac state where hundreds of billions of dollars have disappeared into the pockets of the ruling elite over the past fifteen years, while everybody else endures shortages of everything from jobs and houses to water and electricity.

The popular rage against the political class that came to power in 2003 explains why the movement led by the populist-nationalist cleric Muqtada al-Sadr, which demands political and social reform and is allied to the Iraqi Communist Party, topped the poll in the parliamentary election in May. But the low turnout of 44.5 percent underlined a conviction on the part of many that nothing much is going to change, whatever the makeup of the next government—something still being patched together in snail's pace negotiations between the parties. "Even friends of mine who did vote are disillusioned and say they will not vote again," one Baghdad resident told me. It is impossible to exaggerate the frustration of Iraqis who know they live in a potentially rich country, the second-largest oil producer in OPEC, but see its wealth being stolen in front of their eyes year after year.

I was in Ramadi looking at the war damage when I met Muthafar Abdul Ghafur, sixty-four, a retired engineer who had just finished rebuilding his house which had been destroyed in an air strike. "I did it all myself and got no compensation from the government," he said, adding bitterly that some whose houses were largely intact had received compensation because, unlike him, they bribed the right officials. "Write that Iraq has no government!" he shouted at me. "It has only thieves!" Back in Baghdad, I visited the upper-middle-class districts of Mansour and Yarmouk to talk to a real estate dealer, Safwat Abdul Razaq, who said he was doing good business. The price of property in this area had doubled in the past two years, but he was less optimistic about the future because of the weak government and, above all, because of the pervasive state corruption. "The government has no credibility," he said. "Wherever you go, they ask you for a bribe." He added that a contractor invariably had to pay off officials to win a contract and one of the three businessmen sitting in the office said that this could easily be 50 percent of the contract price. There was plenty of private money in Iraq, but little of it was invested there because corruption made any business activity insecure: "that is why I buy property in Jordan but not in Iraq."

These are well-off people, but I heard the same complaints in the Shia working-class stronghold of Sadr City, where heaps of rubbish lie uncollected in the streets. "The young people are a lost generation, who can't afford to get married because they have no jobs and no prospects unless they know somebody in the government," said a local paramilitary. Water and electricity were in short supply and expensive to buy privately. Grotesque examples of official theft have been frequent since a new class of leaders, mostly Shia and Kurdish, took power in Iraq after the US invasion. When the Iraqi government was supposedly fighting for its life militarily in 2004–2005, the entire $1.3 billion (£980 million) military procurement budget disappeared. A few years later, police at checkpoints in Baghdad were trying to detect car bombs with a useless device that cost a few dollars to make and which the government had bought for tens of thousands. How did successive Iraqi governments get away with such blatant thefts for so long? For years they diverted attention away from their looting of Iraq's oil revenues by claiming that the struggle against al-Qaeda in Iraq and later Isis was the only thing that mattered. They appealed to the sectarian solidarity of the Shia and, in northern Iraq, to the ethnic solidarity of the Kurds.

But a year after Isis suffered a decisive defeat in the siege of Mosul, these excuses no longer work. Security is better than at any time since the fall of Saddam Hussein, so Iraqis are more conscious than ever before of the failings of a parasitic leadership and a semi-functional state machine. A word of caution here: Iraqis like to think of their country as uniquely cursed by corruption with billions of dollars paid to shell companies for projects in which not a single brick is placed on top of another. But Iraq is not alone in this since all the states whose wealth is drawn entirely from the exploitation of their natural resources—usually oil—operate similarly. In each case, members of a predatory ruling elite—from Angola to Saudi Arabia and Iraq—plug into state revenues and grab as much as they can get their claws on.

Obscenely excessive expenditure by the ruling circles in these countries is notorious, but they are not the sole beneficiaries. All these resource-rich states have vast patronage systems whereby a large chunk of the population gets jobs, or receives salaries, though no work may be necessary. Iraqis and Saudis may denounce corruption at the top but millions of them have a stake in the system, which gives it a certain stability. In Iraq, for instance, some 4.5 million Iraqis work for the state and these are the plum jobs that others would like to have. Though political leaders in Baghdad talk about reforming this system, it is politically dangerous to do so because the networks of corruption and patronage established themselves too long ago and involve too many powerful people and parties. "Anti-corruption campaigns"—in Iraq as in Saudi Arabia—are often just one group of super-rich trying to displace another. The patronage system is the only way that many Iraqis and Saudis get a share of the oil revenues and they will resist being deprived of this in the supposed interest of creating a more functional system.

In Iraq, the mechanics of corruption operate in a slightly different way than elsewhere because of the role of the political parties. Mudher Salih, a financial adviser to Prime Minister Abadi, told me that "unless the political system is changed it is impossible to fight corruption." He said that the reason for this is that parties use the government ministries they control as cash cows and patronage machines through which they sustain their power. This way of doing things is probably too ingrained, and in the interests of too many people, to be radically changed.

Corruption cannot be eliminated in Iraq, but it can be made less destructive. When Abadi became prime minister in 2014, Isis was advancing on Baghdad and oil prices were well. Salih said that in response to the crisis the government "cut expenditure by 37 percent by removing 'fishy' items— money being spent for nothing at all." Corruption will stay, but in the future, Iraqis can at least hope to get something for their money.

28 September 2019

It about midnight on 20 September, a young man got off a white minibus at the entrance to the Shia shrine city and pilgrimage centre of Karbala, south-west of Baghdad. A few minutes later, he pressed a remote control, detonating the explosives he had left in a bag under his seat on the bus. The bomb killed twelve people and injured a further five: footage shows the bus engulfed in flames and a voice screaming that "people are dying." Iraqi security sources say that the alleged bomber was swiftly identified from CCTV pictures and was arrested with two other men, whose families hail from the Sunni town of Jurf al-Sakhar. Isis claimed responsibility for the attack.

The bombing made an impact out of proportion to its size because, for the last two years, Iraqi cities have been largely free from the devastating bombings by Isis, the worst of which once killed hundreds of civilians at a time. The latest attack is a sign that Isis is not completely destroyed and is trying to rebuild its strength. "They have lost their territory, but they still have core supporters," says Ali al-Talkani, a researcher at the Centre for Security in Karbala. "They will try to win back the support of those who were temporarily Isis at the height of its power."

Among those whom it particularly seeks to recruit are those from Sunni communities that suffered badly during the ferocious civil war that raged in Iraq between about 2013 and 2017 and which has left a legacy of deprivation and hatred. It is this legacy that makes the place of origin of the three-member Isis cell that allegedly carried out the Karbala bombing so significant. Jurf al-Sakhar, which once had a population of 90,000, was one of the few Sunni towns south of Baghdad and was notorious as a stronghold of al-Qaeda and later of Isis. They exploited its strategic position close to Baghdad and on the main route to Shia southern Iraq to launch bomb attacks in the capital and against Shia targets in and around Karbala.

The town was stormed by Shia paramilitary groups in 2014 and the entire Sunni population was expelled—many families who had once owned large farms being reduced over the last five years to living in shacks or being packed into a single room. Jurf al-Sakhar became a ghost town, largely occupied by hard-line Shia militias. Its inhabitants have long been asking for permission to go home, but this basic privilege is unlikely to be granted any time soon. The representatives of the majority Shia population in surrounding Hilla province, much relieved that Isis no longer has a territorial base close to them, have threatened legal action against any politician who calls for the people of Jurf al-Saakhar to be allowed to return to their old town.

People living in Karbala say that at least the latest bombing did not penetrate the city's outer defences. A crucial test of security will come in the next few weeks as millions of Shia pilgrims from all over the world take part in the Arbaeen religious walk to Karbala. The gigantic columns of marchers waving religious flags are vulnerable to bombers but have been relatively safe in recent years because of tight security. Karbala itself is in the middle of a construction boom, with cranes everywhere, particularly around the shrines to Imam al-Hussein and Imam al-Abbas, whose golden domes and walls covered with mosaics dominate the centre of the city. Officials say that "we have to build places to stay for the millions of people who come to the shrine." As a result, construction machinery is everywhere and there are giant holes in the ground where foundations for hotels and hostels are being built.

The shrines employ great numbers of black-clad young men—15,000 at the Imam Hussein shrine and 7,000 at the al-Abbas shrine—to safely shepherd the great masses of pilgrims from place to place. They do not always do so with success: on 10 September, a stampede by crowds at the entrance to the Imam Hussein shrine left thirty-one crushed to death and 100 injured. It happened during Ashura, the climax of the commemoration of the death of Imam Hussein and his family, when a traditional run called the Twareej takes place over the last hundred metres before the pilgrims enter the shrine. On this occasion, an old man tripped and fell just by the al-Raja gate. The crowd was particularly dense as only two of the shrine's doors were open—construction work meant the other eight were closed or inaccessible, leaving pilgrims trapped in the narrow entrance.

The physical expansion of the shrines of Karbala and the millions of pilgrims from the rest of Iraq, and from across the Shia world, marks the triumph of the Shia majority in Iraq since the US invasion overthrew Saddam Hussein. In 1991, the Shia shrines in Karbala were the last bastion of resistance against Saddam as his tanks and Republican Guard stamped out the Shia uprising with massacres and destruction. Iraqi tanks—British Challengers captured from Iran during the Iran-Iraq War—were positioned outside the shrines and Iraqi soldiers were encamped within its precincts, where they put up pictures of Saddam to celebrate their victory.

Almost thirty years later, it is the loss of Sunni towns like Jurf al-Sakhar, and the partial destruction of Sunni cities like Mosul, which are the main feature of the new order of things in Iraq. Even if there are more Isis bombings like the one in Karbala last weekend, this order will not change.

30 September 2019

Lieutenant General Abdul Wahab al-Saadi was the great Iraqi military hero of the war against Isis, leading the assault on Mosul, which recaptured the de facto Isis capital after a nine-month siege in 2017. But at the weekend, he was suddenly removed as the commander of the Counter Terrorism Service shock troops by Prime Minister Adel Abdul-Mahdi. He was instead given what the general considered to be a non-job at the Defence Ministry.

Saadi has refused to accept the move against him and described his new posting as an "insult" and a "punishment." His effective demotion has provoked a wave of popular support for arguably Iraq's most esteemed general, on the streets as well as on social media. "He won the people's friendship but the politicians' hatred," reads one slogan being shared online; another warns that "there is no longer any room for a patriot in this country." His removal is all the more significant because it takes place at a time when there is an intense struggle for influence in Iraq between the US and Iran. This tension is leading to fears, almost certainly exaggerated, that it could escalate into armed conflict.

There is uncertainty over why exactly Saadi was removed: one interpretation for the sidelining is that he was considered to be too close to the Americans by pro-Iran factions, but a more convincing motive may have been his aggressive campaign against corruption in the CTS which had reportedly alienated other senior officers. The military corruption in the CTS took its usual shape in the Iraqi armed forces of money for food and other supplies being diverted into private pockets, soldiers paying kickbacks to avoid fighting in the front line, or being permanently AWOL. Corruption became more rampant when the CTS recaptured the oil city of Kirkuk from the Kurds on 17 October 2017, after which some CTS officers worked with others in positions of authority to sell oil on the black market.

Some Iraqi commentators agree that Saadi was unfairly treated, but argue that he himself was in the wrong by refusing to accept his orders from the prime minister. "He made a huge mistake in going on television to denounce the decision," says Abbas Khadim, director of the Iraq Initiative at the Atlantic Council. But Khadim, currently in Baghdad, says that it is too crude to analyse all political developments in Iraq as being tied to the Iran-US confrontation. However, if the simmering tensions do descend into armed conflict, then Iraq would be one of the battlefields where it will be fought out, so the final loyalties of the armed forces, regular and irregular, will be of importance.

In addition to the turmoil over Saadi's dismissal as head of the CTS, there is an ongoing struggle over control of the Hashd al-Shaabi. Comprising some thirty different groups with a total of 65,000 to 85,000 fighters, many of the Hashd groups have a history which far predates the ascent of Isis. The Hashd as a whole is to be more closely integrated into the regular armed forces as of 30 September, under a decree issued by the prime minister. This has led to disagreements within the Hashd coalition, which is strongly represented in parliament, as to how far they should give up their autonomy. The US, Saudi Arabia, and the Gulf states have traditionally seen the Hashd as being Iranian proxies, though this view is incorrect or, at best, overly simplistic, according to experts on the movement.

Some groups such as the Kata'ib Hezbollah openly look to Iran as the leader of resistance to the US, Israel, and the Gulf states and says it will attack US bases in Iraq if there is a US-Iran war. But most of the Hashd has never been a proxy of Iran and its soldiers are paid by the Iraqi state. This money used to go to the leaders of the different armed factions in the coalition, but is now paid directly to their men. "That makes a big difference," says one Hashd official, because it means that Hashd fighters will owe their loyalty to the state and be less closely bound to different groups and commanders as their paymasters. "It is a mistake to think that there is somehow an 'Iranian Iraq' and an 'American Iraq,'" says Qais al-Khazali, the leader of Asa'ib Ahl al-Haq, once seen as under the control of Iran, in an interview with me.

Dr. Khadim agrees, saying that Washington's obsession with the Hashd as being the long arm of Iran is self-fulfilling. He believes that the US has unwisely promoted the Hashd as the biggest problem of the Iraqi government, which it is not true—he says the biggest problem for Iraqis is getting an adequate supply of electricity. But American pressure to dissolve or otherwise marginalise the Hashd could create a problem similar to those which arose when the US occupation authorities had the disastrous idea of dissolving the Iraqi army after the 2003 invasion: "suddenly you had 400,000 angry trained soldiers on the streets."

Turmoil in the Iraqi security forces, either in the senior ranks of the CTS with the removal of Saadi or over the future of the Hashd, could open the door to the re-emergence of Isis. Without the tens of thousands of experienced Hashd soldiers, regular government forces would be hard-pressed to prevent an Isis comeback due to a lack of numbers and well-trained units. Iraq has been largely quiet since the fall of Mosul, but the peace is still fragile.

PART IX. TURKEY INVADES ROJAVA

Mass expulsion or the physical extermination of an entire ethnic or religious community—ethnic cleansing—is usually treated by the media in one of two different ways: either it receives maximum publicity as a horror story about which the world should care and do something about, or it is ignored and never reaches the news agenda.

It appeared at first that the ethnic cleansing of the Kurds by Turkey after its invasion of northern Syria on 9 October 2019 would belong to the first category. There was an angry condemnation of the forced displacement of 190,000 Kurds living close to the Syrian-Turkish border as Turkish soldiers, preceded by the Syrian National Army (SNA), in reality, ill-disciplined anti-Kurdish Islamist militiamen, advanced into Kurdish-held areas. Videos showed fleeing Kurdish civilians being dragged from their cars and shot by the side of the road and reporters visiting hospitals saw children dying from the effects of white phosphorus that eats into the flesh and had allegedly been delivered in bombs or shells dropped or fired by the advancing Turkish forces.

People wonder why armies with complete military superiority should resort to such horrific weapons that are both illegal under international law or, at the very least, guarantee the user a lot of bad publicity. The explanation often is that "terror" weapons are deployed deliberately to terrify the civilian population into taking flight.

In the case of the Turkish invasion of Syria, the motive is not a matter of speculation: William V. Roebuck, a US diplomat stationed in north-east Syria at the time, wrote an internal memo about what he was seeing for the State Department that later leaked. It is one of the best-informed analyses of what happened and is titled: "Present at the Catastrophe: Standing By as Turks Cleanse Kurds in Northern Syria and De-Stabilise our D-Isis [sic] Platform in the Northeast."

Roebuck, with access to US intelligence about Turkish intentions, has no doubt that Ankara would like to expel the 1.8 million Kurds living in their semi-independent state of Rojava. He says: "Turkey's military operation in northern Syria, spearheaded by armed Islamist groups on its payroll, represents an…effort at ethnic cleansing, relying on widespread military conflict targeting part of the Kurdish heartland along the border and benefiting from several widely publicised, fear-inducing atrocities these forces committed."

Later in the memo, Roebuck notes that the SNA irregulars had formerly been allied to al-Qaeda and Isis and that Turkish President Recep Tayyip Erdogan had openly broadcast, in a speech at the UN, Turkey's intention to fill de-populated Kurdish areas with Syrian Arabs from other parts of Syria who are currently refugees in Turkey. Roebuck's reference to the extreme jihadi links of the SNA is certainly correct since its members have videoed themselves denouncing Sunni Muslim Kurds, Yazidis, and Christians as infidels along with threats to kill members of the People's Protection Units that lost 11,000 dead fighting Isis in a coalition with the US.

October 2019

9 October 2019

In a field beside a disused railway station on the plain just south of the Syrian-Turkish frontier, a brigade of Syrian Kurdish soldiers were retraining in order to resist an invasion by the Turkish army. "We acted like a regular army when we were fighting Daesh," Rojvan, a veteran Kurdish commander of the YPG, told me. "But now it is we who may be under Turkish air attack and we will have to behave more like guerrillas."

Rojvan and his men had just returned from fighting Isis for forty-five days in their last strongholds in eastern Syria. I had met him first in a cemetery in Qamishli, where he was burying one of his men who had been killed by an Isis rocket when driving a bulldozer to build field fortifications in the middle of a battle. But now he and his men were learning new tactics to combat the Turkish military units that were beginning to mass on the Turkish side of the border. Rojvan was a very experienced soldier and not given to false optimism, saying: "We are mainly armed with light weapons like the Kalashnikov and the RPG launcher and light machine guns, but we will be resisting tanks and aircraft."

Rojvan was speaking eighteen months ago after the Turkish army and its Syrian Arab allies had invaded the Syrian Kurdish enclave of Afrin, forced most of its inhabitants to flee, and was preparing to replace them with Arab settlers. What happened then may have been a preview of what we are about to see repeated on a much wider scale in north-east Syria after President Trump's incoherent announcement that the US would not stand in the way of a Turkish invasion. He has rowed back a little on this in the face of a deluge of criticism, but his basic message—that the US wants out, and does not object to the Turks coming in—has developed its own momentum and will be difficult to stop at this stage.

We are already on the downslope leading to the ethnic cleansing of up to two million Kurds in the vast triangle of land which the Kurds call Rojava in north-east Syria. Much of the Kurdish population lives in cities and towns like Qamishli, Kobani, and Tal Abyad just south of the Syrian-Turkish frontier. They are unlikely to wait to see what a Turkish occupation, backed by bands of Syrian Arab paramilitaries with links to al-Qaeda type groups, is like. Trump's support for America's Kurdish allies was always rickety, but the brazenness of the final betrayal is still breathtaking. All the credit for defeating Isis is given to US forces under Trump's wise leadership, while in reality, the US role was almost entirely confined to air strikes and artillery fire.

Speaking of the Kurdish role as the military core of the SDF in the crucial battle for Raqqa, Brett McGurk, the former presidential envoy to the anti-Isis coalition, says on Twitter: "The SDF suffered thousands of casualties in the Raqqa battle. Not a single American life was lost." Overall, 11,000 Syrian Kurds were killed fighting Isis over the last five years. McGurk denies that the Kurds ever received lavish supplies of military hardware from the US: "The weapons provided were meagre and just enough for the battle against Isis. (The SDF cleared IEDs by purchasing flocks of sheep.)"

Since 2015 I have been visiting Rojava watching the YPG soldiers advance west and south and always wondering what would happen when Isis was defeated and the US did not need them anymore. The Kurds, who are no political neophytes, wondered the same thing, but there was little they could do to change the direction of events, except hope that the US would not entirely let them down. It seems that, in the event, their most pessimistic assumptions are being fulfilled, though—such is the nature of the Trump White House—the extent of American betrayal is unclear.

The most important feature by far of the US military presence in Syria is airpower and not the small number of troops on the ground. Will the US maintain an air umbrella over Rojava and, if so, does this mean that the Turks will not be able to deploy their air force against the YPG? If this is indeed the case, it will give the 25,000 battle-hardened YPG troops more of a military option, though, even so, their chances of long-term success are limited. It is unclear how far the Turks will advance: their attack could at first be in a limited area between the towns of Tal Abyad and Ras al-Ayn. But the White House statement spoke of Turkey taking responsibility for Isis prisoners, most of whom are in a camp at al-Hol that is deep inside Rojava, close to the Iraqi border. Taking over this would mean the Turks seizing much of north-east Syria.

Do the Kurds have any political options? The only obvious one—supposing the Kurdish alliance with the US to be a broken reed—is to look to President Bashar al-Assad and to Russia. The Kurds do not like the Syrian government, which persecuted and marginalised them for years before 2011, but they do prefer them to Turkish control and probable expulsion. The problem here is that the Kurds may have left it too late. So long as they were allied to the US, they could not seriously negotiate with Damascus. Now they appear to have the worst of all possible worlds: neither Washington nor Moscow nor Damascus is going to protect them. But the options were never quite as simple as that: the Syrian army has never been strong enough to fight Turkey. Presidents Putin and Assad do not want a Turkish invasion, but they will also be glad to see the back of the American forces.

Rojava could swiftly disintegrate under the impact of a Turkish incursion. A scramble for its territory is already beginning: Syrian and Turkish army units are reportedly racing each other to take over Manbij. A new chaotic phase in the Syrian war is beginning.

11 October 2019

"Never get into a well with an American rope" goes the saying spreading across the Middle East, as the US abandons its Kurdish allies in Syria to a Turkish invasion force. People in the region are traditionally cynical about the loyalty of great powers to their local friends, but even they are shocked by the speed and ruthlessness with which Donald Trump greenlit the Turkish attack.

According to the UN and human rights groups, tens of thousands of Kurdish refugees are in flight from their border towns and are being targeted by Turkish air strikes and artillery fire. Most leaders contemplating ethnic cleansing keep quiet about it, but Turkey's President Erdogan is openly declaring that he will settle two million Syrian Arab refugees from other parts of Syria on Kurdish lands (he says he's discovered that the land is not really Kurdish).

Every news dispatch from the new war zone is full of ironies. Trump says that Turkey will be responsible for securing the thousands of Isis prisoners held by the Kurdish People's Protection Units. But Brett McGurk, as the former presidential adviser to the anti-Isis coalition—and the source for the saying about the unreliability of US rope—notes that in the past it was Turkey which had rejected "any serious cooperation on Isis even as 40k foreign fighters flowed through its territory into Syria." Other ironies are still to come. At about the same moment that the Turkish army was crossing the Syrian frontier to attack the YPG on Wednesday, these Kurdish forces were under attack from a different enemy: in the former de facto Isis capital of Raqqa, two Isis fighters with automatic rifles, grenades, and suicide belts opened fire on the YPG, who have controlled the city since they captured it from Isis in 2017. On this occasion, the two Isis men were surrounded by the YPG, who ultimately came out on top. But in future, their soldiers—it is absurd to call them militiamen since they are some of the most experienced soldiers in the Middle East—will face a more difficult task. In addition to battling Isis at ground level, they will also have to scan the sky for hostile Turkish aircraft that are already hitting YPG positions to the north of Raqqa. Inevitably, parts of the old caliphate will soon start to slip back under Isis rule.

The resurgence of Isis and the fate of the thousands of Isis prisoners held by the YPG has been the focus of much self-centred speculation in the US and Europe. But this is only one consequence of the chaos brought about by the Turkish invasion; there will be no like-for-like replacement of Kurdish/American control with Turkish control. In this vast area—the 25 percent of Syria that lies east of the Euphrates—Turkey will be a big player, but it will not be an all-powerful one. It may try to carve its way through north-east Syria salami-style, one slice at a time, though this will still have a great effect on the Kurds since 500,000 of them live close to the border. In effect, the frontier between Turks and Kurds will simply be pushed further south and will be a great deal hotter than it was before. In other words, the inevitable outcome of President Trump greenlighting the Turkish action—in this case, the absence of a red light was the same as a green one—is a fragmentation of power. This fragmentation will clear an ideal breeding ground for a renewed Isis, and the attack in Raqqa mentioned above is evidence that this rebirth is already beginning.

Another feature of the present crisis favours Isis and the al-Qaeda-type paramilitaries acting as Turkish proxies. Maps showing north-east Syria as

"Kurdish-controlled" mask the fact that the demographic balance between Arab and Kurd in this region is fairly equal. Ethnic rivalries and hatreds are the substance of local politics and will become even more venomous and decisive as communities have to choose between Turks and Kurds. It is this sort of broken political terrain in which Isis and al-Qaeda have traditionally flourished.

The balance of power in Syria has been changed by the Turkish invasion and by the American unwillingness or inability to stop it. Trump makes clear that he wants out of the Syrian war. "USA should never have been in Middle East," he tweeted this week. "The stupid endless wars, for us, are ending." Despite this, the world has been curiously slow to take his isolationism and dislike of military action seriously. When it comes to Syria, Trump's policy—though so incoherent that it is closer to a set of attitudes—may be treacherous towards the Kurds, but it contains a cold-hearted nugget of realism. The US position in Syria is weak and not really sustainable in the long term. Minimal US forces could not hope to indefinitely prop up a de facto Kurdish statelet squeezed between a hostile Turkey to the north and an almost equally hostile Syrian government to the south and west. The US foreign policy establishment may be aghast at Trump giving up on the Kurds and keen for him to instead confront Russia and President Assad of Syria. But this could only have been done with a much greater US military and political commitment—something that both Congress and the US public do not want.

McGurk is probably right in believing that sales of US rope as a means of escaping from deep wells will be sold at a heavy discount in the Middle East from now on. In the eyes of the rest of the world, the US has suffered a serious defeat in Syria. The sight of convoys of terrified Kurds in flight recalls pictures of desperate Vietnamese, who had worked so closely with the Americans, trying to escape Saigon in 1975. The Kurds were always privately cynical about their alliance with the US, but they believed they had no other option. Even so, they did not expect to be discarded quite so totally and abruptly. Yet it may be that the crudity and unfairness of US actions, and the furore this has provoked at home and abroad, will do the Syrian Kurds some good. Certainly, the anger expressed all round is in sharp contrast to the international disinterest when Turkey took over and ethnically cleansed the small Kurdish enclave of Afrin in north-west Syria last year.

But there is a broader lesson to be learned from the latest phase in the Syrian crisis. For a while, it seemed that the violence was ebbing as winners and losers emerged, but now a whole fresh cycle of Turkish-Kurd violence is beginning. It is only when all the multiple conflicts in Syria are brought to an end at about the same time that the country will cease to generate new crises.

14 October 2019

It is the endgame of the eight-year-old Syrian war: the Turkish-Kurd confrontation was the most serious crisis still to be resolved, something that is now happening in the cruellest way possible. The Turkish priority, which was to destroy anything even resembling self-determination for the two to three million Syrian Kurds, has been achieved. The Kurds have no option but to throw themselves into the embrace of Assad to protect themselves from a Turkish advance that is likely to mean ethnic cleansing for Kurds and has already created 130,000 displaced people. What is doubly sad about this is that Rojava was the only part of Syria in which the outcome of the 2011 uprising had produced an improved life for many people—particularly if you were a Kurd or a woman. In every other part of Syria, Mr. Assad's government and his opponents seemed to vie with each other in their violence and corruption.

Syrian army troops are racing to take up positions in Kurdish-controlled cities, towns, and villages before the Turkish army and its allied Arab militiamen can reach them. The idea is that Syrian soldiers will provide a *cordon sanitaire* to stop the Turkish advance. This would save Kobani, the Kurdish city at the western end of Rojava and Qamishli, the de facto Kurdish capital, 320 kilometres (200 miles) to the east. Syrian troops are establishing a presence in Hasakah, which Isis fought hard to capture, north of the oil fields that will now presumably come under Mr. Assad's control once again. Kurdish leaders say that their agreement with Damascus is only military and they will still have political control, but there is no doubt that the balance of power has swayed significantly and irrevocably towards the central government in Damascus. The Kurdish authorities will remain a strong force where they are the majority, but not in the middle Euphrates Valley, where they held Sunni Arab cities like Raqqa and Manbij. The Kurds could never have permanently held these areas where they were never accepted by the Arabs—the dislike was mutual.

"They have always been fascists around here," volunteered a Kurd to me as we drove into Raqqa last year. The Kurds have lost much but not everything: they still have a powerful army of 25,000 experienced YPG fighters that now presumably shift to the government side. Mr. Assad will have to pay some attention to what the Kurds want in terms of autonomy. It is the Kurds who will pay the greatest price for President Trump's decision two weeks ago to publicly abandon his YPG allies. But there is also a heavy cost to the US in terms of loss of trust on the part of others who have hitherto relied on Washington to support them. After seeing what happened to the Syrian Kurds, pro-American leaders around the world will wonder if the same thing might happen to them. Unsurprisingly, President Putin is currently receiving a particularly warm welcome on an official visit to Saudi Arabia. The discrediting of the US as a leader and an ally will have an immediate impact in the Middle East. President Trump was seeking to create a coalition to confront and exert "maximum pressure" on Iran, which he had accused of trying to spread its malign influence throughout the region. But the total failure of the US in Syria and the swift and frivolous abandonment of the Kurds makes the Iranians look like reliable friends and determined enemies by comparison. Washington was never going to have a success in Syria, but Mr. Trump's humiliating scuttle maximises the damage to US credibility.

And Russia will be a primary beneficiary of the latest events. It stuck by Mr. Assad since 2011, became his active military ally in 2015, and, instead of being sucked into the Syrian swamp as many had predicted, emerges on the winning side. This is the greatest Russian political and military success since before the collapse of the Soviet Union in 1991 and goes far to re-establish Moscow as a superpower. Russia is now seeking to re-establish Mr. Assad's authority over most of north-east Syria, while not offending its ally Turkey, close cooperation with which is one of Russia's gains from the Syrian war. It will most likely succeed: Turkey does not have the military forces to push far into the vast plains of this part of Syria. It has had a big success since its invasion started last week in bringing an end to Rojava. Anything more would be complicated and bring diminishing returns. There are flashpoints—like who will control the Syrian Arab city of Manbij, which has been a vital link between Mr. Assad's territory and the Kurdish held zone—but Turkey would be overplaying its hand to try to fight the Syrian government as well as the Kurds.

Another one of Syria's multiple civil wars has yet to play out: this is the fate of Idlib and the surrounding land, the last bastion of the Syrian armed opposition, where three million people are trapped and are under the Syrian government and Russian air and artillery attack. Turkey looks increasingly acquiescent in the gradual extinction of this enclave, so long as its population does not flee across the Turkish border and become refugees in Turkey. The Syrian government, Russia, and Iran are the main winners and the US and its allies the main losers. Among the latter are Saudi Arabia and the Sunni oil states of the Gulf that played a central role in the Syrian crisis between 2011 and 2015. They were committed to getting rid of Mr. Assad and rolling back Iranian influence and failed in both attempts. Saudi Arabia's influence in the region is bound to decline because of this indirect failure in Syria, but also because of its lack of success in Yemen and its vulnerability to Iranian-inspired pinprick attacks like the drone assault on its oil facilities on 14 September.

Syria became the arena in which conflicts that have little to do with Syria were fought out. In terms of world politics, President Trump has ensured that the US is emerging as the great loser, not least because of his erratic tweets over the last two weeks—accusing the Kurds of not taking part in the Normandy landings and other weird allegations—look ever more demented and self-destructive.

15 October 2019

Turkey's Syrian venture is rapidly turning sour from President Erdogan's point of view. The Turkish advance into the north-east is moving slowly, but Turkey's military options are becoming increasingly limited as the Syrian army, backed by Russia, moves into Kurdish-held cities and towns that might have been targeted by Turkish forces. It is unlikely that Mr. Erdogan will risk taking on Syrian government troops, even if they are thin on the ground if this involves quarrelling with Russia. In the seven days since he launched Operation Peace Spring, Turkey has become more diplomatically isolated than Ankara might have envisaged when President Trump appeared to greenlight its attack.

A week later, after that implicit OK of Turkey's offensive, Mr. Trump is imposing economic sanctions on Ankara after a wild zig-zag in US policy—bizarre even by Trumpian standards. Almost the entire world is condemning the Turkish invasion and, having achieved the objective of eliminating the Kurdish statelet of Rojava, Turkey will have great difficulty in making any more gains. "Now that the Kurds and Damascus have come to an agreement, I do not think that Ankara will dare to open a new front against Assad forces," writes the Turkish military commentator Metin Gurcan.

Even token numbers of Syrian troops in cities like Manbij and Kobani close to the Euphrates, and Qamishli and Hasakah close to the Iraqi border, will leave Turkish soldiers and allied Arab militiamen confined to a rectangle of territory between the towns of Ras al-Ayn and Tal Abyad, possibly extending twenty miles south to the M4 highway—which is the strategic spine of Rojava. The YPG have avoided costly engagements but could become more of a threat if backed by Syrian army artillery and tanks.

Focus now is on the 160,000 Kurdish refugees fleeing the Turkish advance, publicity is given to the murder of prisoners by the pro-Turkish Arab militiamen, and mention is made of their Isis and al-Qaeda backgrounds. President Erdogan and Turkey are, for the moment at least, replacing Assad and his regime as the leading international pariahs. Suddenly, there are pictures everywhere of Isis captives fleeing their prisons as their Kurdish guards try to stem the Turkish advance. Mr. Trump's suggestion that Turkey, which only a few years ago had tolerated the great influx of foreign Isis fighters across its borders into the so-called caliphate, would replace the Kurds in suppressing Isis, provoked general derision and dismay.

In terms of domestic Turkish public opinion, the emphasis is still on Turkish military success, but, from now on, this will bring no political benefits to Mr. Erdogan. He must try to operate without allies and is being squeezed by the US and Russia. Turkish troops and their Arab allies are still pushing forward, but Turkey has lost the diplomatic and propaganda wars. In the end, it will have no option but to declare a famous victory and retreat.

18 October 2019

I was driving a year ago past a giant cement factory in north-east Syria, which was then the military headquarters of the US forces fighting alongside the Kurds to defeat Isis. I did not want to loiter—in the land of the vehicle-borne suicide bomber, the soldiers inside such facilities keep a suspicious eye on any car or truck that gets too close to them. It was this same Lafarge cement plant, close to the Euphrates, that was bombed by two US F-I5 jets last week after being hastily abandoned by US forces, to destroy stores of ammunition that had been left behind. The air strike on the former US headquarters is a symbol of the US failure in Syria, just as a helicopter crammed with terrified Vietnamese lifting off from the roof of the American embassy in Saigon in 1975 became a symbol of the US defeat in Vietnam.

People across the Middle East are asking how far the US pull-out from Syria changes the balance of power in the region, as Russia, Turkey, Iran, and Assad all, in their different ways, move to fill the vacuum left by the US. Does it mean, for instance, that Donald Trump's policy of confronting Iran, which was already in trouble, is close to being capsized entirely? Trump's efforts to escape a mess of his own making keep making it worse. On Thursday night in Ankara, US Vice President Mike Pence announced that after tough negotiating with Erdogan, he had persuaded the Turks to agree to a five-day truce in Syria. It turns out that he had achieved this negotiating masterpiece by giving the Turks everything they wanted, such as a permanent Turkish occupation of a 300-mile long and twenty-mile wide swathe of Kurdish-inhabited north-east Syria.

Turkish military forces are supposedly pausing their offensive for five days while the YPG withdraws. This agreement was succinctly described by Robert Malley of the International Crisis Group as "a capitulation dressed up as a win [for the US]." Its real purpose is to enable Trump to claim to have ended the war in northern Syria through astute diplomacy—though reporters at Pence's press conference in the Turkish capital were already asking him if this was "a second betrayal of the Kurds." Nothing in this deal is what it seems to be: even treachery requires some strength to influence events and the US no longer has the power in Syria to carry out a further act of betrayal of their former allies.

The YPG commanders say that they will abide by the ceasefire in the narrow corridor of territory between the towns of Ras al-Ayn and Tal Abyad, already largely under Turkish control. But this is only 20 percent of the "safe zone" that Erdogan says he has been promised by the US, which is no longer in a position to pressure the Kurds into making territorial concessions to Turkey. As for the ceasefire (or "pause," as the Turks like to call it), this could go the way of many another Middle East truce that never quite got off the ground. Erdogan says that fighting has ceased, but the YPG says that they are still holding out in Ras al-Ayn, a largish town on the border, and they have cleared Arab paramilitaries under Turkish command from the M4 highway that runs east to west across northern Syria.

The truth is that Trump and Erdogan both need to get off the hook in Syria and pretend to their domestic audiences to have won triumphant successes. Turkey wants to claim a non-existent military victory and Mr. Trump is saying that he ended a war that he is accused of fecklessly initiating. Syrian Kurdish claims to have been horrified and surprised by Trump stabbing them in the back should be taken with a fairly large pinch of salt. When interviewing the Syrian Kurdish leaders in north-east Syria in recent years, I was struck that these were not people who trusted anybody very much, a trait born of grim historical experience.

The speed and efficiency with which Russian and Syrian forces rushed into the main cities of north-east Syria as soon as the Turkish offensive began ten days ago indicate pre-planning, and torpedoed Turkish hopes of seizing important Kurdish-controlled cities. The Turkish invasion force is, in any case, far too small to penetrate far beyond the frontier or defeat the YPG.

25 October 2019

The sectarian and ethnic civil wars that have ravaged a large part of the Middle East over the past forty years are coming to an end. Replacing them is a new type of conflict in which protests akin to popular uprisings rock kleptocratic elites that justify their power by claiming to be the defenders of communities menaced by extreme violence or extinction. It is a period of transition and one should never underestimate the ability of embattled communal leaders to press the right sectarian buttons in order to divide opposition to their predatory misrule.

I first went to the region in 1975, fresh from sectarian warfare in Northern Ireland, in order to report on the beginning of the Lebanese civil war between a mosaic of communities defined by religion and ethnicity. In later years in Iraq, I watched divisions between Sunni and Shia grow and produce sectarian bloodbaths after the fall of Saddam Hussein. Popular protests in Syria in 2011 swiftly turned into a sectarian and ethnic civil war of extraordinary ferocity that may now be coming to an end. This is not because combatants on all sides have come to see the error of their ways or that they have suddenly noticed for the first time that their leaders are for the most part criminalised plutocrats. It is rather because winners and losers have emerged in these conflicts, so those in power can no longer divert attention from their all-embracing corruption by claiming that their community is in danger of attack from merciless foes.

Victors and vanquished have long been identifiable in Lebanon and became clear in Iraq with the capture of Mosul and the defeat of Isis in 2017. The winners and losers in the Syrian civil war have become ever more apparent over the last month as Bashar al-Assad, Russia, and Iran take control of almost the whole country. The Iraqi and Syrian Kurds had been able to create and expand their own quasi-states when central governments in Baghdad and Damascus were weak and under assault by Isis. The statelets were never going to survive the defeat of the Isis caliphate: the Iraqi Kurds lost the oil province of Kirkuk to the Iraqi army in 2017 and the Syrian Kurds have just seen their quasi-state of Rojava squeezed to extinction by the Turks on one side and the Syrian government on the other.

The fate of the Kurds is a tragedy but an inevitable one. Once Isis had been defeated in the siege of Raqqa in 2017, there was no way that the US was going to maintain a Kurdish statelet beset by enemies on every side. For all their accusations of American treachery, the Kurdish leaders knew this, but they did not have an alternative protector to turn to, aside from Russia and Assad, who were never going to underwrite a semi-independent Kurdish state.

A problem in explaining developments in the Middle East over the last three years is that the US foreign policy establishment supported by most of the US and European media blame all negative developments on President Trump. This is a gross over-simplification when it is not wholly misleading. His abrupt and cynical abandonment of the Kurds to Turkey may have multiplied their troubles, but extracting the small US military from eastern Syria was sensible enough because it was over-matched by four dangerous and determined opponents: Turkey, Iran, Russia, and the Assad government.

The final outcome of the multiple Syrian wars is now in sight: Turkey will keep a small, unstable enclave in Syria, but the rest of the Syrian-Turkish border will be policed by Russian and Syrian government troops who will oversee the YPG withdrawal twenty-one miles to the south. The most important question is how far the Kurdish civilian population, who have fled the fighting, will find it safe enough to return. A crucial point to emerge from the meeting between Vladimir Putin and Recep Tayyip Erdogan in Sochi last Tuesday is that Turkey is tiptoeing towards implicitly recognising the Assad government backed by Russia as the protector of its southern border against the YPG. This makes it unlikely that Ankara will do much to stop a Russian-Syrian government offensive from taking, probably a slice at a time, the last stronghold of the Syrian armed opposition in Idlib.

The ingredient that made communal religious and sectarian hatreds so destructive in the past in Lebanon, Syria, and Iraq is that they opened the door to foreign intervention. Local factions became the proxies of outside countries pursuing their own interests, which armed and financed them. For the moment at least, no foreign power has an interest in stirring the pot in this northern tier of the Middle East, the zone of war forty-four years, and there is just a fleeting chance of a durable peace.

PART X. AN UPRISING IN IRAQ

The mass street protests that began in Baghdad on October 1, 2019 caught me entirely by surprise, as they did everybody else. This was not lack of a political foresight on anybody's part, but because the small scale demonstrations would not have turned into a mass movement without the violent overreaction of the Iranian-directed parts of the Iraqi government security apparatus and the paramilitaries. I was in Baghdad on the day of the first protest that had been billed as a low-key affair, starting in Tahrir Square not far from my hotel. I had met some jobless university graduates who were planning to attend, but they did not expect much to happen. I was writing in my hotel room that evening when I first heard the sound of shots that I thought might be celebrating some football match triumph or a wedding, but they turned out to be the security forces, supplemented by paramilitary snipers, shooting dead at least ten protesters and wounding many more. I was swiftly informed about this by a doctor in the Medical City hospital complex who said the real number of fatalities was greatly understated, going by the number of bodies he had seen.

The protesters were demanding jobs, a better supply of electricity and water, and an end to corruption, but the ballooning size of the demonstrations was essentially repression-driven, making them different from other mass street protests in Baghdad and Basra since 2016. It was Iranian General Qasem Soleimani who had initiated this disastrous over-reaction, probably having an exaggerated idea of the threat posed by the protests. He would not be the first general to convince himself that a "whiff of grapeshot" would put an end to any outward show of popular discontent. Twice before as a journalist, I had seen security services fuel the growth of a resistance movement: the first occasion was in Northern Ireland at the start of The Troubles after 1968 when the British Army, along with the Royal Ulster Constabulary, treated Catholic civil rights marchers as if they were dangerous terrorists—thereby becoming the unwitting recruiting sergeants for the Provisional IRA. I saw similar counter-productive repression in Iraq after the US-led invasion of 2003, when the foreign forces, supposedly in the country only to remove Saddam Hussein, transformed into an occupying army intent on imposing its rule. In all three cases, military commanders convinced themselves that the only thing wrong with the use of physical force was that not enough of it was being used.

The mass street protests that spread through Shia Iraq in the last three months of 2019 could not be suppressed despite horrendous casualties and took on a strong anti-Iranian flavour. The crucial question now is if they will be marginalised by the US killing of General Soleimani and Abu Mahdi al-Muhandis, the leader of the Kat'aib Hezbollah paramilitary group and the deputy head of the Popular Mobilisation Forces. Their deaths have been portrayed as a body-blow to Iran and the pro-Iranian paramilitaries, but, because both leaders had been pursuing disastrous policies, their removal may, perversely, have done Iran and the paramilitaries a favour. Muqtada al-Sadr, previously supportive of the protests, met with the leaders of the paramilitary groups in mid-January 2020 and called for a million-strong march against the presence of US troops. The unity of the very diverse groups taking part in the protests, previously very impressive, was beginning to fray. Optimists in Iraq hope there might just be a moment when their country can escape the domination of both Iran and the US. Pessimists fear that, on the contrary, they will be trampled on by both these foreign powers as they struggle for supremacy in Iraq.

October–November 2019

1 October 2019

Security forces opened fire on protesters in central Baghdad on Tuesday evening, with some witnesses saying more than ten people had been killed and some 286 wounded. Riot police used live rounds as well as stun grenades and rubber bullets to stop demonstrators from crossing a bridge over the Tigris River to the Green Zone from Tahrir Square, where they had been protesting against unemployment, government corruption, and lack of electricity and water. Many ministers, senior officials, and government are located in the Green Zone.

A doctor at Medical City, a nearby hospital complex, told me that he had seen four bodies, but that the total number of dead admitted to his hospital was at least ten. This figure was confirmed off the record later in the evening by a government adviser, citing a confidential news system used by government officials to which he had access. The sound of machine gun fire could be heard rippling across the city long after darkness had fallen, with main roads closed by the security services. By 22.30 local time [19.30 GMT] shots could no longer be heard and sparse traffic was running.

It was the worst civil violence seen in years in the Iraqi capital, although it had become well used to devastating bomb blasts that have tailed off since 2016. This year there has also been a noticeable lack of mass protests against the electricity shortage and the lack of jobs which peaked last year in Basra where protesters took over the city. The demonstration in Baghdad on Tuesday was small by Iraqi standards—about 3,000 people—but the overreaction by the security services could lead to a new wave of demonstrations in the next few days. It may be that the government is minimising casualty figures in order to avoid a popular backlash. As people converged on the square chanting anti-government slogans, riot policemen tried to disperse them, scattering the mostly young male protesters, some of whom covered their face with scarves. Other protesters responded by throwing stones at security forces and waved Iraqi flags above the water cannon. Young men were seen carried away, some of them bleeding.

In a tweet, Muqtada al-Sadr called on government leaders to launch an investigation into Tuesday's clashes. In the past, tens of thousands of his followers have joined the anti-corruption protests, making it impossible for the government to suppress them. A joint statement issued by the Iraqi interior and health ministries said two people were killed and 200 injured, including forty members of the security forces in Baghdad and other cities. It said it "regretted" the violence that accompanied the protests in Baghdad and several other provinces, blaming "a group of rioters," while calling for calm and restraint.

University graduates had already been demonstrating outside ministries, saying that they were being denied jobs for which they were qualified. These were being given instead to candidates for their party loyalty or religion, they said. Outside the Foreign Ministry, a group of political science graduates said they had set up a small camp forty-three days earlier to demand employment but had got nowhere. They were intending to join the demonstration that ended so violently on Tuesday.

The shooting of the protesters could provoke a crisis for Prime Minister Adel Abdul-Mahdi, who has lasted longer in office than was expected. He was already under pressure because of the dismissal last Friday of Lieutenant General Abdul-Wahab al-Saadi.

2 October 2019

A man is lying dead or injured on the pavement beside a road leading into Tahrir Square. Soldiers and police are running towards him, while Iraqi soldiers on the other side of the square are penning into a corner a group of a hundred or so protesters, some holding Iraqi flags, and chanting "Peaceful" and "For Iraq." The protesters are more numerous than first appears because they have broken up into groups that are permanently on the move. There is the sharp crack of automatic rifle fire, with all the shots being supposedly fired into the air. Black smoke is rising from burning tyres on one road and others are blocked off by police in their green and yellow cars, along with regular soldiers in uniform and black-clad members of the Counter Terrorism Service. As night falls, the situation deteriorates.

"At least eight or ten districts in Baghdad have sealed themselves off with barricades and burning tyres," says one informant. Groups of youths are trying to block the motorways as the authorities struggle to retain control. If the Iraqi government had made a plan at the beginning of this week to turn sparsely attended demonstrations against corruption and lack of jobs into a mass movement, then it is doing very nicely. The government claims that only two people were killed and several hundred injured on Tuesday, though hospital doctors, who treated the injured, say that the real figure is much higher.

"We were caught by surprise by the toughness of the security services' response to a peaceful demonstration," says Haider, who trained as a lawyer and has helped organise the demonstrations against joblessness—particularly among graduates of whom 307,000 are unemployed—for the last three months. The protests had not been getting much traction until the police and army violently attacked protesters on Tuesday, saying that they were under orders to defend the Green Zone at all costs. Haider says that the committees and NGOs organising the demonstrations want to stage a big one on Friday, 4 October. They had tried to call off the protest at 7 p.m. because it was getting out of their control and a Turkish restaurant had been burned down, he adds.

The overreaction by the government is continuing: on Wednesday, heavily armed troops in black ski masks were milling about near Tahrir Square and giving the impression that they were there to repel a foreign invasion force. All the airline offices on Sadoon Street are closed, as are the clinics in al-Nidal Street. The traffic is very limited by Baghdad standards and there are not many pedestrians to be seen. Municipal workers had cleaned up Tahrir Square overnight, spraying the street with water while bulldozers removed rubbish. As they did so, a car was distributing water to protesters and soldiers alike. "We are not against you; you are our brothers," one activist told a soldier as he offered him a cold bottle of water. In Zaafaraniya, south-east of Baghdad, at least five people were treated for shortness of breath after police used tear gas to break up a small protest.

Police also used tear gas in al-Shaab, north of Baghdad. Security officials said five people were arrested in al-Shaab and three in Zaafaraniya.

The protests are the most serious challenge against Prime Minister Abdul-Mahdi's government since it was formed nearly a year ago. It had got through the height of the summer, when the shortage of electricity for air conditioning causes intense popular rage, without major protests along the lines of those that paralysed Basra in 2018 and led to the fall of the previous prime minister, Haider al-Abadi. The demonstrations and marches had been tame and their leaders wanted to avoid being identified with any political party. The followers of Muqtada al-Sadr were asked not to take part. Using social media to coordinate, people rallied against corruption and lack of basic services, with university students in particular complaining that their academic credentials did not help them get jobs. Similar protests and confrontations took place in other provinces, including in the cities of Basra and Nasiriyah in the south. In Nasiriyah, one protester was killed and around twenty people wounded, according to hospital officials.

What is significant here is that all the protests are in Shia provinces, which is important in a country that has a Shia majority and a predominantly Shia government. The problem is that the government is corrupt at every level and the allocation of jobs in ministries—and jobs within them—depends on party allegiance and religious affiliation.

3 October 2019
Iraq is on the edge of a mass popular uprising, which the government is seeking to stifle through a strictly imposed open-ended curfew and an enforced internet blackout. Protests, met with a fierce response from the authorities, have gripped Baghdad and spread since Tuesday to southern Iraqi provinces. So far, nineteen people have been reported killed, including one policeman, according to authorities. The real total could be higher.

The closing down of the internet has not stopped the protests but has led to them becoming more disorganised and focused in districts of Baghdad away from the centre. Protesters in the Shia working-class stronghold of Sadr City in east Baghdad attacked municipal offices and set fire to the Dawa Party headquarters. Doctors said some 600 people had been injured on Thursday alone, mostly by rubber bullets fired at the neck or chest. Sources said that thousands of people from Sadr City had begun a march towards Tahrir Square on Thursday evening. The curfew was also being imposed in provincial cities across Shia provinces south of Baghdad. Iraqi medical officials say ten people were killed in southern Iraq overnight.

Iran closed a border crossing with Iraq, citing the "situation" in its neighbouring country. An Iraqi official says the Khesro border in the eastern province of Diyala will remain closed until further notice.

"I was in Tahrir Square talking to the protesters and they are making all the demands that people have been making since 2003," Hiwa Osman, an Iraqi commentator, told me. "Against corruption, the political parties, the quota system (for different sects and ethnic groups), the lack of education, health concerns, and jobs."

Most of the demonstrators are twenty or under, which means they do not remember a time before the fall of Saddam Hussein. The uprising has no discernible leadership, except at a local level, which means that the government has no one to talk to, even if it wanted to. Parliament Speaker Mohammed al-Halbusi invited representatives of the protesters to come to the parliament to discuss their demands, state media reported on Thursday—but it was unclear to whom the invitation was directed.

Muqtada al-Sadr has tweeted that he supports the movement but "does not want to politicise it," and is not directly calling on his followers to take part. He is likely acutely aware that the involvement of his followers could alienate many other potential protesters. The demonstrators appear to have strong support among all sections of society, from working-class Shia slum districts in east Baghdad to doctors and engineers sending supportive messages.

The streets are almost entirely empty, apart from the occasional bus, potentially used by the security forces. And the occasional bicyclist—one telling me that while vehicles and pedestrians had been banned, the authorities had said nothing about cycling. So far, the uprising has been confined to Shia parts of Baghdad and Shia cities, but there is talk of a demonstration in the Sunni city of Mosul on Friday. Friday is likely to be a crucial moment for the protests, as it is the traditional day for demonstrations.

The motives for the government's hard-line actions are mysterious, with speculation that Abdul-Mahdi is being advised by hawkish military officers, with no understanding of Iraqi politics. The government has made few conciliatory statements or concessions, and Iraqi journalists say that officials are failing to recall their calls.

4 October 2019

Iraq is poised at a turning point in its modern history as its people wait to see if the government curfew and close down of the internet will end the ongoing demonstrations. I am staying in the Baghdad Hotel, off Sadoon Street in central Baghdad, not far from Tahrir Square, the focus of most protest movements in Iraq. On Tuesday, I was expecting to visit Iraqi army bases north of Baghdad to find out if Isis was still a threat and what the chances were of it making a comeback.

I never went: on Tuesday afternoon at about 4 p.m. I began to hear the "put-put" of rifle fire in the distance, which at first I disregarded, thinking there might be a wedding or some other celebration. But the sound got louder and soon there was the sharp crack of weapons being fired close by. In the lobby of my hotel, a man stopped me and said, "There are ten dead already and the fighting is going to get worse."

It is noticeable that the government has failed to make any concessions since it made its first mistakes on Tuesday. "The prime minister should have done something like announcing that he would arrest the hundred most corrupt members of his government," said one friend. Instead, ministers have been saying that they will inquire into the reasons for the protests, but these are glaringly obvious and known to the whole country: corruption, joblessness, and lack of services. What will happen next? The government cannot maintain a total lockdown on Baghdad, a city of seven million people, for very long. Already people are beginning to move on the streets around my hotel and many of them heading for Tahrir Square.

The government may find it difficult to suppress the Shia, their own base support, using armed forces that are themselves mostly Shia. The government's legitimacy was low to begin with and is sinking by the day. Ali Sistani, the revered religious leader of the Shia, may come out against the government's actions. Even government spokespeople are refusing to talk to Iraqi journalists, probably because they do not want to be seen approving the government's tactics. In other words, unless the prime minister can bring the crisis under control in the next couple of days, his own administration may begin to implode.

7 October 2019

Iraqi paramilitary groups close to Iran are suspected of joining attacks on protesters in Baghdad and other cities, leading to heavy loss of life among demonstrators. Some 107 people have been killed and over 6,000 wounded in the last six days, though hospital doctors say the government is understating the true number of fatalities. "The pro-Iranian militia have each taken a sector of Baghdad and are responsible for its security," a source, who does not want his name published, told me. He said that snipers belonging to these groups had fired live rounds at protesters, often aiming for the head or heart. Eyewitnesses say that Iraqi soldiers are also firing directly into crowds of the protesters. The gunmen shooting protesters come from pro-Iranian factions of the Hashd al-Shaabi.

The demonstrations in Baghdad and in much of Shia, southern Iraq, are largely spontaneous, but where there are local leaders, they have sometimes been singled out for killing. Haider Karim Al-Saidi, a leading organiser of the protests, was shot dead by a sniper near Al-Mudhafar Square late on Sunday night. Earlier, witnesses had reported that they had seen snipers taking up positions on rooftops overlooking the square. The paramilitaries have assaulted injured protesters in hospital: a doctor working in the Medical City complex in central Baghdad said that members of the paramilitary group Asa'ib Ahl al-Haq, known for its pro-Iranian sympathies, had broken into a hospital ward filled with wounded demonstrators and started hitting them. When he protested, he was told "to mind his own business" and was beaten with a baton.

An Interior Ministry spokesman, Saad Maan, said that 6,107 people had been injured in the unrest, including 1,200 members of the security forces. Public buildings and political party headquarters have also been destroyed. A paramilitary group called Kata'ib Hezbollah is alleged to have ransacked at least ten television stations that had been giving full or sympathetic coverage to the demonstrations. In one case, gunmen in balaclavas arrived in twelve white cars without license plates and wrecked studios, seizing computers, beating up staff, and taking their wallets and mobile phones.

The government has expressed suspicion that a third party is playing a role in provoking greater violence, through using snipers who shoot to kill. Interior Ministry spokesman Saad Maan said at a press conference that "malicious hands" were targeting protesters and security forces alike. This may be true in part but is also a bid by the security forces to evade responsibility for firing directly into crowds, though there is every sign that they have been doing just that. Repressive measures have included a two-day curfew, a continuing ban on the internet, and preemptive arrests.

The demands of the protesters have become more radical since last Tuesday, as the casualty toll has mounted, with growing calls for the fall of the government of Abdul-Mahdi. He has shown himself to be ineffective, making a speech at the weekend in which he outlined a seventeen-point plan including unemployment benefit and subsidised housing, but he made little impression. In his year in office, Mr. Mahdi has failed to introduce any important reforms, so his sudden zeal for change carries little credibility. The signs are, for the moment, that repression will continue but also that it will not succeed. "The protesters are very young and feel they have little to lose," says one observer. "They will go on protesting whatever happens."

The aggressive role of the pro-Iranian paramilitaries is evidence that Tehran fears peaceful anti-government mass protests along the lines of the Green Movement in Iran in 2009 and in Syria in 2011, both of which, at their peak, threatened regime change. "The Iranians want to militarise the situation so it ceases to be a mass movement," says one Iraqi commentator. This would explain the shooting of so many demonstrators. But by overreacting the government and the Iranians may have provoked the very situation that they want to avoid.

10 November 2019
Iraqi security and pro-Iranian paramilitary forces are shooting into crowds of protesters in a bid to drive them from the centre of Baghdad and end six weeks of demonstrations. Police retook three bridges across the Tigris River that lead to the fortified Green Zone on Saturday and are surrounding Tahrir Square, the central focus of the protests.

In al-Rasheed Street, close to the square, police set fire to tents set up by volunteer doctors to treat injured protesters. At least six people were killed in the latest clashes, four of them by bullets and two by heavy-duty tear gas grenades fired directly at the head or bodies of protesters, according to Amnesty International. It says that 264 people taking part in demonstrations have died since 1 October, though the Iraqi High Commission for Human Rights gives a higher figure of 301 dead and 15,000 injured.

The protests—and the merciless government attempt to stamp them out—are the biggest threat to the power of the Iraqi political establishment since Isis was advancing on Baghdad in 2014. In many respects, the danger to the status quo is greater now because Isis was an existential threat to the Shia majority who had no choice but to support their ruling elite, however predatory and incompetent they had proved in office. The slaughter of so many demonstrators is similar to the tactics used by Egyptian President Abdel Fattah el-Sisi in 2013 to crush protests opposing his military coup that had overthrown the elected government. By way of contrast, there was no such violence in response to street demonstrations in Baghdad in 2016, when protesters invaded the Green Zone, or in Basra in 2018, when the government and party offices were set ablaze. Over the last month-and-a-half, however, there has been repeated use of snipers firing at random into demonstrations or targeting local protest leaders.

It is the Iranian leadership, and more especially General Qasem Soleimani, the commander of the Revolutionary Guard's al-Quds force and supremo of Iranian regional policy, who is orchestrating the campaign to smash the protests by sustained use of violence. Precisely why General Soleimani decided to do so is a mystery, since the initial demonstration in Tahrir Square on 1 October was small. The NGOs organising it had been failing for months to generate momentum. It was the unprecedented "shoot-to-kill" policy of the authorities that turned these ill-attended rallies into a mass movement not far from a general uprising.

During the first days of the protests, protest organisers told me they were at first baffled by what had happened, inclining at first to believe that the first day's violence, when at least ten people were killed, might be a one-off overreaction that would not be repeated. But the killing of protesters, counter-productive though it might be, went on. It is unlikely that the wrecking of television stations, assault of injured demonstrators in hospitals, and abduction and threatening of journalists, doctors, and anybody else backing the demonstrations was a pre-arranged plot by the pro-Iranian paramilitaries acting on their own initiative.

I interviewed several of their leaders, whose groups were subsequently known to have supplied snipers to shoot at the street protests. Though they later declared that they had long detected a deep-laid conspiracy by the US, Israel, Saudi Arabia, and the UAE to use the protests to overthrow the political system in Iraq, they did not say so at the time. Qais al-Khazali, the leader of Asa'ib Ahl al-Haq, a powerful paramilitary faction, said that "Iran wants a solution [in the US-Iran confrontation], but it cannot say this itself." He downplayed the idea that a US-Iran war was on the cards. Abu Ala al-Walai, the head of Kata'ib Sayyid al-Shuhada, said in a separate interview that what most concerned him was an Israeli drone attack on a weapons depot at one of his bases on the outskirts of Baghdad. Nevertheless, the speed and cohesion with which these pro-Iranian Shia paramilitary groups reacted—or overreacted—to the protests suggests a detailed contingency plan.

"The Iranians always have a plan," notes one Iraqi commentator. Nor did the paramilitaries act alone: no distinct boundary line divides the Hashd from state security institutions. The Hashd may number about 85,000, are paid their salaries by the Iraqi government and their chairman Faleh al-Fayyad, the government's national security adviser. The interior minister always belongs to the Iran-supported Badr Organisation and the ministry's Emergency Response Division, for instance, is reported to have provided snipers to shoot protesters.

In the weeks since the first peaceful march was met with extreme violence, the intensity of the repression has escalated in Baghdad and across southern Iraq. In the Shia holy city of Karbala on one day, snipers killed eighteen people and survivors were detained by pop-up checkpoints as they fled through the alleyways. Kidnapping, disappearances, intimidation—a whole apparatus of repression—has been put in place and is unlikely to be dismantled.

Pro-Iranian pro-status quo individuals and institutions within the Iraqi political system are becoming more dominant. Critics of the status quo, like Muqtada al-Sadr, whose coalition is the largest grouping in parliament, have fallen silent. Grand Ayatollah Ali al-Sistani called last Friday for the security forces to refrain from using "excessive force," but there is no sign of this having any impact. Adel Abdul-Mahdi, the Iraqi prime minister for the last year, has come out of the crisis looking ineffectual.

The Iraqi political class as a whole have evidently decided that they must stamp out the protests to preserve their interests. The protesters in the streets—the radicalism of whose demands and their vagueness about how they might be achieved resembles French students during the 1968 events in France—are not able to say what they would put in place of the present corrupt and dysfunctional government. As for those carrying out the repression, they are so steeped in blood that it will be impossible for them to reverse course, not that they show any sign of wanting to do so.

AFTERWORD

The Peace of the Grave: The Cemeteries of Iraq

11 October 2018

Apart from witches, who come here to bury spells, few people visit the British North Gate cemetery in Baghdad. The witches believe that words written on paper and placed in the ground between the graves of non-Muslims, particularly old graves, have enhanced magical powers. North Gate, in the Waziriyah district, is a large quadrilateral of burned grass fringed by palm trees. There are 511 graves with tombstones, almost all of them dating from the calamitous British campaign in 1914–18 when 40,620 soldiers from the British and Indian armies died fighting the Ottoman Turks. British military cemeteries, looked after by the Commonwealth War Graves Commission, are dotted around Iraq. Looking for somebody to let me into North Gate this summer, I asked a group of women standing outside their house by the cemetery if they shared the superstition, common in Iraq, that it was unlucky to live near such a place. They said they didn't mind the cemetery but didn't like "the witches who climb over the fence in the middle of the night so they can carry on their works among the dead." One of them said that whenever she saw witches, she would phone the cemetery's caretaker, Sayid Jassim, and he would come and drive them away.

Sorcery is well established in Iraq and belief in its power has grown since the US-led invasion of 2003: living in conditions of extreme insecurity, many Iraqis believe they can do with all the miraculous assistance they can get. The police estimate that there are around 3,000 sorcerers in Baghdad, male and female, their activities often advertised on television and Facebook. Many of them are alleged to belong to the ancient Sabean sect whose worshippers give primacy as a prophet to John the Baptist. Depending on the nature of what they are asked to do, I'm told, witches and sorcerers charge at least $400 for a spell or a curse, though the better-known ones can command up to $6,000. Spells relate to marriage, love, divorce, good health, job opportunities, and promotion. Costlier spells may be sold to politicians seeking re-election, or to those who ask a sorcerer to exercise magical influence over a government official to force him to sign or refrain from signing a document—not an uncommon need, given that Iraqis spend large amounts of time wrestling with a corrupt and impenetrable bureaucracy. Many of the most famous sorcerers are employed by clients from other Arab countries; payment is in advance and by bank transfer. For the extra potency they give to spells, non-Muslim cemeteries are preferred, but the vast Shia cemetery Wadi us-Salaam ("Valley of Peace") in the holy city of Najaf is sometimes used.

Iraq has been engulfed by wars and crises since 1979, when Saddam Hussein established absolute rule, starting the Iran-Iraq War a year later. The years of chronic instability since then, during which Iraqis have felt at the mercy of events beyond their control, have boosted the belief that good and evil spirits can be influenced to affect human affairs. Many today blame increased credulity about magic on plunging standards of education and, since 2003, on the shortage of good doctors, many of whom fled the country after the invasion because they were a particular target of kidnappers, with the result that sick people have increasingly resorted to witches and faith healers for cures.

Sometimes a whole district is infested by evil spirits and ghosts. Sunni Arabs living in the Abu Ghraib district of west Baghdad, close to the notorious prison, complained that the physical, psychological, and sexual abuse carried out there during the US occupation meant that, long after the Americans had gone, the tormented ghosts of prisoners still roamed the streets and cried out in the night. They said that their children couldn't sleep and became mentally disturbed because of the spirits. According to an account by the Institute for War and Peace Reporting, farmland fell out of use, school enrolment dropped, and 70 percent of the 450 houses near the prison were abandoned. By 2010, they were for sale at a quarter of their previous price. Waled Hamid, a newcomer who did buy a house, later sued the seller, claiming the property was haunted, and that he should have been warned of this in advance. "I didn't know anything about the history of this area," Hamid was quoted as saying. "Now we are frightened in the house. At night, everything gets creepy and the dogs and cats act strange." He lost the case because the provincial court decided that the law did not recognise superstitions. According to a local sheikh, some of those stuck with unsaleable property in Abu Ghraib have paid sorcerers tens of thousands of dollars to perform an exorcism.

I started visiting British cemeteries in Iraq in the run-up to the Gulf War in 1991 as a distraction from current events. These visits put the latest all-absorbing crisis—Saddam's defeat in Kuwait in 1991, or the US/UK invasion of 2003, or the victories of Isis in 2014—in the broader context of Iraqi and world history. It's easy to explain in general terms why Iraq has been such a dangerous place over the last hundred years: it is an oil state, whose fate is important to the great powers, and which is surrounded by regional players—Iran, Turkey, the Arab world—which fuel and manip- ulate existing divisions between Sunni, Shia, and Kurd. But quite how lethal the country has been, particularly for interventionist foreign powers, becomes far more vivid when one stands a few feet away from the neatly incised gravestone in North Gate of Driver T.R. Morris of the Royal Horse Artillery, who died on 13 October 1917, or that of Captain S.O. Robinson, who died on 5 November 1917. In the centre of the cemetery is a monu- ment to General Sir Stanley Maude, who captured Baghdad in 1917 and died of cholera six months later. The long rows of graves carry the message: that, however bad the current crisis in Iraq, it is only the latest in a long series. Victories here are always temporary.

The changing appearance of the cemetery is a crude barometer of the state of security in Baghdad; when things are bad, the grass is long, and rubbish is strewn around. The mainly Sunni district of Waziriyah has sometimes been hard to get to, as in 2007, when a suicide bomber blew up a truck and destroyed the central spans of the bridge across the Tigris. In 2009, the blast from a nearby car bomb knocked down or smashed many of the headstones. Over the last two years, as the Iraqi government has tightened its grip on Baghdad, the grounds have once again begun to look spruce and the Commonwealth War Graves Commission has replaced most of the lost and damaged stones.

But for me the chief fascination of these cemeteries—whether in Baghdad, Kut, Amara, or Basra—is the sheer immensity of the disaster they commemorate, and the extent to which it has been forgotten. Unlike the defeat at Gallipoli and the slaughter on the Somme, the Mesopotamian campaign has faded from British memory, despite the national obsession with the First World War. According to the War Graves Commission, 85,000 British and Indian soldiers were killed, wounded, or captured, but this is probably an underestimate: the commission notes that the cemetery in Amara on the lower Tigris "commemorates some five thousand servicemen of the Indian Army, of whom only nine are identified as no comprehensive records of the burials were kept by the military authorities." I visited Amara in 2003, when beyond a ruined archway, the cemetery was being used as a dumping ground for broken-down buses.

The Mesopotamian campaign was grotesquely mismanaged, even by the low standards of the First World War, and those responsible had no wish to recall it. After the publication of a damning official report in 1917, Lord Curzon, a member of the war cabinet, suggested that "a more shocking exposure of official blundering and incompetence has not in my opinion been made, at any rate since the Crimean War." The intervention began on a small scale in 1914, initially intended to protect the oil fields in south-west Iran from attack by the Ottoman Turks. By 1918, the campaign had ballooned into the biggest British military action outside Europe. In 1915, an overambitious advance, which underestimated the Turks' fighting strength, aimed at capturing Baghdad to counterbalance the failure at Gallipoli earlier that year. Heavy casualties in a battle at Salman Pak led to a precipitate retreat to Kut, a ramshackle Shia city on a bend in the Tigris a hundred miles south-east of Baghdad. Commanded by Sir Charles Townshend, an insanely egocentric general, 13,000 British and Indian soldiers were besieged there for 147 days between December 1915 and 29 April 1916. Townshend appears deliberately to have allowed his troops to be surrounded: he wanted to make his reputation through a heroic and successful defence of Kut even though he knew his forces were far from their supply base in Basra while the Turks were close to theirs in Baghdad. In order to accelerate the arrival of the British-led forces coming to relieve him, he sent misleading information about how long he could hold out, forcing them to attack prematurely and suffer 23,000 casualties while failing to dislodge the well-entrenched Turks. Injured soldiers, their wounds gangrenous and filled with maggots, were crammed into slow-moving river boats and lay in their own excreta for the two weeks it took to reach Basra.